DOES IT BELONG IN THE NEW TESTAMENT?

Omissions from the New Testament

Roderick L. Ross, VDS

Does It Belong in the New Testament: Omissions from the New Testament is copyright ©2019, Roderick L. Ross. All rights reserved.

Published in the United States of America by:

Cobb Publishing
704 E. Main St.
Charleston, AR 72933
(479) 747-8372
CobbPublishing@gmail.com
www.CobbPublishing.com

Table of Contents

The Preface

This volume is dedicated to those who seek the truth. Truth is not determined by the majority. Truth is not determined by popularity. Truth is not determined by influence. Truth is determined by God.

My search for truth has been complimented and supplemented by my wife. Her encouragement, her support and her help throughout the years we have spent together (we were married in 1975) have been invaluable.

May each and every reader find someone to help them and encourage them in their pursuit of the truth.

The Introduction

During Bible class in Benson, Arizona a gentleman asked me a question: "Why is your Bible different from my Bible?"

At the age of twenty, I did not know. But I told him I would find out.

The research to answer his question led my wife and I to examine twenty-nine translations, comparing them to each other and to the United Bible Society 3rd Edition Greek New Testament that I had from college.

What I, at first, thought was a difference in translation, I began to see as a difference in text. The translations were different because they were not translating the same thing. It was the same basic story, but there was a difference in the textual basis of what was said.

This lead me to study the history of Textual Criticism.

I am an incessant researcher. I consumed everything I could put my hands on about textual criticism from every viewpoint. This book, in connection with my book THE PRESERVATION OF THE NEW TESTAMENT: A study in Textual Criticism, is the result of that research.

In 2012, I suffered a stroke that did not affect anything other than my sight. The neurological ophthalmologist determined that I would never read, drive nor work again. My eyesight has not improved, but I found a way around it – partially. I have not driven since that day in 2012, nor have I worked for a wage. I have, however, found a way to read (at a much slower rate) and to write. Audible books, digital books and speech-to-text have been a great help. But, even with technical help and advances, I am restricted in the amount of time that I can function. The amount of concentration (expulsion of mental energy) wears me out quickly. I function as Isaiah said, "Line upon line, precept upon precept, here a little, there a little ..."

This book is a compilation of the work that I did over thirty years ago, that I had hoped to expand – but now realize that I shall never be able to do that. Hopefully, those who come after me will be able to do what I could not, and cannot, in completing a textual commentary on the New Testament, dealing with every omission that is seen in the more modern translations from the more traditional text.

I used the United Bible Society 3rd Edition Greek New Testament that I used in college for the information.

My conclusion was that even those who rejected these verses, did not honestly deal with the evidence that they willingly admit.

I invite you to examine what I found, and see for yourself.

■ August 19, 2019

The Approach to Textual Criticism

Textual Criticism of the New Testament is a close inquiry into what is the genuine Greek the true text of the Holy Gospels, of the Acts of the Apostles, of the Pauline and Apostolic Epistles, and the Revelation. Inasmuch as it concerns the text alone, it is confined to the Lower Criticism according to German nomenclature, just as a critical examination of meaning, with all its attendant references and connexions, would constitute the Higher Criticism. It is thus the necessary prelude of any scientific investigation of the language, the purport, and the teaching of the various books of the New Testament, and ought itself to be conducted upon definite and scientific principles. ...

In the very earliest times much variation in the text of the New Testament, and particularly of the Holy Gospels for we shall treat mainly of these four books as constituting the most important province, and as affording a smaller area, and so being more convenient for the present inquiry : much diversity in words and expression, I say, arose in the Church. In consequence, the school of scientific Theology at Alexandria, in the person of Origen, first found it necessary to take cognizance of the matter. When Origen moved to Caesarea, he carried his manuscripts with him, and they appear to have formed the foundation of the celebrated library in that city, which was afterwards amplified by Pamphilus and Eusebius, and also by Acacius and Euzoius, who were all successively bishops of the place. During the life of Eusebius, if not under his controlling care, the two oldest Uncial Manuscripts in existence as hitherto discovered, known as B and N, or the Vatican and Sinaitic, were executed in handsome form and exquisite calligraphy. But shortly after, about the middle of the fourth century as both schools of Textual Critics agree a text differing from that of B and N advanced in general acceptance ; and, increasing till the eighth century in the predominance won by the end of the fourth, became so prevalent in Christendom, that the small number of MSS. agreeing with B and {Aleph} forms no sort of comparison with the many which vary from those two. Thus the problem of the fourth century anticipated the problem of the nineteenth. Are we for the genuine text of the New Testament to go to the Vatican and the Sinaitic MSS. and the few others which mainly agree with them, or are we to follow the main body of New Testament MSS., which by the end of the century in which those two were produced entered into possession of the field of contention, and have continued in occupation of it ever since ? This is the problem which the following treatise is intended to solve, that is to say, which of these two texts or sets of readings is the better attested, and can be traced back through the stronger evidence to the original autographs. [Traditional Text; pp. 1-4]

Westcott and Hort based their Greek text upon the readings of **A, B, ALEPH, C, D**. Upon the basis of a handful of documents, they rejected 48 whole verses from the New Testament text, and made, according to one estimate 2,288 differences affecting translation [EVALUATING VERSIONS OF THE NEW TESTAMENT; Everett W. Fowler; Maranatha Baptist Press, Maranatha Baptist College; Watertown, WI; 1981; p. 68], and a total number of 5,788 differences in the text according to other sources [THE ENGLISH BIBLE FROM KJV TO NIV: A HISTORY AND EVALUATION; Jack Lewis; Baker Book House: Grand Rapids, MI; 1982; pp. 69 and 335].

The readings of the TEXTUS RECEPTUS were termed Syrian by Westcott and Hort, and of them they said, *"… the range of documents which attest it may be safely rejected at once."* [THE NEW TESTAMENT IN THE ORIGINAL GREEK; 1891; p. 554]. Thus, with the wave of the hand 95-96% of Greek manuscripts extant are dismissed, not to be considered in determining the text by Westcott and Hort.

Those textual scholars which have followed in the twentieth century, have accepted the basic concept of textual criticism utilized by Westcott and Hort; although there have been minor changes in the method applied to the sorting of texts into "families" or text-types. Thus, the UNITED BIBLE SOCIETIES' GREEK NEW TESTAMENTS and NESTLE'S GREEK NEW TESTAMENT are based upon the philosophy of approach used by Westcott and Hort.

It should not be thought, however, that the TRADITIONAL TEXT has been without its champions. Both Dean J.W. Burgon [12 volumes indexing quotations of the NT by early writers located in the British Museum, THE LAST TWELVE VERSES OF THE GOSPEL ACCORDING TO MARK, THE REVISION REVISED, and posthumously THE CAUSES OF CORRUPTION OF THE TRADITIONAL TEXT OF THE HOLY GOSPELS, and THE TRADITIONAL TEXT OF THE HOLY GOSPELS VINDICATED AND ESTABLISHED], Dean F.H.A. Scrivener [BEZAE CODEX CANTABRIGIENSIS: BEING AN EXACT COPY, IN ORDINARY TYPE, OF THE CELEBRATED UNCIAL GRAECO-LATIN MANUSCRIPT OF THE FOUR GOSPELS AND ACTS OF THE APOSTLES, WRITTEN EARLY IN THE SIXTH CENTURY, AND PRESENTED TO THE UNIVERSITY OF CAMBRIDGE BY THEODORE BEZA, A.D. 1581, WITH A CRITICAL INTRODUCTION, ANNOTATIONS, AND FACSIMILES; A FULL COLLATION OF THE CODEX SINAITICUS WITH THE RECEIVED TEXT OF THE NEW TESTAMENT, TO WHICH IS PREFIXED A CRITICAL INTRODUCTION; THE NEW TESTAMENT IN THE ORIGINAL GREEK, ACCORDING TO THE TEXT FOLLOWED IN THE AUTHORIZED VERSION, TOGETHER WITH VARIATIONS ADOPTED IN THE REVISED VERSION; SIX LECTURES ON THE TEXT OF THE NT; PLAIN INTRODUCTION TO THE CRITICISM OF THE NEW TESTAMENT FOR USE OF BIBLICAL STUDENTS; NOV. TEXT. TEXTUS STEPHANUS] were world class scholars of unquestionable caliber who found against the Westcott/Hort theory of textual criticism from its very beginning. Edward Miller [editor of SCRIVENER'S 4TH EDITION OF PLAIN INTRODUCTION TO THE TEXTUAL CRITICISM OF THE CORRUPTION OF THE TRADITIONAL TEXT OF THE TEXT OF THE HOLY GOSPELS, and his uncle's (J.W. Burgon) posthumous works; and author OF A GUIDE TO THE TEXTUAL CRITICISM OF THE NEW TESTAMENT], Benjamin G. Wilkinson [OUR AUTHORIZED BIBLE VINDICATED], and

David O. Fuller [WHICH BIBLE?, TRUE OR FALSE? THE WESTCOTT-HORT THEORY EXAMINED; AND COUNTERFEIT OR GENUINE? MARK 16 JOHN 8?; all published by Grand Rapids International Publications: Grand Rapids, MI] have championed the RECEIVED TEXT through the 20th century. They have been joined by others: Wilbur N. Pickering [THE IDENTITY OF THE NEW TESTAMENT TEXT, Thomas Nelson, Inc.; 1977], Gordon Clark [LOGICAL CRITICISM OF TEXTUAL CRITICISM], Edward Freer Hills [THE KING JAMES VERSION DEFENDED] and Earnest Cadman Colwell [WHAT IS THE BEST NEW TESTAMENT?; The University of Chicago Press: Chicago; 1952].

John William Burgon stated the difference in approach to the Greek text, between the Majority adherents and the Westcott/Hort theorists, well: *"Does the truth of the Text of Scripture dwell with the vast multitude of copies, uncial and cursive, concerning which nothing is more remarkable than the marvelous agreement which subsists between them? Or is it rather to be supposed that the truth abides exclusively with a very little handful of manuscripts, which at once differ from the great bulk of witnesses, and -- strange to say -- also amongst themselves?*

"The advocates of the Traditional Text urge that the Consent without concert of so many hundreds of copies, executed by different persons, at diverse times, in widely sundered regions of the Church, is a presumptive proof of their trustworthiness, which nothing can invalidate but some sort of demonstration that they are untrustworthy guides after all.

"The advocates of the old uncials -- for it is the text exhibited by one or more of five Uncial Codexes known as A B Aleph C D which is set up with so much confidence -- are observed to claim that the truth must needs reside exclusively with the objects of their choice. They seem to base their claim on "antiquity;" but the real confidence of many of them lies evidently in a claim to subtle divination, which enables them to recognize a true reading or the true text when they see it. Strange, that it does not seem to have struck such critics that they assume the very thing which has to be proved." [THE TRADITIONAL TEXT OF THE HOLY GOSPELS VINDICATED AND ESTABLISHED; pp. 16,17]

The contrast between the two systems is seen in the Preface to THE OXFORD DEBATE ON THE TEXTUAL CRITICISM OF THE NEW TESTAMENT, HELD AT NEW COLLEGE ON MAY 6, 1897 [London; George Bell & Sons; 1897], in the words of advocates of each system.

PREFACE

The debate, of which the following pages contain a report, was the result of an offer courteously made by the Rev. Dr. Sanday, Lady Margaret Professor of Divinity, when I asked him whether those who are devoted to the study of Theology in Oxford would be ready to hear an explanation from me of the system of Textual Criticism advocated by the late Dean Burgon and myself, in order to the removal of misconceptions of it.

The speeches made in the debate have been referred both in manuscript and in type to the several speakers for their approval and corrections. In compliance with a thoughtful suggestion, the ensuing descriptions of the two present systems have been prefixed to the Report of the discussion, for the purpose of reference in the case of readers who have not a familiar acquaintance with them ready for use. And it is hoped that, taken together with the debate, they may form an easy means to many students of the Bible of learning some of the chief points in a very important study and controversy. The former of these two descriptions, according to Dr. Sanday's suggestion, has been taken with the kind leave of the author from *Our Bible and the Ancient Monuments*, by Frederick G. Kenyon, M.A., D.Litt., of the British Museum. Dr. Kenyon's description has received special praise from Mr. Hort in the Life of his illustrious father. The second I have prepared especially for this little book.

I. Dr. Hort's System.

' Westcott and Hort's Theory.

' One critic of earlier days, Griesbach by name, at the end of the last century, essayed the task of grouping, and two distinguished Cambridge scholars of our own day. Bishop Westcott and the late Professor Hort, have renewed the attempt with much greater success. They believe that by far the larger number of our extant MSS. can be shown to contain a revised (and less original) text ; that a comparatively small group has texts derived from manuscripts which escaped, or were previous to, this revision ; and that, consequently, the evidence of this small group is almost always to be preferred to that of the great mass of MSS. and versions. It is this theory, which has been set out with conspicuous learning and conviction by Dr. Hort, that we propose now to sketch in brief ; for it appears to mark an epoch in the history of New Testament criticism.

' Groups of MSS. in New Testament.

An examination of passages in which two or more different readings exist shows that one small group of authorities, consisting of the uncial manuscripts B, N, L, a few cursives such as Evan. 33, Act. 61, and the Memphitic and Thebaic versions, is generally found in agreement; another equally clearly marked group consists of D, the Old Latin and Old Syriac versions, and cursives 13, 69, 81 of the Gospels, 44, 137, and 180 of the Acts, and Evst. 39, with a few others more intermittently; while A, C (generally),the later uncials, and the great mass of cursives and the later versions form another group, numerically overwhelming. Sometimes each of these groups will have a distinct reading of its own ; sometimes two of them will be combined against the third; sometimes an authority which usually supports one group will be found with one of the others. But the general division into groups remains constant and is the basis of the present theory.

'Combined or "Conflate" Readings.

Next, it is possible to distinguish the origins and relative priority of the groups. In the first place, many passages occur in which the first group described above has one reading, the second has another, and the third combines the two. Thus in the last words of St. Luke's Gospel (as the Variorum Bible shows), K, B, C, L, with the Memphitic and one Syriac version, have " blessing God " ; D and the Old Latin have "praising God"; but A and twelve other uncials, all the cursives, the Vulgate and other versions, have " praising and blessing God." Instances like this occur, not once nor twice, but repeatedly.. Now it is in itself more probable that the combined reading in such cases is later than, and is the result of, two separate readings.

It is more likely that a copyist, finding two different words in two or more manuscripts before him, would put down both in his copy, than that two scribes, finding a combined phrase in their originals, would each select one part of it alone to copy, and would each select a different one. The motive for combining would be praiseworthy—the desire to make sure of keeping the right word by retaining both ; but the motive for separating would be vicious, since it involves the deliberate rejection of some words of the sacred text. Moreover we know that such combination was actually practised; for, as has been stated above, it is a marked characteristic of Lucian's edition of the Septuagint.

At this point the evidence of the Fathers becomes important as to both the time and the place of origin of these combined (or as Dr. Hort technically calls them "conflate") readings. They are found to be characteristic of the Scripture quotations in the works of Chrysostom, who was bishop of Antioch in Syria at the end of the fourth century, and of other writers in or about Antioch at the same time ; and thenceforward it is the predominant text in manuscripts, versions, and quotations. Hence this type of text, the text of our later uncials, cursives, early printed editions, and Authorized Version, is believed to have taken its rise in or near Antioch, and is known as the " Syrian " text. The type found in the second of the groups above described, that headed by D, the Old Latin and Old Syriac, is called the " Western " text, as being especially found in Latin manuscripts and in those which (like D) have both Greek and Latin texts, though it is certain that it had its origin in the East, probably in or near Asia Minor. There is another small group, earlier than the Syrian, but not represented continuously by any one MS. (mainly by C in the Gospels, A, C, in Acts and Epistles, with certain cursives and occasionally K and L), to which Dr. Hort gives the name of" Alexandrian." The remaining group, headed by B, may be best described as the " Neutral" text.

The "Syrian" Readings latest.

'Now among all the Fathers whose writings are left to us from before the middle of the third century (notably Irenaeus, Hippolytus, Clement, Origen, Tertullian, and Cyprian), we find readings belonging to the groups described as Western, Alexandrian, and Neutral, but no distinctly Syrian readings'. On the other hand, we have seen that in the latter part of the fourth century, especially in the region of Antioch, Syrian readings are found plentifully. Add to this the fact that, as stated above, the Syrian readings often show signs of having been derived from a combination of non-Syrian readings, and we have strong confirmation of the belief, which is the corner-stone of Dr. Hort's theory, that the Syrian type of text originated in a revision of the then existing texts, made about the end of the third century in or near Antioch. The result of accepting this conclusion obviously is, that where the Syrian text differs from that of the other groups, it must be rejected as being of later origin, and therefore less authentic; and when it is remembered that by far the greater number of our authorities contain a Syrian text, the importance of this conclusion is manifest. In spite of their numerical preponderance, the Syrian authorities must be relegated to the lowest place.

'The "Western" Group.

'Of the remaining groups, the Western text is characterized by considerable freedom of addition, and sometimes of omission. Whole verses, or even longer passages, are found in manuscripts of this family, which are entirely absent from all other copies. Some of them will be found enumerated in the following chapter in the description of D, the leading manuscript of this class. It is evident that this type of text must have had its origin in a time when strict exactitude in copying the books of the New Testament was not regarded as a necessary virtue. In early days the copies of the New Testament books were made for immediate edification, without any idea that they would be links in a chain for the transmission of the sacred texts to a distant future ; and a scribe might inno-cently, insert in the narrative additional details which he believed to be true and valuable. Fortunately the literary conscience of Antioch and Alexandria was more sensitive, and so this tendency did not spread very far, and was checked before it had greatly contaminated the Bible text. Western manuscripts often contain old and valuable readings, but any variety which shows traces of the characteristic Western vice of amplification or explanatory addition must be re-jected, unless it has strong support outside the purely Western group of author-ities.

-The "Alexandrian" Group.

' There remain the Alexandrian and the Neutral groups.

The Alexandrian text is represented, not so much by any individual MS. or ver-sion, as by certain readings found scattered about in manuscripts which else-where belong to one of the other groups. They are readings which have neither Western nor Syrian characteristics, and yet differ from what appears to be the earliest form of the text ; and being found most regularly in the quotations of Or-igen, Cyril of Alexandria, and other Alexandrian Fathers, as well as in the Mem-phitic version, they are reasonably named Alexandrian. Their characteristics are such as might naturally be due to such a centre of Greek scholarship, since they affect the style rather than the matter, and appear to rise mainly from a desire for correctness of language. They are consequently of minor im-portance, and are not always distinctly recognisable.

'The "Neutral " Group.

' The Neutral text, which we believe to represent most nearly the original text of the New Testament, is chiefly, recognisable by the absence of the various forms of aberration noticed in the other groups. Its main centre is at Alexandria, but it also appears in places widely removed from that centre. Sometimes sin-gle authorities of the Western group will part company with the rest of their family and exhibit readings which are plainly both ancient and non-Western, showing the existence of a text preceding the Western, and on which the West-ern variations have been grafted. This text must therefore not be assigned to any local centre. It belonged originally to all the Eastern world. In many parts of the East, notably in Asia Minor, it was superseded by the text which, from its transference to the Latin churches, we call Western. It remained pure longest in Alexandria, and is found in the writings of the Alexandrian Fathers, though even here slight changes of language were introduced, to which we have given the name of Alexandrian. Our main authority for it at the present day is the great Vatican manuscript known as B, and this is often supported by the equally an-cient Sinaitic manuscript (N), and by the other manuscripts and versions named above (p. vi). Where the readings of this Neutral text can be plainly discerned, as by the concurrence of all or most of these authorities, they may be accepted with confidence in the face of all the numerical preponderance of other texts ; and in so doing lies our best hope of recovering the true words of the New Tes-tament.'

Reference may also be made, for a short account, to the Life and Letters of Fen-ton John Anthony Hort, by his Son (Macmillan & Co.), vol. ii. pp. 344-353 ; and for more information, to Dr. Hort's celebrated Introduction (Macmillan & Co.) published in 1881.

II. BURGON AND MILLER'S SYSTEM.

§ 1. The True Text.

The great object of the Textual Criticism of the New Testament is the ascertainment of the actual or genuine words of the original autographs of the writers. Such an ascertainment can only be made with soundness and rest upon a broad basis, if all the evidence that can be collected be sifted and taken into account, and in the case of readings where the evidence is not consistent a balance be struck with all impartiality and justice. The words thus ascertained must constitute the True Text, of which the following must be the essential characteristics :

—I. It must be grounded upon an exhaustive view of the evidence of Greek copies in manuscript in the first place; and in all cases where they differ so as to afford doubt, of Versions or Translations into other languages, and of Quotations from the New Testament made by Fathers and other early writers.

3. It must have descended from the actual composition of Books of the New Testament, and must thus possess the highest possible antiquity.

3. It must be the outcome, not of one stem of descent, but of many. Consentient copies, made by successive transcription in the different countries where the Holy Scriptures were used, revered, and jealously watched, must confirm and check one another.

4. The descent must be continuous, without break or failure, or it would be no real descent, but a fragmentary or stunted line of genealogy, broken up or prematurely closed.

5. The Readings, or Text, must be such as to commend themselves to the enlightened judgement of Christendom.

' A. The Neutral Text.

Judged by these canons, the 'Neutral' Text of Dr. Hort must be rejected :

—

(1) It rests upon a very few documents arbitrarily selected, and is hopelessly condemned by the vast majority, it cannot reckon, therefore, number or variety. Aspiring to be the expression of the standard work of the Catholic Church, it fails in catholicity.

(2) As a collection of readings, apart from separate readings of early date, we maintain that it does not go further back than the School of Caesarea, and that in consequence it does not as a Text possess the highest antiquity.

(3) It has only one stem by hypothesis,—the probable archetype of B and K (the Vatican and Sinaitic), which Dr. Hort—gratuitously in our contention—thrusts back into the second century.

(4) It fails in continuity, because {a) there is thus a break or chasm in the earliest period, and [b) because by the admission of Dr. Hort himself it was superseded by the Traditional Text, by him termed ' Syrian,' before the end of the century (fourth) in which the latter Text acquired permanent expression.

(5) We contend that the Text itself is strangely blurred by numerous omissions of more or less length, including in feomie instances passages held by its supporters to be genuine extracts from the words of life of our Lord, and by other blemishes.

B. The Received Text.

The Textus Receptus, which was adopted in the revival of Greek learning, though it agrees substantially with our Canons, fails under the first, which is the virtual embodiment of them all ; because some of its readings are condemned by the balance struck upon all the evidence which has been assembled under the unprecedented advantages afforded in this century. There remains therefore, in accordance with the Canons already laid down, only

C. The Traditional Text.

We maintain, then, that the Traditional Text, duly ascertained according to all the evidence with all fairness of judgement, will represent the Text •which issued from the pens of the writers of the New Testament and was used all over the Church; and which after contracting corruption to a large extent, perhaps in most places, was gradually purged in the main as years went on, though something is left still to be done.

In the ascertainment of this Text or these Readings, guidance is to be sought under seven Notes of Truth, viz.

1. Antiquity of witnesses

2. Number „

3. Variety

4. Weight

5. Continuity „

6. The Context of Passages

7. Internal Evidence.

These Seven Notes of Truth, which are essential to the Traditional Text, sufficiently exhibit the agreement of it with the Canons laid down. In fact, coincidence with the first Canon implies coincidence with all the rest. But the age and the uninterrupted existence of the Traditional Text must be further proved.

Now Dr. Hort has admitted that the Traditional Text has existed ever since the later years of the fourth century. The question remains only as to the period between that date and the issue of the autographs. That the Traditional Text existed in that period is proved, in the absence of contemporaneous MSS. (except B and Aleph in the same century),

(1) By its undeniable prevalence afterwards. Such an almost universal prevalence implies a previous existence widely disseminated, and carried down in numerous stems of descent.

(2) The verdict of contemporaneous Fathers proves this position amply.

(3) The witness of the Peshitto and Old Latin Versions confirm it, to say nothing of occasional witness to separate readings found in the Egyptian Versions.

PREFACE XV

§ 2, Origin and Prevalence of Corruption.

We hold that Corruption arose at the very first propagation of stories or accounts, of our Lord's Life, probably even before the Gospels were written. It must have infected teaching spread from mouth to mouth, as well as writings more or less orderly, and more or less authorized. From this source mistakes must have crept in course of time, and in constant process of copying, into the authorized copies. In early though in later days as well, when or where education was not universal in the Church, and Christians had not yet imbibed familiarity with the words of Holy Scripture, Corruption spread further. A great deal of such Corruption, as we believe, found its way into the Vatican and Sinaitic manuscripts. It was persistent and multiform; and has been analyzed and explained in our second volume.

§ 3. Dr. Hori's disagreement with us.

(1) We entirely traverse the assertion, that * no distinctly Syrian (i. e. Traditional) readings ' are found amongst the earliest Fathers. Very many of the readings in the Traditional Text which are rejected by the other school are supported by those Fathers : and there is no evidence, as we maintain, to show that Thuy pertain to the other side or to any other Text rather than to us, or that readings confessedly old and found in the Traditional Text did not belong to that Text.

(2) We deny the existence of any Neutral Text, except as a collection, chiefly in B and Aleph, of corrupt readings, though we admit that many of those readings, if not most of them, are of very high antiquity. Considerable danger must attend all systems founded upon Texts or Groups,—valuable as these classifications are for subsidiary employment,—because they open the way more or less to speculation and are apt to foster a shallow and delusive sciolism instead of a judicial view of evidence. Readings depending upon actual evidence afford the only true basis, though study of the causes of corruption, as well as other investigations, sheds light upon the matter.

(3) Important points of contention exist with reference to the age of the Peshitto or great Syriac Version (as to which the age of the Curetonian or Lewis is mainly A distinct question), the Theory of the Western Texts and the Latin Versions (or Version), and of Texts in general, as will be seen in the Report of the debate.

For more information, reference may be made to The Traditional Text, Burgon and Miller (George Bell St Sons), 1896, and The Causes of Corruption (Bells), 1896. Also to Burgon's The Revision Revised, 1883 (John Murray), and to Miller's Textual Guide (Bells), 1885, and upon the question of the Peshitto, to an article in the Church Quarterly Review for April, 1895,

E. M.
9, Bradmore Road, Oxford,
May 24, 1897.

This is the question which underlies the text of the New Testament in the English translations. This is the determining factor in deciding whether the text underlying the King James Version is inadequate, or satisfactory. This is the pivotal point in the inclusion or omission of 48 verses in the New Testament, as well as portions of many others.

J.W. Burgon

There can be no Science of Textual Criticism, I repeat – and therefore no security for the Inspired Word – so long as the subjective judgment, which may easily degenerate into individual caprice, is allowed ever to determine which readings shall be rejected, which retained.

Begin with the evidence. When beginning an investigation, the question is how do you proceed. First gather the evidence, examine it, then draw your conclusion.

Textual Criticism as it has been practiced in the Critical Era has degenerated into a mind-reading exercise. "Internal Evidence" determines the result before objective evidence is examined. It is the equivalent of making up your mind what the results should be, then finding evidence to support your position rather than utilizing the evidence to come to your conclusion. Notice Greenlee's statement: *"... so that one's thinking from the first will not be unduly influenced by the evidence of the mss."* When you are attempting to come to a conclusion, unless you are not concerned about coming to the truth, how can you be *"unduly influenced by the evidence"?* Isn't the evidence exactly what you want to be influenced by? Yet, this has been the prevailing approach taken toward the text since the time of Westcott/Hort.

1. *Antiquity or Primitiveness;*

In taking a look at the witnesses, what do they date from? How old are they?

2. *Consent of Witnesses, or Number;*

How many witnesses are there? Count the number. Textual Criticism is not merely counting the number, but if the witnesses overwhelmingly favor a reading, there must be strong evidence to reject it.

3. *Variety of Witnesses, or Catholicity;*

Is the reading found in a variety of witnesses? Is it found in all regions the evidence comes from? Or, is it limited to the witnesses from a particular location? The truth is not limited to a certain location.

4. *Respectability of Witnesses, or Weight;*

If the witnesses are of similar number, what is the character of that witness? Are they reliable on other readings, or have they shown themselves to contain a corrupt text on a consistent basis? Where were the witnesses found? Were they taken out of a trash can because they were considered corrupt? All this has a bearing upon what weight should be granted to a witness in determining the validity of a reading they provide.

5. *Continuity, or Unbroken Tradition;*

When you string the witnesses together, do they portray a history which spans the ages, or do they merely represent an aberration in the history of the text?

6. *Evidence of the Entire Passage, or Context;*

After considering the witnesses, consider the flow of the text. Is there something about the context of the reading that tips the scale one way or another?

7. *Internal Considerations, or Reasonableness.*

Lastly consider the "internal considerations" which are more subjective than objective.

Operating with this procedure, the results of textual criticism achieves a different result than the "textual criticism" of the critical era.

J. Harold Greenlee

… there may be some advantage in considering internal evidence first, since it is more subjective, so that one's thinking will not from the first be unduly influenced by evidence of the mss.

It is more important to determine the possibilities for the individual variants than to examine what the witnesses say, so as not to be "unduly influenced by evidence of the mss."

for Deciding Internal Evidence

The following sets forth the process upon which the internal evidence is considered. These are the same concepts championed by Westcott/Hort, and developed by Lachman, Greisbach and Semler.

(i) *The shorter reading is often preferable…*

Assuming that scribes would always embellish the text rather than omit something from the text, accept the shorter reading.

(ii) *The harder reading is often preferable…*

Assuming that scribes would always attempt to simplify the text, accept the more difficult reading as the better.

(iii) *The reading from which the other readings in a variant could most easily have been derived is preferable…*

Assuming that you know what the copyists did or would do, accept the reading you can best guess the explanation of.

(iv) *The reading which is characteristic of the author is generally preferable…*

Assuming that you know what the author would have said, accept the reading that that you guess he would have written.

Procedure for Deciding External Evidence

The following is the process to be used to determine the use of hard evidence.

   (i) Divide the manuscripts into text-types.

Assuming you know the history of the manuscripts, divide them into various text types (although few in any manuscripts are purely one of the text-types that are determined to be used).

   (ii) "The characteristics of the individual witnesses to a text-type must likewise be considered."

Each reading found in the evidence should be categorized by text-type, not just the evidence as a whole (even though the text-type is invented).

   (iii)"Which reading has the best mss. Support by text-types and/or parts of text-types."

Having artificially divided the manuscripts and evidence into categories, and having determined which category has priority over the others, see which reading is best supported by those manuscripts which you have predetermined were the best.

   (iv)Weigh the evidence against the internal evidence.

Take this evidence and conclusion and weigh it against the internal evidence to determine the accepted reading.

CONCLUSION

The question comes down to this: ***Should the evidence or the opinion of the critic decide the text of the New Testament?*** Is the text of the New Testament a matter of objective study, or is it a subjective conclusion? Should you allow the evidence to lead you to the conclusion, or should you conclude what you think is right, and manipulate the evidence to reach your conclusion?

Significant Portions & Whole Verses Omitted From the New Testament

Sometimes the question arises, "Is there really any difference in the Greek texts and translations in the English language?" This chart will show the major differences between the Greek texts which are used. There is even more difference in the manner the words are translated in these verses, and other verses.

**Significant Portions Of & Whole Verses Omitted
From the New Testament**

If AV space is blank, the entire verse is missing.

Matt.	AV/TR [words omitted]	WH	N	BS	AS	NAS	NIV	RSV	NKJ	CEB	ESV
5:27	*By them of old time*	O	O	O	O	O	O	O	--	O	O
5:44	*Bless them that curse you, do good to them that hate you*	O	O	O	O	O	O	O	--	O	O
5:44	*Despitefully use you, and*	O	O	O	O	O	O	O	--	O	O
6:13*	*For thine is the kingdom, and the power, and the glory, for ever. Amen*	O	O	O	O	SB	O	O	--	O	O
12:47		O	S B	S B	--	--	--	O	--	--	O

Verse	Phrase										
13:51*	*Jesus saith unto them*	O	O	O	O	O	O	O	--	--	O
15:6	*Or his mother*	O	-	O	O	--	O	O	--	O	O
15:8*	*Draweth nigh unto Me with their mouth, and*	O	O	O	O	O	O	O	--	O	O
17:21		O	O	O	O	O	O	O	--	O	O
18:11		O	O	O	O	S	O	O	--	O	O
19:9	*And whoso marrieth her which is put away doth commit adultery*	O	O	O	--	O	O	O	--	O	O
19:20	*From my youth*	O	O	O	O	O	O	O	--	O	O
20:7	*And whatsoever is right, that shall ye receive*	O	O	O	O	O	O	O	--	O	O
20:16	*For many be called, but few chosen*	O	O	O	O	O	O	O	--	O	O
20:22*	*And to be baptized with the baptism that I am baptized with*	O	O	O	O	O	O	O	--	O	O
20:23*	*And be baptized with the baptism that I am baptized with*	O	O	O	O	O	O	O	--	O	O
21:44		SB	SB	DB	--	SB	O	O	--	--	--
22:13	*And take him away*	O	O	O	O	O	O	O	--	O	O
23:4	*And grievous to be borne*	O	O	SB	--	O	O	--	--	O	O
23:5	*Of their garments*	O	O	O	--	--	--	O	--	--	O
23:14		O	O	O	O	SB	O	O	--	O	O
25:13*	*Wherein the Son of man cometh*	O	O	O	O	O	O	O	--	O	O
26:3	*And the scribes*	O	O	O	O	O	O	O	--	O	O
26:60	*Yet found they none*	O	O	O	O	O	O	O	--	O	--

27:35*++	That it might be fulfilled which was spoken by the prophet, They parted my garments among them, and upon my vesture did they cast lots	O	O	O	O	O	O	O	--	O	O
28:2	From the door	O	O	O	O	O	O	O	--	O	O
28:9*	As they went to tell His disciples	O	O	O	O	O	O	O	--	O	O

Mark	AV [words omitted]	WH	N	BS	AS	NAS	NIV	RSV	NKJ	CEB	ESV
1:1*++	The Son of God	O	O	SB	--	--	--	--	--	--	--
1:14	Of the kingdom	O	O	O	O	O	O	O	--	O	O
1:42*	As soon as He had spoken	O	O	O	O	O	O	O	--	O	O
3:5	Whole as the other	O	O	O	O	O	--	O	--	O	O
3:15	To heal sicknesses, and	O	O	O	O	O	O	O	--	O	O
6:11*	Verily I say unto you, It shall be more tolerable for Sodom and Gomorrha in the day of judgment, than for that city	O	O	O	O	O	O	O	--	O	O
6:33*	And came together unto Him	O	O	O	O	O	O	O	--	O	O
6:36	For they have nothing	O	O	O	O	O	O	O	--	O	O
7:2	They found fault	O	O	O	O	O	O	O	--	O	O
7:8	As the washing of pots and cups: and many other such things ye do	O	O	O	O	O	O	O	--	O	O
7:16		O	O	O	O	O	O	O	--	O	O
8:9	They that had eaten	O	O	O	O	O	O	O	--	O	O

8:26	*Nor tell it to any in the town*	O	O	O	O	O	O	O	--	O	O
9:38	*And he followeth not us*	O	--	O	O	O	O	O	--	--	--
9:44		O	O	O	O	O	O	O	--	O	O
9:45	*Into the fire that never shall be quenched*	O	O	O	O	O	O	O	--	O	O
9:46		O	O	O	O	O	O	O	--	O	O
9:49	*And every sacrifice shall be salted with salt*	O	O	O	O	O	O	O	--	O	O
10:7	*And cleave to his wife*	O	O	SB	--	O	--	--	--	--	O
10:21	*Take up the cross*	O	O	O	O	O	O	O	--	O	O
10:24++	*Them that trust in riches*	O	O	O	--	O	O	O	--	O	O
11:8	*And strawed them in the way*	O	O	O	O	O	O	O	--	--	--
11:10*	*In the name of the Lord*	O	O	O	O	O	O	O	--	O	O
11:23	*Whatsoever he saith*	O	O	O	O	O	O	O	--	O	O
11:26		O	O	O	O	O	O	O	--	O	O
12:23	*Therefore, when they shall rise*	O	--	SB	O	--	O	O	--	--	--
12:29	*Of all the commandments*	O	O	O	O	O	O	O	--	O	O
12:30	*This is the first com-mandment*	O	O	O	O	O	O	O	--	O	O
12:33	*And with all the soul*	O	O	O	O	O	O	O	--	O	O
13:11	*Neither do ye premedi-tate*	O	O	O	O	O	O	O	--	O	O
13:14	*Spoken of by Daniel the prophet*	O	O	O	O	O	O	O	--	O	O
14:19	*And another said, Is it I?*	O	O	O	O	O	O	O	--	--	O
14:27*	*Because of Me this night*	O	O	O	O	O	O	O	--	O	O

		WH	N	BS	AS	NAS	NIV	RSV	NKJ	CEB	ESV
14:68	And the cock crew	O	O	SB	--	O	O	O	--	--	--
14:70	And thy speech agreeth thereto	O	O	O	O	O	O	O	--	O	O
15:3*	But He answered nothing	O	O	O	O	O	O	O	--	O	O
15:28*		O	O	O	O	O	O	O	--	--	O
16:9-20		DB	DB	DB	--	SB	--	O	--	S^ DB	DB

Luke	AV [words omitted]	WH	N	BS	AS	NAS	NIV	RSV	NKJ	CEB	ESV
1:28	Blessed art thou among women	O	O	O	O	O	O	O	--	O	O
1:29	When she saw him	O	O	O	O	O	O	O	--	O	O
2:42	Up to Jerusalem	O	O	O	O	O	O	O	--	--	O
4:4*	But by every word of God	O	O	O	O	O	O	O	--	O	O
4:5	Into an high mountain	O	O	O	O	O	O	O	--	O	O
4:8*	Get thee behind Me, Satan	O	O	O	O	O	O	O	--	O	O
4:18	To heal the brokenhearted	O	O	O	O	O	O	O	--	O	O
5:38	And both are preserved	O	O	O	O	O	O	O	--	O	O
6:45	Treasure of his heart (bringeth forth ... evil)	O	O	O	O	O	--	--	--	O	O
7:31*	And the Lord said	O	O	O	O	O	O	O	--	O	O
8:43	And spent all her living upon physicians	O	O	S B	--	O	O	O	--	--	--
8:45	And they that were with Him	O	O	O	--	O	O	O	--	O	O
845*	And sayest thou, Who touched Me?	O	O	O	O	O	O	O	--	O	O

8:48	*Be of good comfort?*	O	O	O	O	O	O	O	--	O	O
8:54	*Put them all out, and*	O	O	O	O	O	O	O	--	O	O
9:10	*A desert place*	O	O	O	O	O	O	O	--	O	O
9:54	*Even as Elias did?*	O	O	O	O	O	O	O	--	O	O
9:55	*And said, Ye know not what manner of spirit ye are of*	O	O	O	O	O	O	O	--	O	O
9:56*	*For the Son of man is not come to destroy men's lives, but to save them*	O	O	O	O	O	O	O	--	O	O
10:38	*Into her house*	--	--	O	--	--	--	--	--	O	--
11:2*	*Which art in heaven*	O	O	O	O	O	O	O	--	O	O
11:2*	*Thy will be done, as in heaven, so in earth*	O	O	O	O	O	O	O	--	O	O
11:4	*But deliver us from evil*	O	O	O	O	O	O	O	--	O	O
11:11	*Bread of any of you ... will he give him a stone? Or if he ask*	O	O	O	--	O	O	O	--	O	O
11:44	*Scribes and Pharisees, hypocrites*	O	O	O	O	O	O	O	--	O	O
11:54*	*That they might accuse Him*	O	O	O	O	O	O	O	--	O	O
12:39	*He would have watched, and*	--	O	O	--	O	O	O	--	O	O
17:9*	*Him? Trow not*	O	O	O	O	O	O	O	--	O	O
17:24*	*In His day*	O	--	S B	--	--	--	--	--	O	--
17:36		O	O	O	O	O	O	O	--	O	O
18:24	*That he was very sorrow-ful*	O	O	S B	O	O	O	O	--	O	--
19:45	*Therein, and them that bought*	O	O	O	O	O	O	O	--	O	O

20:13	*When they see him*	O	O	O	O	O	O	O	--	O	O
20:23*	*Why tempt ye Me?*	O	O	O	O	O	O	O	--	O	O
20:30	*Took her to wife, and he died childless*	O	O	O	O	O	O	O	--	O	O
22:20		DB	DB	--	--	--	--	O	--	--	--
22:43		DB	DB	DB	--	--	--	--	--	--	--
22:44		DB	DB	DB	--	--	--	--	--	--	--
22:31*	*And the Lord said*	O	O	O	O	O	O	O	--	O	O
22:64*	*They struck Him on the face*	O	O	O	O	O	O	O	--	O	O
22:68*	*Me, nor let Me go*	O	O	O	O	O	O	O	--	O	O
23:17		O	O	O	O	O	O	O	--	O	O
23:23	*And of the chief priests*	O	O	O	O	O	O	O	--	O	O
23:38	*Written ... in letters of Greek, and Latin, and Hebrew*	O	O	O	O	O	O	O	--	O	O
24:1	*And certain others with them*	O	O	O	O	O	O	O	--	O	O
24:12*		DB	O	--	--	SB	--	O	--	--	--
24:36*	*And saith unto them, Peace be unto you*	DB	O	--	--	O	--	O	--	--	--
24:40*		DB	O	--	--	O	--	O	--	--	--
24:42	*And of an honeycomb*	O	O	O	O	O	O	O	--	O	O
24:46	*And thus it behooved*	O	O	O	O	O	O	O	--	O	O
24:51*++	*And carried up into heaven*	DB	O	--	--	O	--	O	--	--	--
24:52*	*Worshipped Him*	DB	O	--	--	O	--	O	--	--	--

John	AV [words omitted]	WH	N	BS	AS	NAS	NIV	RSV	NKJ	CEB	ESV
1:27*++	Is preferred before me	O	O	O	O	O	O	O	--	O	O
3:13*++	Which is in heaven	O	O	O	--	O	O	O	--	O	O
3:15	Should not perish, but	O	O	O	O	O	O	O	--	O	O
5:3	Waiting for the moving of the water	O	O	O	O	O	O	O	--	O	O
5:4		O	O	O	O	O	O	O	--	O	O
5:16*	And sought to slay Him	O	O	O	O	O	O	O	--	O	O
6:11	To the disciples, and the disciples	O	O	O	O	O	O	O	--	O	O
6:22*	That one whereinto His disciples were en-tered	O	O	O	O	O	O	O	--	O	O
6:47*++	On Me	O	O	O	O	O	O	O	--	O	O
6:51*	Which I will give	O	O	O	--	--	--	--	--	--	O
7:46	Like this Man	O	--	O	O	--	--	--	--	O	--
7:53-8:11		O	O	O	O	O	O	O	--	DB	SB/DB
8:9	Being convicted by their own conscience	O	O	O	O	O	O	O	--	O	O
8:9	Even unto the last	O	O	O	--	O	O	O	--	O	O
8:10	And saw none but the woman	O	O	O	O	O	O	O	--	O	O
8:10	Those thine accusers?	O	O	O	O	O	O	O	--	O	O
8:59*++	Going through the midst of them, and so passed by	O	O	O	O	O	O	O	--	O	O
9:6	Of the blind man	O	O	O	O	O	O	O	--	O	O
10:13	The hireling fleeth	O	O	O	--	--	--	--	--	O	O
10:26	As I said unto you	O	O	O	O	O	O	O	--	O	O

11:41	Where the dead was laid	O	O	O	O	O	O	O	--	O	O
12:1	Which had been dead	O	O	O	O	O	O	O	--	O	O
13:32*	If God be glorified in Him	O	--	S B	O	--	--	--	--	--	--
16:16*	Because I go to the Father	O	O	O	O	O	O	O	--	O	O
17:12	In the world	O	O	O	O	O	O	O	--	O	O
19:16	And led Him away	O	O	O	O	O	O	O	--	O	O

Acts	AV [words omitted]	WH	N	BS	AS	NAS	NIV	RSV	NKJ	CEB	ESV
2:30*	According to the flesh, He would raise up Christ	O	O	O	O	O	O	O	--	O	O
2:47	To the church	O	O	O	O	--	--	--	--	O	O
3:11	The lame man which was healed	O	O	O	O	O	O	O	--	O	O
7:37*	Him shall ye hear	O	O	O	O	O	O	O	--	O	O
8:37		O	O	O	O	O	O	O	--	O	O
9:5	It is hard for thee to kick against the pricks	O	O	O	O	O	O	O	--	O	O
9:6*	And he trembling and astonished said, Lord, what would Thou have me to do? And the Lord said unto him,	O	O	O	O	O	O	O	--	O	O
10:6	He shall tell thee what thou oughtest to do	O	O	O	O	O	O	O	--	O	O
10:12	And wild beasts	O	O	O	O	O	O	O	--	O	O
10:21	Which were sent unto him from Cornelius	O	O	O	O	O	O	O	--	O	O
10:32	Who, when he cometh, shall speak unto thee	O	O	O	O	O	O	O	--	O	O

13:42	*The Jews ... out of the synagogue, the Gentiles*	O	O	O	O	O	O	O	--	O	O
15:18*	*Unto God are all His works*	O	O	O	O	O	O	O	--	O	O
15:24	*Saying, you must be circumcised,* *And keep the law*	O	O	O	O	O	O	O	--	O	O
15:34		O	O	O	O	O	O	O	--	O	O
18:21	*I must by all means keep this feast that cometh in Jerusalem*	O	O	O	O	O	O	O	--	O	O
20:15	*And tarried at Trogyllium*	O	O	O	O	O	O	O	--	O	O
21:8	*That were of Paul's company*	O	O	O	O	O	O	O	--	O	O
21:22	*The multitude must needs come together: for*	O	O	O	O	O	O	O	--	O	O
21:25	*That they observe no such thing, save only*	O	O	O	O	O	O	O	--	O	O
22:20	*Unto his death*	O	O	O	O	O	O	O	--	O	O
22:29	*And were afraid*	O	O	O	O	O	O	O	O	O	O
23:9*	*Let us not fight against God*	O	O	O	O	O	O	O	--	O	O
24:6	*And would have judged according to our law*	O	O	O	O	O	O	O	--	O	O
24:8	*Commanding his accusers to come unto thee*	O	O	O	O	O	O	O	--	O	O
24:26	*That he might loose him*	O	O	O	O	O	O	O	--	O	O
26:30	*And when he had thus spoken*	O	O	O	O	O	O	O	--	O	O

28:16	The centurion delivered the prisoners to the captain of the guard	O	O	O	O	O	O	O	--	O	O

Rom.	AV [words omitted]	WH	N	BS	AS	NAS	NIV	RSV	NKJ	CEB	ESV
1:16*	Of Christ	O	O	O	O	O	O	O	--	O	O
8:1*	Who walk not after the flesh, but after the Spirit	O	O	O	O	O	O	O	--	O	O
9:28	In righteousness: because a short work	O	O	O	O	O	O	O	--	O	O
10:15	Preach the gospel of peace	O	O	O	O	O	O	O	--	O	O
11:6	But if it be of works, then is it no more grace: otherwise work is no more work	O	O	O	O	O	O	O	--	O	O
13:9	Thou shalt not bear false witness	O	O	O	O	O	O	O	--	O	O
14:6*	He that regardeth not the day, to the Lord he doeth not regard it	O	O	O	O	O	O	O	--	O	O
14:21	Or is offended, or is made weak	O	O	O	O	O	O	O	--	O	O
15:24	I will come to you	O	O	O	O	O	O	O	--	--	O
15:29	Of the gospel	O	O	O	O	O	O	O	--	O	O
16:24		O	O	O	O	O	O	O	--	O	O

1 Cor.	AV [words omitted]	WH	N	BS	AS	NAS	NIV	RSV	NKJ	CEB	ESV
6:20*	And in your spirit, which are God's	O	O	O	O	O	O	O	--	O	O

10:28*	For the earth is the Lord's and the fullness thereof	O	O	O	O	O	O	O	--	O	O
11:24	Take, eat	O	O	O	O	O	O	O	--	O	O
15:54	This corruptible shall have put on corruption, and	O	-	-	-	-	-	-	--	--	O

Gal.	AV [words omitted]	WH	N	BS	AS	NAS	NIV	RSV	NKJ	CEB	ESV
3:1	That ye should not obey the truth	O	O	O	O	O	O	O	--	O	O

Eph.	AV [words omitted]	WH	N	BS	AS	NAS	NIV	RSV	NKJ	CEB	ESV
3:14*	Of our Lord Jesus Christ	O	O	O	O	O	O	O	--	O	O
5:30*	Of His flesh, and of His bones	O	O	O	O	O	O	O	--	O	O

Phil.	AV [words omitted]	WH	N	BS	AS	NAS	NIV	RSV	NKJ	CEB	ESV
3:16	By the same rule, let us mind the same thing	O	O	O	O	O	O	O	--	O	O
3:21	That it may be	O	O	O	-	O	-	O	--	--	O

Col.	AV [words omitted]	WH	N	BS	AS	NAS	NIV	RSV	NKJ	CEB	ESV
1:2*	And the Lord Jesus Christ	O	O	O	O	O	O	O	--	O	O
1:14*++	Through His blood	O	O	O	O	O	O	O	--	O	O
3:6	On the children of disobedience	O	O	S B	-	O	O	O	--	--	O

1 Thess.	AV [words omitted]	WH	N	BS	ASV	NAS	NIV	RSV	NKJV	CEB	ESV
1:1*	*From God our Father, … Jesus Christ*	O	O	O	O	O	O	O	--	O	--

1 Tim.	AV [words omitted]	WH	N	BS	AS	NAS	NIV	RSV	NKJ	CEB	ESV
3:3	*Not greedy of filthy lucre*	O	O	O	O	O	O	O	--	O	--
6:5	*From such withdraw thy-self*	O	O	O	O	O	O	O	--	O	O
6:7	*It is certain*	O	O	O	O	O	O	O	--	O	O

Heb.	AV [words omitted]	WH	N	BS	AS	NAS	NIV	RSV	NKJ	CEB	ESV
2:7*	*And didst set him over the works of Thy hands*	SB	O	O	-	-	O	O	--	O	O
3:6	*Firm unto the end*	SB	S B	O	-	-	O	O	--	O	O
7:21	*After the order of Mel-chisedec*	O	O	O	O	O	O	O	--	O	O
8:12	*And their iniquities*	O	O	O	O	O	O	O	--	O	O
10:30*	*Saith the Lord*	O	O	O	O	O	O	O	--	O	O
10:34	*In heaven*	O	O	O	O	O	O	O	--	O	O
11:11	*Was delivered of a child*	O	O	O	O	O	O	O	--	--	O
11:13	*And were persuaded of them*	O	O	O	O	O	O	O	--	O	O
12:20	*Or thrust through with a dart*	O	O	O	O	O	O	O	--	O	O

1 Pet.	AV [words omitted]	WH	N	BS	AS	NAS	NIV	RSV	NKJ	CEB	ESV
1:22*	*Through the Spirit*	O	O	O	O	O	O	O	--	O	O
4:3	*Of our life*	O	O	O	O	O	O	O	--	O	O

4:14*	On their part He is evil spoken of, but on your part He is glorified	O	O	O	O	O	O	O	--	O	O
5:2	Taking the oversight thereof	O	O	S B	-	O	-	O	--	--	--

2 Pet.	AV [words omitted]	WH	N	BS	AS	NAS	NIV	RSV	NKJ	CEB	ESV
3:10	In the night	O	O	O	O	O	O	O	--	O	O

1 John	AV [words omitted]	WH	N	BS	AS	NAS	NIV	RSV	NKJ	CEB	ESV
4:3*++	Christ is come in the flesh	O	O	O	O	O	O	O	--	O	O
5:7		O	O	O	O	O	O	O	--	O	O
5:13*	And that ye may believe on the name of the Son of God	O	O	O	O	O	O	O	--	O	O

Rev.	AV [words omitted]	WH	N	BS	AS	NAS	NIV	RSV	NKJ	CEB	ESV
1:8*++	The Beginning and the Ending	O	O	O	O	O	O	O	--	O	O
1:11*++	I am the Alpha and Omega, the First and the Last: and	O	O	O	O	O	O	O	--	O	O
1:11	Which are in Asia	O	O	O	O	O	O	O	--	O	O
5:14	Him that liveth for ever and ever	O	O	O	O	O	O	O	--	O	O
11:1	And the angel stood	O	O	O	O	O	O	O	--	O	O
11:17*++	And art to come	O	O	O	O	O	O	O	--	O	O
14:5*	Before the throne of God	O	O	O	O	O	O	O	--	O	O

		AV	WH	N	BS	ASV	NAS	NIV	RSV	NKJV	CEB	ESV
15:2	*Over his mark*	O	O	O	O	O	O	O	--	O	O	
21:24	*Of them which are saved*	O	O	O	O	O	O	O	--	O	O	

AV=Authorized Version [King James Version]; WH= Westcott/Hort Greek Text; N=Nestle/Aland Greek Text; BS=United Bible Society Greek Text; ASV=American Standard Version; NAS=New American Standard; NIV=New International Version; RSV=Revised Standard Version; NKJV=New King James Version; CEB=Common English Bible; ESV=English Standard Version

O=Omits; -- = includes; SB=Single Bracket (of dubious origin and included); DB=Double Bracket (was not in the original, but included anyway); S=Set aside; ^=inserts

Does Matthew 12:47 Belong in the New Testament?

This is the first of the whole verses omitted by WESTCOTT/HORT *in their Greek text*. It is also single bracketed [indicating a dubious origin] by NESTLES *and the* UNITED BIBLE SOCIETIES GREEK TEXTS, and is omitted by the original REVISED STANDARD VERSION.

Passage	TR	W/H	NT	UBS	MT	KJV	ASV	RSV	TEV	LB	NAS	NIV	NKJ
Mt. 12:47	-	O	S	S	-	-	-	O	-	-	-	-	-

The verse will be examined according to the method proposed by J.W. Burgon and Edward Miler.

Antiquity of witnesses

FOR	AGAINST
2ND CENTURY	
Diatessaron version	Curetorian Syriac version (II-VII)
Peshitta Syriac version (II-VII)	Sinaitic Syriac version (II-VII)
Harclean Syriac version (II-VII)	
3RD CENTURY	
Origen	Sahidic Coptic version (III-VI)
Bohairic Coptic version (III-VI)	
4TH CENTURY	
{Aleph} Sinaiticus uncial	{Aleph} Sinaiticus uncial

Vercellensis Old Latin version	B Vaticanus uncial
Vulgate version	Bobiensis Old Latin version (IV/V)
Armenian version (IV/V)	

Number

There are forty-four manuscripts which include the verse. UBSIII has four Greek manuscripts listed against it: Aland lists more, four uncials and three cursives – ℵ* B L Γ 579 597 1009. Still the number is forty-four to either four or seven: overwhelmingly in favor of the verse.

The versions, overwhelmingly eighteen to five, favor it.

Five early writers include the verse, zero omit it.

Numerically, the evidence is in favor of the inclusion of the verse.

FOR   AGAINST

GREEK MSS.	VERSIONS	EARLY WRITERS	BYZ. MSS.	TEXT	BYZ. MSS	EARLY WRITERS	VERSIONS	GREEK MSS.
44	18	3	+	Mt. 12:47	-	0	5	4

Variety

In terms of types of evidence, the uncials, the cursives, the versions and early writers all speak of the inclusion of the verse. Whereas, no early writer stands in favor of the exclusion of the verse, and only a handful of versions and Greek manuscripts. The only manuscripts omitting this verse are {Aleph} Sinaiticus, {B} Vaticanus and {L} Regius, along with a singular cursive manuscript {1009} from the 13th Century. The only versions omitting the verse are two older Syriac versions, and two Old Latin versions (Bobiensis and Corbiensis I).

Therefore, variety – both in type and location – undoubtedly and overwhelmingly indicates the inclusion of the verse.

Weight

The manuscripts which exclude the verse are (according to Aland) {Aleph} {B} {L} {Γ} 579 597 1009. As Hoskier's study proves, backed by the statements of Burgon, Miller, and Scrivener (among others), {Aleph} and {B} are corrupt and unreliable texts, although early and full texts. {L} or the Regius is known for its agreement with the older uncials, namely {Aleph} Sinaiticus and {B} Vaticanus. That is why Lachmann prized it so highly. Then it is omitted by three 13th Century cursives.

The majority of the uncials, cursives, lectionaries and all the writers who say anything about the passage include it. The combined testimony of the church throughout the ages in all the best manuscripts, both uncial and cursive, and some of the not so good, include the verse.

The weight of the evidence is for the inclusion of the verse.

Continuity

In the 2ND through 4TH Centuries, the evidence is somewhat even.

In the 2ND Century, the Diatessaron along with the Peshitta Syriac version and Harclean Syriac version (dated somewhere between the 2ND and the 7TH Centuries) include the verse; while the Curetorian Syriac and the Sinaitic Syriac versions (dated somewhere between the 2ND and the 7TH Centuries) omit the verse.

In the 3RD Century Origen notes the verse belongs along with the Bohairic Coptic version (which is dated somewhere between the 3RD and 6TH Centuries); while the Sahidic Coptic version (which is dated somewhere between the 3RD and 6TH Centuries) excludes it.

In the 4TH Century, the Sinaiticus (Aleph) uncial gives mixed testimony, cited by the UBS for both the inclusion and exclusion of the verse. In addition, the Vercellensis Old Latin version, the Vulgate version, and the Armenian version (dated either the 4TH or 5TH Century) include the verse; while the Vaticanus (B) uncial and the Bobiensis Old Latin Version (dated either the 4TH or 5TH Century) omit the verse.

From this point, the weight of the evidence is overwhelming. One uncial, one Old Latin version, one minuscule and one lectionary omit the verse – every other witness includes the verse.

In the 5TH Century, two uncials (Ephraemi Rescriptus {C}, the Freer Gospels {W}), four Old Latin versions (the Veronensis, the Bezae Cantabrigiensis, the Corbiensis II, and the Claromontanus), the Georgian version and the early writer Chrysostom all include the verse.

In the 6TH Century, one uncial (D), the Brixianus Old Latin version and the Ethiopic version include the verse.

In the 7TH Century, three Old Latin versions include the verse (the Aureus, the Monacensis, the Rhedigeranus).

In the 8TH Century, the lone uncial Regius (L) omits the verse.

In the 9TH Century, four uncials (K, Δ, Θ, Π); along with three minuscules (33, 565, 892), and one Old Latin version (the Sangermanensis) include the verse.

In the 10TH Century, one uncial (X) and one minuscule (1079) include the verse, while one lone Old Latin version (Corbiensis I) excludes the verse.

In the 11TH Century, seven minuscules (28, 700, 1216, 124, 230, 174, 788) include the verse.

In the 12TH Century, thirteen minuscules (1010, 1071, 1195, 1230, 1344, 1365, 1646, 1, 346, 543, 826, 828, 983) and one Old Latin version (Colbertinus) include the verse.

In the 13TH Century, five minuscules (1242, 1546, 118, 13, 1689) include the verse, and one minuscule (1009) and one lectionary (L12) omit the verse.

In the 14TH Century, four minuscules (2148, 2174, 131, 209) include the verse.

In the 15TH Century, two minuscules (1253, 69) include the verse.

THE EVIDENCE FOR MATTHEW 12:47

FOR	AGAINST
2ND CENTURY	
Diatessaron version	Curetorian Syriac version (II-VII)
Peshitta Syriac version (II-VII)	Sinaitic Syriac version (II-VII)

Harclean Syriac version (II-VII)

3RD CENTURY

Origen

Bohairic Coptic version (III-VI)

Sahidic Coptic version (III-VI)

4TH CENTURY

Aleph Sinaiticus uncial

Vercellensis Old Latin version

Vulgate version

Armenian version (IV/V)

Aleph Sinaiticus uncial

B Vaticanus uncial

Bobiensis Old Latin version (IV/V)

5TH CENTURY

C Ephraemi Rescriptus uncial

W Freer Gospels uncial

Veronensis Old Latin version

Bezae Cantabrigiensis Old Latin version

Corbiensis II Old Latin version

Claromontanus Old Latin version

Georgian version

Chrysostom

6TH CENTURY

D uncial

Brixianus Old Latin version

Ethiopic version

7TH CENTURY

Aureus Old Latin version

Monacensis Old Latin version

Rhedigeranus Old Latin version

8TH CENTURY

L Regius uncial

9TH CENTURY

K uncial

Delta uncial

Theta uncial

Pi uncial

33 minuscule

565 minuscule

892 minuscule

Sangermanensis Old Latin version

10TH CENTURY

X uncial

1079 minuscule

Corbiensis I Old Latin version

11TH CENTURY

28 minuscule

700 minuscule

1216 minuscule

124 minuscule

230 minuscule

174 minuscule

788 minuscule

12TH CENTURY

1010 minuscule

1071 minuscule

1195 minuscule

1230 minuscule

1344 minuscule

1365 minuscule

1646 minuscule

1 minuscule

346 minuscule

543 minuscule

826 minuscule

828 minuscule

983 minuscule

Colbertinus Old Latin version

13TH CENTURY

1242 minuscule

1546 minuscule

118 minuscule

13 minuscule

1689 minuscule

1009 minuscule

L12 lectionary

14TH CENTURY

2148 minuscule

2174 minuscule

131 minuscule

209 minuscule

15TH CENTURY

1253 minuscule

69 minuscule

The evidence for the omission of the verse is spotty. No evidence (no manuscript, no version, no lectionary, no early writer) is cited for the 5th, 6th, 7th, 9th, 11th, 12th, 14th, and 15th centuries. There is no continuity to the evidence. It is missing in too many centuries.

The Context of Passage

"While he yet talked to the people, behold, his mother and his brethren stood without, desiring to speak with him. Then one said unto him, Behold, thy mother and thy brethren stand without, desiring to speak with thee. But he answered and said unto him that told him, Who is my mother? and who are my brethren? And he stretched forth his hand toward his disciples, and said, Behold my mother and my brethren! For whosoever shall do the will of my Father which is in heaven, the same is my brother, and sister, and mother." (MATTHEW 12:46-50 KJV)

Jesus had answered the accusations of the Pharisees, and has just finished rebuking the scribes and the Pharisees for seeking after a sign. While He was conversing with these men, His mother and brothers came to the location where He was, and wished to talk with him.

The verse in question has someone bringing this to His attention.

The following verse begins, "But he answered and said unto him that told him, ..." If the verse is omitted, Jesus answers an address that was never made to Him. Our Lord here directs His remarks in answer to the remark that was made. There is no impotence for the answer if there is no comment.

Christ utilizes the opportunity that He is given here to make a point. It is not physical relations that make the greatest importance; it is the spiritual. Yes, the woman waiting outside to speak to Him may have given Him birth, and the men waiting outside may be the closest of kin; but, His purpose here on the earth was to do His Father's business. He had at a young age already stated this point rather emphatically. [see LUKE 2:49]. To make His point at this time, He waves His hand toward the disciples (those to whom he is talking) and says, *"Behold my mother and my brethren! For whosoever shall do the will of my Father which is in heaven, the same is my brother, and sister, and mother."*

The verse fits into the flow of the passage wonderfully.

Internal Evidence.

There appears to be no objection internally to the verse.

The conclusion

Metzger, in writing for the editors of the United Bible Societies Greek New Testament says:

"The sentence, which seems to be necessary for the sense of the following verses, apparently was accidentally omitted because of homoeoteleuton (λαλησαι ... λαλησαι). In view, however, of the age and weight of the diverse text-types that omit the words, the Committee enclosed the words within square brackets in order to indicate a certain amount of doubt concerning their right to stand in the text." [p.32]

This verse becomes an excellent example of how selective some textual critics are when it comes to evaluating the evidence. Undue weight is given to the Sinaiticus uncial {Aleph} and the Vaticanus uncial {B}.

When the seven points of truth are examined, all seven (**1. Antiquity, 2. Number, 3. Variety, 4. Weight, 5. Continuity, 6. Context of the Passage,** and **7. Internal Considerations**) are in favor of the inclusion of the verse.

Does Matthew 17:21 Belong in the New Testament?

This verse is included by THE TEXTUS RECEPTUS, THE MAJORITY TEXT, THE KING JAMES VERSION, THE LIVING BIBLE, THE NEW KING JAMES VERSION, and omitted by the WESTCOTT/HORT, THE NESTLE, AND THE UNITED BIBLE SOCIETIES' GREEK TEXTS, as well as BY THE AMERICAN STANDARD VERSION, THE REVISED STANDARD VERSION, THE NEW ENGLISH BIBLE, THE NEW AMERICAN STANDARD, THE NEW INTERNATIONAL VERSION, THE COMMON ENGLISH VERSION, THE ENGLISH STANDARD VERSION.

Passage	TR	W/H	NT	UBS	MT	KJV	ASV	RSV	TEV	LB	NAS	NIV	NKJ	CEV	ESV
Mt. 17:21	-	O	O	O	-	-	O	O	S	-	O	O	-	O	O

The verse will be examined according to the method proposed by J.W. Burgon and Edward Miler.

Antiquity of witnesses

The verse is attested for in the 2nd, 3rd and 4th centuries by versions ranging from the Syriac (Peshitta and Harclean) to the Armenian to the Bohairic Coptic, along with the Diatessaron, the Vulgate and Vercellensis Old Latin. Other Syriac versions (Curetonian, Sinaitic, and Palestinian – all younger than the Peshitta), and the Coptic Versions omit the verse.

Of the early writers, Origen, Hilary, Basil and Ambrose include the verse. One rejects it, Eusebius.

Two manuscripts from the 1st four centuries omit the verse: the Sinaiticus and the Vaticanus.

The verse unquestionably has ancient evidence for its inclusion.

FOR	AGAINST
2ND CENTURY	
Peshitta Syriac version (II-VII)	**Curetonian Syriac version (II-VII)**
Diatessaron version	**Sinaitic Syriac version (II-VII)**
	Palestinian Syriac (II-VI)
3RD CENTURY	
Bohairic Coptic version (III-VI)	**Sahidic Coptic version (III-VI)**
Origen	**Bohairic Coptic version (III-VI)**
4TH CENTURY	
Harclean Syriac version	
Armenian version (IV/V)	
Hilary	**Aleph Sinaiticus uncial**
Basil	**B Vaticanus uncial**
Ambrose	**Eusebius**
Vulgate version	
Vercellensis Old Latin version	

Number

There are forty-four Greek manuscripts which include the verse, and five which exclude it.

There are eighteen Versions which include the verse, and eight which exclude it.

There are three early writers which include the verse, and zero who exclude it.

It is found in the Byzantine Manuscripts, which text type the vast majority of Greek manuscripts are place in.

There is not a category in which the numbers do not favor the inclusion of the verse.

FOR   AGAINST

GREEK MSS.	VERSIONS	EARLY WRITERS	BYZ. MSS.	TEXT	BYZ. MSS	EARLY WRITERS	VERSIONS	GREEK MSS.
44	18	3	+	Mt. 17:21	-	0	8	5

Variety

The verse is testified by Greek manuscripts (both Uncial and Minuscule) from every area that they are extant. It is included in versions coming from various areas and influences. The early writers who testify to its inclusion are few, but they do not waver. It is not found just in the New Testaments in a particular area, but is found universally.

Weight

The five Biblical manuscripts which exclude the verse are: the Sinaiticus, the Vaticanus, Korideth Theta uncial (from the 9th century), plus the 33 minuscule and 892 minuscule (both from the 9th century). The aberrations of the 9th century can easily be dismissed when you consider the type and character of the Sinaiticus and Vaticanus manuscripts. Both are early and complete manuscripts, but the multiple hands which corrected them, and the multiple times that they cannot come to agreement as to the text, show that they though of great interest are not trustworthy. That would leave only the witness of manuscripts from the 9th century alone for the omission of the verse. These can hardly be sufficient evidence to overthrow the testimony of manuscripts which predominate from the 5th century on.

Although the version evidence for the omission of the verse is stronger. The number and universality of the versions which include it would outweigh its exclusion. In the early centuries, the Peshitta is a better translation than the other Syriac (some modern scholars notwithstanding).

The testimony of early writers is slightly more credible for the inclusion of the verse.

Continuity

In the 2ND Century, the Diatessaron and the Peshitta Syriac version (dating somewhere between the 2ND and 7TH Centuries) include the verse, while three Syriac versions (the Curetonian, the Sinaitic, the Palestinian) (dating somewhere between the 2ND and 7TH Centuries) omit the verse.

In the 3RD Century, Origen includes the verse, the Sahidic Coptic version (dating between the 3RD and 6TH Centuries) omits the verse, and the Bohairic Coptic version (dating somewhere between the 3RD and 6TH Centuries) gives mixed testimony both including and omitting the verse.

From the 4TH Century on, the weight of the evidence clearly sides with the inclusion of the verse.

In the 4TH Century, four versions (the Harclean Syriac, the Armenian {IV/V}, the Vulgate, the Vercellensis Old Latin), along with Hilary, Basil and Ambrose all include the verse. It is omitted by two uncials (Sinaiticus {Aleph}, Vaticanus {B}) and Eusebius.

In the 5TH Century, two uncials (Ephraemi Rescriptus {C}, Freer Gospels {W}), four Old Latin versions (Veronensis, Bezae Cantabrigiensis, Corbeiensis II, Sangallensis), and two early writers (Chrysostom, Augustine) which include the verse. The Georgian version is listed as split testimony, both including and excluding the verse. The Palatinus Old Latin version omits Matthew 7:21.

In the 6TH Century, one uncial (Bezae Cantabrigiensis {D}) and two versions (Brixianus Old

Latin & Pell Platt & Praetorius Ethiopic) include the verse, while one version (Rome Ethiopic) omits it.

In the 7TH Century, four Old Latin versions (Aureus, Monacensis, Usserianus I, Rhedigeranus or Legionensis {dated either the 7TH or the 8TH Century}) include the verse.

In the 8TH Century, one uncial (Regius {L}) includes the verse.

In the 9TH Century, three uncials (K, Δ, Π), one minuscule (565), and one version (Sanger-manensis Old Latin) include the verse. One minuscule (892) includes the verse in the margin but omits it in the text. One uncial (Koridethi Θ) and one minuscule (33) omit the verse.

In the 10TH Century, one uncial (X) and one minuscule (1079) include the verse.

In the 11TH Century, seven minuscules (28, 700, 1216, 124, 174, 230, 788) include the verse.

In the 12TH Century, fourteen minuscules (1010, 1071, 1195, 1230, 1241, 1344, 1365, 1646, 1, 346, 543, 826, 828, 983) and the Colbertinus Old Latin version (dated either the 12TH or 13TH Century) include the verse.

In the 13TH Century, six minuscules (1009, 1242, 1546, 118, 13, 1689) include the verse while some manuscripts of the Ethiopic version {dated either 13TH or 14TH Century) omit it.

In the 14TH Century, four minuscule (2148, 2174, 131, 209) include the verse.

In the 15TH Century, two minuscules (1253, 69) include the verses.

THE EVIDENCE FOR MATTHEW 17:21

FOR	AGAINST
2ND CENTURY	
Peshitta Syriac version (II-VII)	Curetonian Syriac version (II-VII)
Diatessaron version	Sinaitic Syriac version (II-VII)
	Palestinian Syriac (II-VI)
3RD CENTURY	
Bohairic Coptic version (III-VI)	Sahidic Coptic version (III-VI)
Origen	Bohairic Coptic version (III-VI)
4TH CENTURY	
Harclean Syriac version	Aleph Sinaiticus uncial
Armenian version (IV/V)	B Vaticanus uncial
Hilary	Eusebius

Basil

Ambrose

Vulgate version

Vercellensis Old Latin version

5TH CENTURY

C Ephraemi Rescriptus uncial

W Freer Gospels uncial

Veronensis Old Latin version

Bezae Cantabrigiensis Old Latin version

Corbeiensis II Old Latin version

Sangallensis Old Latin version

Georgian version

Chrysostom

Augustine

Palatinus Old Latin version

Georgian version

6TH CENTURY

D Bezae Cantabrigiensis uncial

Brixianus Old Latin version

Pell Platt & Praetorius Ethiopic version

Rome Ethiopic version

7TH CENTURY

Aureus Old Latin version

Monacensis Old Latin version

Usserianus I Old Latin version

Rhedigeranus or Leionensis Old Latin version (VII/VIII)

8TH CENTURY

L Regius uncial

9TH CENTURY

K uncial

Delta uncial

Pi uncial

565 minuscule

Margin of 892 minuscule

Sangermanensis Old Latin version

Korideth Theta uncial

33 minuscule

892 minuscule

10TH CENTURY

X uncial

1079 minuscule

11TH CENTURY

28 minuscule

700 minuscule

1216 minuscule

124 minuscule

174 minuscule

230 minuscule

788 minuscule

12TH CENTURY

1010 minuscule

1071 minuscule

1195 minuscule

1230 minuscule

1241 minuscule

1344 minuscule

1365 minuscule

1646 minuscule

1 minuscule

346 minuscule

543 minuscule

826 minuscule

828 minuscule

983 minuscule

Colbertinus Old Latin version (XII/XIII)

13TH CENTURY

1009 minuscule

1242 minuscule

1546 minuscule

118 minuscule

Ethiopic version (XIII-XIV)

13 minuscule

1689 minuscule

14TH CENTURY

2148 minuscule

2174 minuscule

131 minuscule

209 minuscule

15TH CENTURY

1253 minuscule

69 minuscule

The majority of lectionaries in the Synaxarion (the so-called "movable year" beginning with Easter) and in the Menologian (the "fixed year" beginning with September 1) include the verse.

The majority of Byzantine manuscripts include this verse.

The 2nd century sees the evidence slightly in favor of the omission of the verse, but beginning with the 3rd century the inclusion evidence is equal. From that point the inclusion evidence is always predominate, with no evidence for the omission of the verse in the 7th, 8th, 10th, 11th, 12th, 14th, or 15th centuries cited. Such holes in the evidence for the omission of the verse give one great pause as to the validity of the argument.

The Context of Passage

And when they were come to the multitude, there came to him a certain man, kneeling down to him, and saying, Lord, have mercy on my son: for he is lunatick, and sore vexed: for oft-times he falleth into the fire, and oft into the water. And I brought him to thy disciples, and they could not cure him. Then Jesus answered and said, O faithless and perverse generation, how long shall I be with you? how long shall I suffer you? bring him hither to me. And Jesus rebuked the devil; and he departed out of him: and the child was cured from that very hour. Then came the disciples to Jesus apart, and said, Why could not we cast him out? And Jesus said unto them, Because of your unbelief: for verily I say unto you, If ye have faith as a grain of mustard seed, ye shall say unto this mountain, Remove hence to yonder place; and it shall remove; and nothing shall be impossible unto you. **Howbeit this kind goeth not out but by prayer and fasting.** (MATTHEW 17:14-21 KJV)

A certain man came to Jesus, pleading with Him to have mercy on his son. He was a "lunatic" and often fell into fire and the water. He had brought his son to the disciples, but they were unable to cure him.

Jesus' reaction was one of frustration. *"O faithless and perverse generation, how long shall I be with you? How long shall I suffer you?"* Jesus rebuked the devil that was in the son, and he was cured immediately.

After the man and his son left, the disciples came to Jesus, and asked why they failed when they attempted to cast out the demon. Jesus' answer was blunt and direct, *"Because of your unbelief ..."* They had been with the Savior, but they still were plagued with unbelief. Faith the size of a grain of mustard seed, a small seed indeed, can move mountains. With faith, nothing is nor would be impossible for the disciples.

There is one final thing which is needed if they were to displace demons like this one: *"Howbeit this kind goeth not out but by prayer and fasting."* The faith they needed would be generated by a time of concentrated prayer, not even interrupted for food.

There is no question but that this verse fits into the flow.

Internal Evidence.

There appears to be no objection internally to the verse.

The conclusion

Metzger says, *"Since there is no good reason why the passage, if originally present in Matthew, should have been omitted, and since copyists frequently inserted material derived from another Gospel, it appears that most manuscripts have been assimilated to the parallel in Mk 9.29."* [p. 43]

Because it is missing from a handful of manuscripts, the verse must have been added? Perhaps, because it is missing from a handful of manuscripts, the verse must have been omitted.

It fits the flow, the literary style, and the evidence is preponderantly in favor of the verse. There is no question that this verse belongs in the Gospel of Matthew.

When the seven points of truth are examined, all seven (**1. Antiquity, 2. Number, 3. Variety, 4. Weight, 5. Continuity, 6. Context of the Passage,** and **7. Internal Considerations**) are in favor of the inclusion of the verse.

Does Matthew 18:11 Belong in the New Testament?

This verse is included by THE TEXTUS RECEPTUS, THE MAJORITY TEXT, THE KING JAMES VERSION, THE LIVING BIBLE, THE NEW KING JAMES VERSION, and omitted by the WESTCOTT/HORT, THE NESTLE, AND THE UNITED BIBLE SOCIETIES' GREEK TEXTS, as well as BY THE AMERICAN STANDARD VERSION, THE REVISED STANDARD VERSION, THE NEW ENGLISH BIBLE, , THE NEW INTERNATIONAL VERSION, THE COMMON ENGLISH BIBLE, THE ENGLISH STANDARD VERSION while it is single bracketed by THE NEW AMERICAN STANDARD AND TODAY'S ENGLISH VERSION.

Passage	TR	W/H	NT	UBS	MT	KJV	ASV	RSV	TEV	LB	NAS	NIV	NKJ	CEB	ESV
Mt. 18:11	-	O	O	O	-	-	O	O	S	-	S	O	-	O	O

The verse will be examined according to the method proposed by J.W. Burgon and Edward Miler.

Antiquity of witnesses

The verse is attested for in the 2nd, 3rd and 4th centuries by versions ranging from the Syriac (Peshitta, Curetorian and Harclean) to the Armenian to the Bohairic Coptic, along with the Diatessaron, the Vulgate and Vercellensis Old Latin. Other Syriac versions (Sinaitic, and Palestinian – all younger than the Peshitta), and the Coptic Versions omit the verse.

Of the early writers, Hilary includes the verse. It is rejected by Origen, Juvenus, Eusebius and the Apostolic Canons.

Two manuscripts from the 1st four centuries omit the verse: the Sinaiticus and the Vaticanus.

The verse has ancient evidence for its inclusion.

FOR	AGAINST
2ND CENTURY	
Harclean Syriac version (II-VII)	
Curetorian Syriac version (II-VII)	Sinaitic Syriac version (II-VII)
Peshitta Syriac version (II-VII)	Palestinian Syriac version (II-VII)
Diastessaron of Tatian	
3RD CENTURY	
	Bohairic Coptic version (III-VI)
Bohairic Coptic version (III-VI)	Sahidic Coptic version (III-VI)
	Origen
4TH CENTURY	
	Aleph Sinaiticus uncial
Vercellensis Old Latin version	B Vaticanus uncial
Vulgate version	Apostolic Canons
Hilary	Juvenus
Armenian version (IV/V)	Eusebius
	Hilary

Number

There are thirty-eight Greek manuscripts which include the verse, and twenty-two which exclude it.

There are twenty Versions which include the verse, and seven which exclude it.

There are four early writers which include the verse, and six who exclude it.

It is found in the Byzantine Manuscripts, which text type the vast majority of Greek manuscripts are placed in.

FOR   AGAINST

GREEK MSS.	VERSIONS	EARLY WRITERS	BYZ. MSS.	TEXT	BYZ. MSS	EARLY WRITERS	VERSIONS	GREEK MSS.
38	20	4	+	Matt. 18:11	-	6	7	22

Variety

The verse is testified by Greek manuscripts (both Uncial and Minuscule) from every area that they are extant. It is included in versions coming from various areas and influences. The early writers who testify to its inclusion are few, but they do not waver. It is not found just in the New Testaments in a particular area, but is found universally.

Continuity

Beginning in the 2nd century three Syriac versions (Peshitta, Harclean and the Curetorian) and the Diatessaron of Tatian include the verse. Two Syriac versions (Sinaitic and Palestinian) omit it.

In the 3rd century, the sole witness to include it is certain copies of the Bohairic Coptic version. Other copies of the Bohairic, along with the Sahidic Coptic version and Origen omit it.

In the 4th century, the Vercellensis old Latin version, the Vulgate, the Armenian version and Hilary include the verse. Two uncials ({Aleph} Sinaiticus and {B} Vaticanus), the Apostolic Canons, Juvenus and Eusebius omit it.

In the 5th century, the evidence begins to overwhelmingly include the verse. Two uncials ({D} Canagrigiensis and {W} the Freer Gospels), four Old Latin versions (Veronensis, Bezae Cantabrigiensis, Corbeiensis II, and Sangallensis), other manuscripts according to the Georgian version, along with the Georgian version, Chrysostom and Augustine include the verse. One old Latin version (Palatinus) and Jerome omit it.

In the 6th century, one uncial (078), the Brixianus old Latin version and the Ethiopic version include it. No witness excludes the verse.

In the 7th century, four old Latin versions (Abureus, Monacensis, Usserianus I, and Rhadigeranus) include the verse. Zero witnesses exclude it.

In the 8th century, no witnesses include the verse. One uncial ({L} Regius) excludes it.

In the 9th century, three uncials (K, Δ, and Π), along with one minuscules (565), one minuscule in the margin (892) and the Sangermonensis old Latin version include the verse. Two uncials (033, {Θ} Korideth) and the text of one minuscule (892) exclude the verse.

In the 10th century, one uncial (X) and one minuscule (1079) include the verse. The old Latin Corbiensis version omits it.

THE EVIDENCE FOR MATTHEW 18:11

FOR	AGAINST
2ND CENTURY	
Harclean Syriac version (II-VII)	Sinaitic Syriac version (II-VII)
Curetorian Syriac version (II-VII)	Palestinian Syriac version (II-VII)

Peshitta Syriac version (II-VII)

Diastessaron of Tatian

3RD CENTURY

Bohairic Coptic version (III-VI)

Bohairic Coptic version (III-VI)

Sahidic Coptic version (III-VI)

Origen

4TH CENTURY

Aleph Sinaiticus uncial

Vercellensis Old Latin version

B Vaticanus uncial

Vulgate version

Apostolic Canons

Hilary

Juvenus

Armenian version (IV/V)

Eusebius

Hilary

5TH CENTURY

D Bezae Cantabrigiensis uncial

W Freer Gospels uncial

Veronensis Old Latin version

Bezae Cantabrigiensis Old Latin version

Corbeiensis II Old Latin version

Palatinus Old Latin version

Sangallensis Old Latin version

Georgian version

Manuscripts according to Georgian version

Jerome

Georgian version

Chrysostom

Augustine

6TH CENTURY

078 uncial

Brixianus Old Latin version

Ethiopic version

7TH CENTURY

Abureus Old Latin version

Monacensis Old Latin version

Usserianus I Old Latin version

Rhadigeranus Old Latin version

8TH CENTURY

L Regius uncial

9TH CENTURY

K uncial

Delta uncial

33 uncial

Pi uncial

892 minuscule

565 minuscule

Korideth Theta uncial

Margin of 892 minuscule

Sangermonensis Old Latin

10TH CENTURY

X uncial

Corbiensis Old Latin version

1079 minuscule

11TH CENTURY

28 minuscule

124 minuscule

700 minuscule

788 minuscule

1216 minuscule

174 minuscule

L374 lectionary

230 minuscule

L185 lectionary

12TH CENTURY

1230 minuscule

1 minuscule

1241 minuscule	346 minuscule
1344 minuscule	543 minuscule
1365 minuscule	826 minuscule
1646 minuscule	828 minuscule
1010 minuscule	983 minuscule
1195 minuscule	
L69 lectionary	
L70 lectionary	
L80 lectionary	
L211 lectionary	
L303 lectionary	
Colbertinus Old Latin (XII/XIII)	

13TH CENTURY

1242 minuscule	
1546 minuscule	
1009 minuscule	
L10 lectionary	118 minuscule
L12 lectionary	13 minuscule
L299 lectionary	1689 minuscule
L950 lectionary	
L1642 lectionary	

14TH CENTURY

2174 minuscule	131 minuscule
2148 minuscule	209 minuscule

15TH CENTURY

1253 minuscule	69 minuscule

The majority of lectionaries in the Synaxarion (the so-called "moveable year" beginning with Easter) and the in the Menologian (the "fixed year" beginning with September 1) include the verse.

The majority of Byzantine manuscripts include the verse.

The 2nd century sees the evidence slightly in favor of the omission of the verse, but beginning with the 3rd century the inclusion evidence is equal. From that point the inclusion evidence is always predominate, with no evidence for the omission of the verse in the 7th, 8th, 10th, 11th, 12th, 14th, or 15th centuries cited. Such holes in the evidence for the omission of the verse give one great pause as to the validity of the argument.

The Context of Passage

Woe unto the world because of offences! for it must needs be that offences come; but woe to that man by whom the offence cometh! Wherefore if thy hand or thy foot offend thee, cut them off, and cast them from thee: it is better for thee to enter into life halt or maimed, rather than having two hands or two feet to be cast into everlasting fire. And if thine eye offend thee, pluck it out, and cast it from thee: it is better for thee to enter into life with one eye, rather than having two eyes to be cast into hell fire. Take heed that ye despise not one of these little ones; for I say unto you, That in heaven their angels do always behold the face of my Father which is in heaven.

<u>*For the Son of man is come to save that which was lost.*</u>

How think ye? if a man have an hundred sheep, and one of them be gone astray, doth he not leave the ninety and nine, and goeth into the mountains, and seeketh that which is gone astray? And if so be that he find it, verily I say unto you, he rejoiceth more of that sheep, than of the ninety and nine which went not astray. Even so it is not the will of your Father which is in heaven, that one of these little ones should perish. (Matthew 18:7-14 KJV).

Jesus, in verses 7 through 11 is speaking of offences, or causing another to sin. Men will be influenced by others to sin, but woe to the man who does so. It is better to enter into heaven missing an eye, or an arm, or a leg, than to enter into hell whole. That is why it is necessary to take care of offending others. It will not go unnoticed. Their angels stand before God and report what is going on.

<u>***For the Son of man is come to save that which was lost.***</u> Jesus came to save those who were lost. He came to save, so make sure you do not cause others to sin.

Do not think that Jesus does not care. Think about it. If a man has a hundred sheep, and ninety-nine come in from the mountain pasture, doesn't he go into the mountains looking for the one sheep? And if he finds it, he is happier at finding that one sheep than he was in seeing the ninety-nine come back from the pasture.

In much the same way, God does not wish that any would go astray, no matter who it is.

Verse 11 is the center of the argument. It explains why and how much the Father is concerned about these little ones. It transitions between the discussion of offence, and the discussion of restoration.

Without it, there is a whole left in the passage.

Internal Evidence.

There appears to be no objection internally to the verse.

The conclusion

Metzger says, *"There can be little doubt that the words* νλθεν γαρ ο ωιοσ του ανθροπου *(ζητησαι και) σωσαι το απολωλοσ are spurious here, being omitted by the earliest witnesses representing several textual types (Alexandrian, pre-Caesarean, Egyptian, Antiochian), and manifestly borrowed by copyists from Lk. 19:10. The reason for the interpolation was apparently to provide a connection between ver. 10 and verses 12-14."* [p.45]

The text-types are artificial categories based upon a presumed history of the text which is based upon the result. There is no basis for the differentiation of the text-types. They are created to obtain the desired result. In this case, the influence of the Egyptian school is predominate in the conclusion reached.

As Metzger notes, it provides *"a connection between ver. 10 and verses 12-14."*

It fits the flow, the literary style, and the evidence is preponderantly in favor of the verse. There is no question that this verse belongs in the Gospel of Matthew.

When the seven points of truth are examined, all seven (**1. Antiquity, 2. Number, 3. Variety, 4. Weight, 5. Continuity, 6. Context of the Passage,** and **7. Internal Considerations**) are in favor of the inclusion of the verse.

Does Matthew 21:44 Belong in the New Testament?

This verse is included by THE TEXTUS RECEPTUS, THE MAJORITY TEXT, THE KING JAMES VERSION, THE AMERICAN STANDARD VERSION, THE NEW KING JAMES VERSION, THE COMMON ENGLISH BIBLE, THE ENGLISH STANDARD VERSION and single-bracketed by the WESTCOTT/HORT, THE NESTLE GREEK TEXTS, AND THE NEW AMERICAN STANDARD and double-bracketed by THE UNITED BIBLE SOCIETIES' GREEK TEXT, as well as omitted by THE REVISED STANDARD VERSION, AND THE NEW INTERNATIONAL VERSION.

Passage	TR	W/H	NT	BS	MT	KJV	ASV	RSV	TEV	LB	NAS	NIV	NKJ	CEB	ESV
Matt. 21:44	--	SB	SB	DB	--	--	--	O	O	O	SB	O	--	--	--

Antiquity of witnesses

The verse is attested for in the 2nd, 3rd and 4th centuries by versions ranging from the Syriac (Peshitta, Curetorian and Harclean) to the Armenian to the Bohairic Coptic, along with the Diatessaron, the Vulgate and Vercellensis Old Latin. Other Syriac versions (Sinaitic, and Palestinian – all younger than the Peshitta), and the Coptic Versions omit the verse.

Of the early writers, Hilary includes the verse. It is rejected by Origen, Juvenus, Eusebius and the Apostolic Canons.

Two manuscripts from the 1st four centuries omit the verse: the Sinaiticus and the Vaticanus.

The verse has ancient evidence for its inclusion.

FOR	AGAINST
2ND CENTURY	
Harclean Syriac version (II-VII)	Sinaitic Syriac version (II-VII)

Curetorian Syriac version (II-VII)	Palestinian Syriac version (II-VII)
Peshitta Syriac version (II-VII)	
Diastessaron of Tatian	

3RD CENTURY

	Bohairic Coptic version (III-VI)
Bohairic Coptic version (III-VI)	Sahidic Coptic version (III-VI)
	Origen

4TH CENTURY

	Aleph Sinaiticus uncial
Vercellensis Old Latin version	B Vaticanus uncial
Vulgate version	Apostolic Canons
Hilary	Juvenus
Armenian version (IV/V)	Eusebius
	Hilary

Number

There are thirty-eight Greek manuscripts which include the verse, and twenty-two which exclude it.

There are twenty Versions which include the verse, and seven which exclude it.

There are four early writers which include the verse, and six who exclude it.

It is found in the Byzantine Manuscripts, which text type the vast majority of Greek manuscripts are placed in.

FOR   AGAINST

GREEK MSS.	VERSIONS	EARLY WRITERS	BYZ. MSS.	TEXT	BYZ. MSS	EARLY WRITERS	VERSIONS	GREEK MSS.
38	20	4	+	Matt. 18:11	-	6	7	22

Variety

The verse is testified by Greek manuscripts (both Uncial and Minuscule) from every area that they are extant. It is included in versions coming from various areas and influences. The early writers who testify to its inclusion are few, but they do not waver. It is not found just in the New Testaments in a particular area, but is found universally.

Continuity

When you consider the character of the evidence, it favors the inclusion of the verses. The majority of the Syriac versions (possibly the first language the New Testament was translated into) include the verse. It is noted by the Coptic. It is included in most known old Latin version (regardless of location). It is included even in the less reliable Vulgate. The more reliable uncials include it (D and W, amongst others). The vast majority of minuscules include it. It is found in both versions of the lectionaries.

The exclusion is based upon mainly witnesses of Egyptian origin or influence: the minority witness of the Syriac, the Sinaiticus and Vaticanus and Regius uncials (whose character rarely agrees with one another), etc.

The reliability and strength of the witnesses for the inclusion is weightier.

Continuity

Beginning in the 2nd century three Syriac versions (Peshitta, Harclean and the Curetorian) and the Diatessaron of Tatian include the verse. Two Syriac versions (Sinaitic and Palestinian) omit it.

In the 3rd century, the sole witness to include it is certain copies of the Bohairic Coptic version. Other copies of the Bohairic, along with the Sahidic Coptic version and Origen omit it.

In the 4th century, the Vercellensis old Latin version, the Vulgate, the Armenian version and Hilary include the verse. Two uncials ({Aleph} Sinaiticus and {B} Vaticanus), the Apostolic Canons, Juvenus and Eusebius omit it.

In the 5th century, the evidence begins to overwhelmingly include the verse. Two uncials ({D} Canagrigiensis and {W} the Freer Gospels), four Old Latin versions (Veronensis, Bezae Cantabrigiensis, Corbeiensis II, and Sangallensis), other manuscripts according to the Georgian version, along with the Georgian version, Chrysostom and Augustine include the verse. One old Latin version (Palatinus) and Jerome omit it.

In the 6th century, one uncial (078), the Brixianus old Latin version and the Ethiopic version include it. No witness excludes the verse.

In the 7th century, four old Latin versions (Abureus, Monacensis, Usserianus I, and Rhadigeranus) include the verse. Zero witnesses exclude it.

In the 8th century, no witnesses include the verse. One uncial ({L} Regius) excludes it.

In the 9th century, three uncials (K, Δ, and Π), along with one minuscules (565), one minuscule in the margin (892) and the Sangermonensis old Latin version include the verse. Two uncials (033, {Θ} Korideth) and the text of one minuscule (892) exclude the verse.

In the 10th century, one uncial (X) and one minuscule (1079) include the verse. The old Latin Corbiensis version omits it.

THE EVIDENCE FOR MATTHEW 18:11

FOR	AGAINST
2ND CENTURY	
Harclean Syriac version (II-VII)	
Curetorian Syriac version (II-VII)	Sinaitic Syriac version (II-VII)
Peshitta Syriac version (II-VII)	Palestinian Syriac version (II-VII)
Diastessaron of Tatian	
3RD CENTURY	
	Bohairic Coptic version (III-VI)
Bohairic Coptic version (III-VI)	Sahidic Coptic version (III-VI)
	Origen
4TH CENTURY	
	Aleph Sinaiticus uncial
Vercellensis Old Latin version	B Vaticanus uncial
Vulgate version	Apostolic Canons
Hilary	Juvenus
Armenian version (IV/V)	Eusebius
	Hilary
5TH CENTURY	
D Bezae Cantabrigiensis uncial	
W Freer Gospels uncial	
Veronensis Old Latin version	
Bezae Cantabrigiensis Old Latin version	Palatinus Old Latin version
Corbeiensis II Old Latin version	Georgian version
Sangallensis Old Latin version	Jerome
Manuscripts according to Georgian version	

Georgian version

Chrysostom

Augustine

6TH CENTURY

078 uncial

Brixianus Old Latin version

Ethiopic version

7TH CENTURY

Abureus Old Latin version

Monacensis Old Latin version

Usserianus I Old Latin version

Rhadigeranus Old Latin version

8TH CENTURY

L Regius uncial

9TH CENTURY

K uncial

Delta uncial

Pi uncial

565 minuscule

Margin of 892 minuscule

Sangermonensis Old Latin

33 uncial

892 minuscule

Korideth Theta uncial

10TH CENTURY

X uncial

1079 minuscule

Corbiensis Old Latin version

11TH CENTURY

28 minuscule

700 minuscule

124 minuscule

788 minuscule

1216 minuscule	174 minuscule
L374 lectionary	230 minuscule
L185 lectionary	

12TH CENTURY

1230 minuscule	
1241 minuscule	
1344 minuscule	
1365 minuscule	
1646 minuscule	1 minuscule
1010 minuscule	346 minuscule
1195 minuscule	543 minuscule
L69 lectionary	826 minuscule
L70 lectionary	828 minuscule
L80 lectionary	983 minuscule
L211 lectionary	
L303 lectionary	
Colbertinus Old Latin (XII/XIII)	

13TH CENTURY

1242 minuscule	
1546 minuscule	
1009 minuscule	
L10 lectionary	118 minuscule
L12 lectionary	13 minuscule
L299 lectionary	1689 minuscule
L950 lectionary	
L1642 lectionary	

14TH CENTURY	
2174 minuscule	131 minuscule
2148 minuscule	209 minuscule

15TH CENTURY	
1253 minuscule	69 minuscule

The majority of lectionaries in the Synaxarion (the so-called "moveable year" beginning with Easter) and the in the Menologian (the "fixed year" beginning with September 1) include the verse.

The majority of Byzantine manuscripts include the verse.

The 2nd century sees the evidence slightly in favor of the omission of the verse, but beginning with the 3rd century the inclusion evidence is equal. From that point the inclusion evidence is always predominate, with no evidence for the omission of the verse in the 7th, 8th, 10th, 11th, 12th, 14th, or 15th centuries cited. Such holes in the evidence for the omission of the verse give one great pause as to the validity of the argument.

The Context of Passage

Woe unto the world because of offences! for it must needs be that offences come; but woe to that man by whom the offence cometh! Wherefore if thy hand or thy foot offend thee, cut them off, and cast them from thee: it is better for thee to enter into life halt or maimed, rather than having two hands or two feet to be cast into everlasting fire. And if thine eye offend thee, pluck it out, and cast it from thee: it is better for thee to enter into life with one eye, rather than having two eyes to be cast into hell fire. Take heed that ye despise not one of these little ones; for I say unto you, That in heaven their angels do always behold the face of my Father which is in heaven.

__For the Son of man is come to save that which was lost.__

How think ye? if a man have an hundred sheep, and one of them be gone astray, doth he not leave the ninety and nine, and goeth into the mountains, and seeketh that which is gone astray? And if so be that he find it, verily I say unto you, he rejoiceth more of that sheep, than of the ninety and nine which went not astray. Even so it is not the will of your Father which is in heaven, that one of these little ones should perish. (Matthew 18:7-14 KJV).

Jesus, in verses 7 through 11 is speaking of offences, or causing another to sin. Men will be influenced by others to sin, but woe to the man who does so. It is better to enter into heaven missing an eye, or an arm, or a leg, than to enter into hell whole. That is why it is necessary to take care of offending others. It will not go unnoticed. Their angels stand before God and report what is going on.

__For the Son of man is come to save that which was lost.__ Jesus came to save those who were lost. He came to save, so make sure you do not cause others to sin.

Do not think that Jesus does not care. Think about it. If a man has a hundred sheep, and ninety-nine come in from the mountain pasture, doesn't he go into the mountains looking for the one sheep? And if he finds it, he is happier at finding that one sheep than he was in seeing the ninety-nine come back from the pasture.

In much the same way, God does not wish that any would go astray, no matter who it is.

Verse 11 is the center of the argument. It explains why and how much the Father is concerned about these little ones. It transitions between the discussion of offence, and the discussion of restoration.

Without it, there is a whole left in the passage.

Internal Evidence.

There appears to be no objection internally to the verse.

The conclusion

Metzger says, *"There can be little doubt that the words* ηλθεν γαρ ο υιοσ του ανθροπου (ζητησαι και) σωσαι το απολωλοσ *are spurious here, being omitted by the earliest witnesses representing several textual types (Alexandrian, pre-Caesarean, Egyptian, Antiochian), and manifestly borrowed by copyists from Lk. 19:10. The reason for the interpolation was apparently to provide a connection between ver. 10 and verses 12-14."* [p.45]

The text-types are artificial categories based upon a presumed history of the text which is based upon the result. There is no basis for the differentiation of the text-types. They are created to obtain the desired result. In this case, the influence of the Egyptian school is predominate in the conclusion reached.

As Metzger notes, it provides *"a connection between ver. 10 and verses 12-14."*

It fits the flow, the literary style, and the evidence is preponderantly in favor of the verse. There is no question that this verse belongs in the Gospel of Matthew.

When the seven points of truth are examined, all seven (**1. Antiquity, 2. Number, 3. Variety, 4. Weight, 5. Continuity, 6. Context of the Passage,** and **7. Internal Considerations**) are in favor of the inclusion of the verse.

Does Matthew 23:14 Belong in the New Testament?

This verse is included by THE TEXTUS RECEPTUS, THE MAJORITY TEXT, THE KING JAMES VERSION, THE NEW KING JAMES VERSION, single-bracketed by THE NEW AMERICAN STANDARD BIBLE, as well as omitted by THE WESTCOTT/HORT, NESTLE, UNITED BIBLE SOCIETY, AND MAJORITY GREEK TEXTS, AND THE AMERICAN STANDARD VERSION, THE REVISED STANDARD VERSION, THE NEW INTERNATIONAL VERSION, THE COMMON ENGLISH BIBLE, AND THE ENGLISH STANDARD VERSION.

Passage	TR	W/H	NT	BS	MT	KJV	ASV	RSV	TEV	LB	NAS	NIV	NKJ	CEB	ESV
Matt. 23:14	--	o	o	o	o	--	o	O	--	--	SB	O	--	o	o

Antiquity of witnesses

Two Syriac versions (Sinaitic and Palestinian [II-VII]) omit the verse from the 2nd century.

The verse is attested for in the 2nd, 3rd and 4th centuries by versions ranging from the Syriac (Peshitta, Curetorian, Harclean, and Palestinian) to the Bohairic Coptic, along with the Clementine Vulgate. The Sahidic Coptic Version omit the verse, while the Bohairic gives split testimony. It is also missing from the Vercellensis Old Latin and the Wordsworth-White Vulgate.

Of the early writers, Hilary includes the verse, Origen both includes and omits the verse, while Eusebius omits the verse.

Two manuscripts from the 1st four centuries omit the verse: the Sinaiticus and the Vaticanus.

The verse has ancient evidence for its inclusion.

	FOR				AGAINST	

2ND CENTURY

FOR	AGAINST
Diatessaron	
Peshitta Syriac version (II-VII)	
Harclean Syriac version (II-VII)	Sinaitic Syriac (II-VII)
Curetorian Syriac version (II-VII)	Palestinian Syriac (II-VII)
Palestinian Syriac (II-VII)	

3RD CENTURY

FOR	AGAINST
	Origen
Origen	Sahidic Coptic version (III-VI)
Bohairic Coptic version (III-VI)	Bohairic Coptic version (III-VI)

4TH CENTURY

FOR	AGAINST
	Aleph Sinaiticus uncial
	B Vaticanus uncial
Clementine Vulgate	Vercellensis Old Latin version
Hilary	Wordsworth-White Vulgate
	Eusebius

Number

There are thirty-nine Greek manuscripts which include the verse, and eight which exclude it. There are fourteen Versions which include the verse, and twelve which exclude it.

There are six early writers which include the verse, and four who exclude it.

It is found in the Byzantine Manuscripts, which text type the vast majority of Greek manuscripts are placed in.

	FOR						AGAINST	
GREEK MSS	VERSIONS	EARLY WRITERS	BYZ MSS	TEXT	BYZ MSS	EARLY WRITERS	VERSIONS	GREEK MSS
39	14	6	+	MT 23:14	-	4	12	8

Variety

The verse is testified by Greek manuscripts (both Uncial and Minuscule) from every area that they are extant. It is included in versions coming from various areas and influences. The early writers who testify to its inclusion are few, but they do not waver. It is not found just in the New Testaments in a particular area, but is found universally.

Continuity

The evidence (excluding the BYZANTINE MANUSCRIPTS) favors the inclusion of the verse.

In the 2ND Century, the DIATESSARON OF TATIAN, and four SYRIAC VERSIONS (PESHITTA, HARCLEAN, CURETORIAN, PALESTINIAN dating somewhere between the 2ND and 7TH Centuries) include the verse. Two SYRIAC VERSIONS (SINAITIC, PALESTINIAN somewhere between the 2ND and 7TH Centuries) exclude it.

In the 3RD Century, the some manuscripts of the BOHAIRIC COPTIC VERSION (dated between the 3RD and 6TH Centuries) and ORIGEN include the verse. ORIGEN, the SAHIDIC COPTIC VERSION and some manuscripts of the BOHAIRIC COPTIC VERSION (both dated between the 3RD and 6TH Centuries) omit the verse.

In the 4TH Century, the CLEMENTINE VULGATE VERSION and HILARY include the verse. Two uncials (SINAITICUS {ALEPH}, VATICANUS {B}), two versions (VERCELLENSIS OLD LATIN, WORDSWORTH-WHITE VULGATE) and EUSEBIUS omit the verse.

In the 5TH Century, one uncial (FREER GOSPELS {W}), three Old Latin versions (CORBEIENSIS II, CLAROMONTANUS, VERONENSIS), and CHRYSOSTOM include the verse. Three versions (GEORGIAN, BEZAE CANTABRIGIENSIS OLD LATIN, PALATINUS OLD LATIN) and JEROME omit the verse.

In the 6TH Century, two versions (ETHIOPIC, BRIXIANUS OLD LATIN) and PS-CHRYSOSTOM include the verse. One uncial (BEZAE CANTABRIGIENSIS {D}) omits the verse.

In the 7TH Century, one uncial (0107) and two OLD LATIN VERSIONS (USSERIANUS I, RHEDIGERANUS – dated either 7TH or 8TH Century) include the verse. The AUREUS OLD LATIN VERSION omits it.

In the 8TH Century, JOHN – DAMASCUS includes the verse, and one uncial (REGIUS {L}) omits it.

In the 9TH Century, four uncials (Δ, Κ, Π, 0138) and two minuscules (892 IN THE MARGIN, 565) include the verse. One uncial (KORIDETHI {Θ}), two minuscules (892 TEXT, 33) and DRUTHMARCUS omit the verse.

In the 10TH Century, one minuscule (1079) includes the verse, and the CORBEIENSIS I OLD LATIN VERSION omits it.

In the 11TH Century, seven minuscules (700, 1216, 124, 28, 174, 230, 788) include the verse.

In the 12TH Century, twelve minuscules (1010, 1071, 1195, 1230, 1241, 1365, 1646, 346, 543, 826, 828, 983), one lectionary (L76) and the COLBERTINUS OLD LATIN VERSION include the verse.

In the 13TH Century, five minuscules (1009, 1242, 13, 1546, 1689) and one lectionary (L547) include the verse.

In the 14TH Century, two minuscules (2174, 2148) include the verse.

In the 15TH Century, one minuscule (69) includes the verse.

The majority of the BYZANTINE MANUSCRIPTS include the verse.

The majority of the lectionaries in the SYNAXARION (the so-called "moveable year" beginning with Easter) and in the MENOLOGIAN (the "fixed year" beginning with September 1) include the verse.

THE EVIDENCE FOR MATTHEW 23:14

FOR	AGAINST
2ND CENTURY	
Diatessaron	
Peshitta Syriac version (II-VII)	
Harclean Syriac version (II-VII)	
Curetorian Syriac version (II-VII)	
Palestinian Syriac (II-VII)	
3RD CENTURY	
Origen	Origen
Bohairic Coptic version (III-VI)	Sahidic Coptic version (III-VI)
	Bohairic Coptic version (III-VI)
4TH CENTURY	
Clementine Vulgate version	Aleph Sinaiticus uncial
	B Vaticanus uncial
Hilary	Vercellensis Old Latin version
	Wordsworth-White Vulgate
	Eusebius
5TH CENTURY	
W Freer Gospels uncial	Georgian version

Corbeiensis II Old Latin version

Bezae Cantabrigiensis Old Latin

Claromontanus Old Latin

Palatinus Old Latin version

Veronensis Old Latin version

Jerome

Chrysostom

6TH CENTURY

Ethiopic version

Brixianus Old Latin

D Bezae Cantabrigiensis uncial

PS-Chrysostom

7TH CENTURY

0107 uncial

Usserianus I Old Latin version

Aureus Old Latin version

Rhedigeranus Old Latin (VII/VIII)

8TH CENTURY

John – Damascus

L Regius uncial

9TH CENTURY

Delta uncial

K uncial

Koridethi Theta uncial

Pi uncial

33 minuscule

0138 uncial

892 minuscule

Margin of 892 minuscule

Druthmarcus

565 minuscule

10TH CENTURY

1079 minuscule

Corbeiensis I Old Latin version

11TH CENTURY

700 minuscule

1216 minuscule

124 minuscule

28 minuscule

174 minuscule

230 minuscule

788 minuscule

12TH CENTURY

1010 minuscule

1071 minuscule

1195 minuscule

1230 minuscule

1241 minuscule

1365 minuscule

1646 minuscule

346 minuscule

543 minuscule

826 minuscule

828 minuscule

983 minuscule

L76 lectionary

Colbertinus Old Latin (XII/XIII)

13TH CENTURY

1009 minuscule

1242 minuscule

13 minuscule

1546 minuscule

1689 minuscule

L547 lectionary

14TH CENTURY

2174 minuscule

2148 minuscule

69 minuscule

The majority of the lectionaries in the Synaxarion (the so-called "moveable year" beginning with Easter) and in the Menologion (the "fixed year" beginning with September 1), include the verse.

The majority of the Byzantine manuscripts include the verse.

The 2nd century sees five witnesses for inclusion to none for omission. The 3rd and 4th centuries are the only times more witnesses include the verse than exclude it. The 8th and 10th centuries see the same number of witnesses for each. Beginning in the 11th century, no witnesses are found which exclude the verse, that's thirty to zilch. No century finds a lack of witnesses which include the verse. Such holes in the evidence for the omission of the verse give one great pause as to the validity of the argument.

The Context of Passage

But woe unto you, scribes and Pharisees, hypocrites! for ye shut up the kingdom of heaven against men: for ye neither go in yourselves, neither suffer ye them that are entering to go in. Woe unto you, scribes and Pharisees, hypocrites! for ye devour widows' houses, and for a pretence make long prayer: therefore ye shall receive the greater damnation. Woe unto you, scribes and Pharisees, hypocrites! for ye compass sea and land to make one proselyte, and when he is made, ye make him twofold more the child of hell than yourselves. Woe unto you, ye blind guides, which say, Whosoever shall swear by the temple, it is nothing; but whosoever shall swear by the gold of the temple, he is a debtor! Ye fools and blind: for whether is greater, the gold, or the temple that sanctifieth the gold? And, Whosoever shall swear by the altar, it is nothing; but whosoever sweareth by the gift that is upon it, he is guilty. Ye fools and blind: for whether is greater, the gift, or the altar that sanctifieth the gift? Whoso therefore shall swear by the altar, sweareth by it, and by all things thereon. And whoso shall swear by the temple, sweareth by it, and by him that dwelleth therein. And he that shall swear by heaven, sweareth by the throne of God, and by him that sitteth thereon. Woe unto you, scribes and Pharisees, hypocrites! for ye pay tithe of mint and anise and cummin, and have omitted the weightier matters of the law, judgment, mercy, and faith: these ought ye to have done, and not to leave the other undone. Ye blind guides, which strain at a gnat, and swallow a camel. Woe unto you, scribes and Pharisees, hypocrites! for ye make clean the outside of the cup and of the platter, but within they are full of extortion and excess. Thou blind Pharisee, cleanse first that which is within the cup and platter, that the outside of them may be clean also. Woe unto you, scribes and Pharisees, hypocrites! for ye are like unto whited sepulchres, which indeed appear beautiful outward, but are within full of dead men's bones, and of all uncleanness. Even so ye also outwardly appear righteous unto men, but within ye are full of hypocrisy and iniquity. Woe unto you, scribes and Pharisees, hypocrites! because ye build the tombs of the prophets, and garnish the sepulchres of the righteous, And say, If we had been in the days of our fathers, we would not have been partakers with them in the blood of the prophets. Wherefore ye be witnesses unto yourselves, that ye are the children of them which killed the prophets. Fill ye up then the measure of your fathers. Ye serpents, ye genera-tion of vipers, how can ye escape the damnation of hell? (MATTHEW 23:13-33 KJV)

The twenty-third chapter of Matthew is a scathing review of the scribes and Pharisees by our Lord. The problem was not what made one a Pharisee (believing in angels and the resurrec-tion), it was the hypocrisy that ran amuck among the Pharisees.

Not only did the scribes and Pharisees refuse to enter the kingdom of God accepting the teachings of Jesus, they did everything that they could to keep others from accepting the Christ. From the time of Jesus through the book of Acts, many of the Jews (especially the scribes and the Pharisees) persecuted the disciples and apostles. However, remember also that thousands of Jews believed in Jesus and obeyed the gospel. But, for those who did not there remained a woe.

Jesus had warned of long prayers to be heard of men in The Sermon on the Mount. Here the Christ rebukes the scribes and Pharisees for using prayer as a religious cover as they mis-used and abused the widows. Their prayer was a farce, a façade to hide their immoral ac-tions. Because of this, they would receive a greater condemnation – damnation.

They were zealous, but the results were to make converts that were even worse than they were themselves, twice as bad.

The scribes and Pharisees were meticulous about tithing, but forgot "the weightier matters of the law, judgment, mercy and faith." They made the same mistake that many do today, think-ing that because they are fulfilling one command, they do not need to obey or even to be con-cerned about another. Jesus showed the folly of this in MATTHEW 28:20 – *"... observe all things whatsoever I have commanded you ..."*

The scribes and Pharisees Jesus addressed were empty shells of faith to be condemned.

The rebuke of misusing and abusing widows while making a pretense of prayer and faking their faith, fits wonderfully in the flow of the context.

Internal Evidence.

There appears to be no objection internally to the verse.

The conclusion

Metzger says,

"That ver. 14 is an interpolation derived from the parallel in Mk 12.40 or Lk 20.47 is clear (a) from its absence in the earliest and best authorities of the Alexandrian, the Western, and the Caesarean types of text, and (b) from the fact that the witnesses which include the passage have it in different places, either after ver. 13 (so the Textus Receptus) or before ver. 13." [p. 60]

There is no question that this verse fits the flow of the context, and that it is the same literary style and quality of the GOSPEL OF MATTHEW.

The question rests solely upon the evidence. If the New Testament texts are divided into groupings, the verse still belongs in the text. Only by tilting the evidence to allow certain manuscripts to outweigh all others can a case be made for its exclusion.

The question of whether it goes before or after verse thirteen is immaterial in the discussion of whether the verse belongs in the text. The position is a discussion after determining whether it belongs, because whether the witness places it before or after verse thirteen, they do place it in the text as being inspired of God.

When the seven points of truth are examined, all (**1. Antiquity, 2. Number, 3. Variety, 5. Continuity, 6. Context of the Passage,** and **7. Internal Considerations**) are in favor of the inclusion of the verse.

Does Mark 7:16 Belong in the New Testament?

This verse is included by THE TEXTUS RECEPTUS, THE MAJORITY TEXT, THE KING JAMES VERSION, AND THE NEW KING JAMES VERSION, and omitted by THE WESTCOTT/HORT, NESTLE, UNITED BIBLE SOCIETY GREEK TEXTS, AND THE AMERICAN STANDARD VERSION, THE REVISED STANDARD VERSION, TODAY'S ENGLISH VERSION, THE LIVING BIBLE, THE NEW INTERNATIONAL VERSION, THE COMMON ENGLISH BIBLE, AND THE ENGLISH STANDARD VERSION.

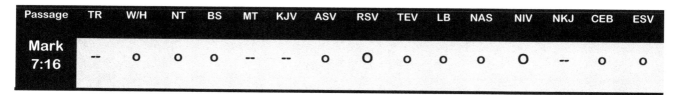

Passage	TR	W/H	NT	BS	MT	KJV	ASV	RSV	TEV	LB	NAS	NIV	NKJ	CEB	ESV
Mark 7:16	--	o	o	o	--	--	o	O	o	o	o	O	--	o	o

Antiquity of witnesses

There is no evidence for the omission of the verse from the 2nd century.

The verse is attested for in the 2nd, 3rd and 4th centuries by versions ranging from the Syriac (Peshitta, Harclean, and Sinaitic) to the Sahidic Coptic and some Bohairic Coptic to Vercellensis Old Latin, the Vulgate, the Gothic version, the Armenian version and the Diatessaron of Tatian. It is omitted by some Bohairic Coptic manuscripts.

Of the early writers, there is no testimony in the first four centuries.

Two manuscripts from the 1st four centuries omit the verse: the Sinaiticus and the Vaticanus.

The verse has ancient evidence for its inclusion.

FOR		AGAINST

2ND CENTURY

Diatessaron of Tatian

Sinaitic Syriac version (II-VII)

Peshitta Syriac version (II-VII)

Harclean Syriac version (II-VII)

3RD CENTURY

Sahidic Coptic version (III-VI)

Bohairic Coptic version (III-VI)   **Bohairic Coptic version (III-VI)**

4TH CENTURY

Vercellensis Old Latin version

Vulgate version   **Aleph Sinaiticus uncial**

Gothic version   **B Vaticanus uncial**

Armenian version (IV/V)

Number

There are forty-eight Greek manuscripts which include the verse, and nine which exclude it.

There are twenty-two Versions which include the verse, and two which exclude it.

There are two early writers which include the verse, and none who exclude it.

It is found in the Byzantine Manuscripts, which text type the vast majority of Greek manuscripts are placed in.

FOR   **AGAINST**

GREEK MSS	VERSIONS	EARLY WRITERS	BYZ MSS	TEXT	BYZ MSS	EARLY WRITERS	VERSIONS	GREEK MSS
48	22	2	+	Mk. 7:16	-	0	2	9

There is no doubt that the numbers are in favor of the verse.

Variety

The verse is testified by Greek manuscripts (both Uncial and Minuscule) from every area that they are extant. It is included in versions coming from various areas and influences. The early writers who testify to its inclusion are few, but they do not waver. It is not found just in the New Testaments in a particular area, but is found universally.

Continuity

The evidence (excluding the BYZANTINE MANUSCRIPTS) favors the inclusion of the verse.

In the 2ND Century, the DIATESSARON OF TATIAN and three SYRIAC VERSIONS (SINAITIC, PESHITTA, HARCLEAN dating somewhere between the 2ND and 7TH Centuries) include the verse.

In the 3RD Century, the SAHIDIC COPTIC VERSION and some manuscripts of the BOHAIRIC COPTIC VERSION include the verse, while certain manuscripts of the BOHAIRIC COPTIC VERSION omit it.

In the 4TH Century, four versions (VERCELLENSIS OLD LATIN, VULGATE, GOTHIC, ARMENIAN {the Armenian dates either 4TH or 5TH Century}) include the verse. Two uncials (SINAITICUS {ALEPH}, VATICANUS {B}) omit it.

In the 5TH Century, two uncials (ALEXANDRINUS {A}, FREER GOSPELS {W}), four OLD LATIN VERSIONS (VERONENSIS, BEZAE CANTABRIGIENSIS, CORBEIENSIS II, SANGELLENSIS), the GEORGIAN VERSION, and AUGUSTINE include the verse. The GEORGIAN VERSION is also sited as a witness against the inclusion of the verse.

In the 6TH Century, one uncial (BEZAE CANTABRIGIENSIS {D}), the BRIXIANUS OLD LATIN VERSION, and the ETHIOPIC VERSION include the verse.

In the 7TH Century, three OLD LATIN VERSIONS (AUREUS, MONACENSIS, USSERIANUS I) and the RHEDIGERANUS OLD LATIN VERSION (dated either the 7TH or 8TH Century) include the verse.

In the 8TH Century, one uncial (REGIUS {L}) omits the verse.

In the 9TH Century, four uncials (K, Δ {CORRECTOR'S HAND}, KORIDETHI {Θ}, P), and three minuscules (33, 565, 892) include the verse. The original hand of one uncial {Δ} omits the verse.

In the 10TH Century, one uncial (X) and one minuscule (1079) include the verse.

In the 11TH Century, four minuscules (124, 788, 700, 1216) and one lectionary (L185) include the verse. One minuscule (28) omits the verse.

In the 12TH Century, fourteen minuscules (1, 346, 543, 826, 828, 983, 1010, 1071, 1195, 1230, 1241, 1344, 1365, 1646), the COLBERTINUS OLD LATIN VERSION (dated either 12TH or 13TH Century), and one lectionary (L76) include the verse. One lectionary (L1127) is listed in part including and in part omitting the verse.

In the 13TH Century, six minuscules (118, 13, 1689, 1009, 1242, 1646) include the verse. Two lectionaries (L333, L950) are cited as both including and omitting the verse in part.

In the 14TH Century, four minuscules (131, 209, 2174, 2148) and one lectionary (L313) include the verse.

In the 15TH Century, two minuscules (69, 1253) include the verse.

The majority of the Byzantine manuscripts include the verse.

The majority of the lectionaries in the SYNAXARION (the so-called "moveable year" beginning with Easter) and in the MENOLOGIAN (the "fixed year" beginning with September 1) omit the verse.

THE EVIDENCE FOR MARK 7:16

FOR	AGAINST
2ND CENTURY	
Diatessaron of Tatian	
Sinaitic Syriac version (II-VII)	
Peshitta Syriac version (II-VII)	
Harclean Syriac version (II-VII)	
3RD CENTURY	
Sahidic Coptic version (III-VI)	Bohairic Coptic version (III-VI)
Bohairic Coptic version (III-VI)	
4TH CENTURY	
Vercellensis Old Latin version	
Vulgate version	Aleph Sinaiticus uncial
Gothic version	B Vaticanus uncial
Armenian version (IV/V)	
5TH CENTURY	
A Alexandrinus uncial	
W Freer Gospels uncial	
Veronensis Old Latin version	
Bezae Cantabrigiensis Old Latin version	
Corbeiensis II Old Latin version	Georgian version
Sangallensis Old Latin version	
Georgian version	
Augustine	

6TH CENTURY

D Bezae Cantabrigiensis uncial

Brixianus Old Latin version

Ethiopic version

7TH CENTURY

Aureus Old Latin version

Monacensis Old Latin version

Usserianus I Old Latin version

Rhedigeranus Old Latin (VII/VIII)

8TH CENTURY

L Regius uncial

9TH CENTURY

K uncial

Delta (corrector's hand) uncial

Theta Koridethi uncial

Pi uncial   **Delta (original hand) uncial**

33 minuscule

565 minuscule

892 minuscule

10TH CENTURY

X uncial

1079 minuscule

11TH CENTURY

124 minuscule

788 minuscule

700 minuscule   **28 minuscule**

1216 minuscule

L185 lectionary

12TH CENTURY

1 minuscule

346 minuscule

543 minuscule

826 minuscule

828 minuscule

983 minuscule

1010 minuscule

1071 minuscule

1195 minuscule   L1127 (in part) lectionary

1230 minuscule

1241 minuscule

1344 minuscule

1365 minuscule

1646 minuscule

L76 lectionary

L1127 (in part) lectionary

Colbertinus Old Latin (XII/XIII)

13TH CENTURY

118 minuscule

13 minuscule

1689 minuscule

1009 minuscule   L333 (in part) lectionary

1242 minuscule   L950 (in part) lectionary

1546 minuscule

L333 (in part) lectionary

14TH CENTURY

131 minuscule

209 minuscule

2174 minuscule

2148 minuscule

L313 lectionary

15TH CENTURY

69 minuscule

1253 minuscule

The 2nd century sees four witnesses for inclusion to none for omission. The 3rd century sees two witness for, and one against. The 4th century has four witnesses for, and two against. From the 5th century on the witnesses for far outnumber the omissions. Only one witness omits the verse in the 5th, 8th, 9th, 11th, and 12th centuries. Two witnesses omit it in the 13th century. However, it is included in eight witnesses from the 5th century, three in the 6th century, four in the 7th century, seven in the 9th century, two in the 10th century, five in the 11th century, seventeen in the 12th century, eight in the 13th century, five in the 14th century, and two in the 15th century. Only the 8th century finds a lack of witnesses which include the verse. Such holes in the evidence for the omission of the verse give one great pause as to the validity of the argument.

The Context of Passage

"Then came together unto him the Pharisees, and certain of the scribes, which came from Jerusalem. And when they saw some of his disciples eat bread with defiled, that is to say, with unwashen, hands, they found fault. For the Pharisees, and all the Jews, except they wash their hands oft, eat not, holding the tradition of the elders. And when they come from the market, except they wash, they eat not. And many other things there be, which they have received to hold, as the washing of cups, and pots, brasen vessels, and of tables. Then the Pharisees and scribes asked him, Why walk not thy disciples according to the tradition of the elders, but eat bread with unwashen hands? He answered and said unto them, Well hath Esaias prophesied of you hypocrites, as it is written, This people honoureth me with their lips, but their heart is far from me. Howbeit in vain do they worship me, teaching for doctrines the commandments of men. For laying aside the commandment of God, ye hold the tradition of men, as the washing of pots and cups: and many other such like things ye do. And he said unto them, Full well ye reject the commandment of God, that ye may keep your own tradition. For Moses said, Honour thy father and thy mother; and, Whoso curseth father or mother, let him die the death: But ye say, If a man shall say to his father or mother, It is Corban, that is to say, a gift, by whatsoever thou mightest be profited by me; he shall be free. And ye suffer him

no more to do ought for his father or his mother; Making the word of God of none effect through your tradition, which ye have delivered: and many such like things do ye. And when he had called all the people unto him, he said unto them, Hearken unto me every one of you, and understand: There is nothing from without a man, that entering into him can defile him: but the things which come out of him, those are they that defile the man. If any man have ears to hear, let him hear." (Mark 7:1-16 KJV)

The verse in question ends the paragraph where Jesus addresses why His disciples did eat wash their hands before eating.

The Pharisees washed their hands (up to the elbow according to Theoplylact) not for cleanliness nor sanitary considerations, but "holding to the tradition of the elders." The Gentiles, any possible contact with the Gentiles and anything the Gentiles might have touched must be washed off of their hands, cups, pots, brazen vessels and tables. Ceremonial cleanliness must be maintained by such a ritual according to tradition.

When they saw Jesus' disciples did not hold with this tradition, they asked Jesus why they ate their food "with unwashen hands?"

Jesus answered more than they wanted to hear. Quoting from the prophet Isaiah (29:13), Christ calls them hypocrites, saying, "This people honoureth me with their lips, but their heart is far from me." It is one thing to give God lip service, another to honor Him with their hearts. They were empty in presenting that honour and worship, because they were "teaching for doctrines the commandments of men." The law of God did not require the washing they were upset about, but one could "reject the commandment of God" and keep their tradition and they were fine with that.

For example, Moses called for honoring, caring for and obeying one's parents, but if a present was made, they freed the person from any responsibility. Thus, they negated the Word of God through their tradition, not only in this one example, but in many things.

He then explains to them why their tradition was wrong. It is not what is eaten, but what is done "that defile the man." It is not what goes in, but what comes out.

In conclusion, Jesus tells them, "If any man have ears to hear, let him hear." It is the punctuation of the lesson.

The verse in question unquestionably fits the flow. With it, Jesus clearly makes His point.

Internal Evidence.

There appears to be no objection internally to the verse.

The conclusion

Metzger says,

"This verse, though present in the majority of witnesses, is absent from important Alexandrian witnesses (Aleph B L ⬚ al). It appears to be a scribal gloss (derived perhaps from 4.9 or 4.23), introduced as an appropriate sequel to ver. 14."* [pp. 94, 95]

It is admitted that the weight of the evidence "the majority of the witnesses" is for the inclusion of the passage. Our examination shows this is true from the earliest writings on. The difficulty is seen in two areas: 1) giving an undue emphasis to certain manuscripts, and 2) giving primary consideration to perceived subjective internal evidence.

There is no reason to reject the verse, and every reason to accept it.

When the seven points of truth are examined, all seven (**1. Antiquity, 2. Number, 3. Variety, 5. Continuity, 6. Context of the Passage,** and **7. Internal Considerations**) are in favor of the inclusion of the verse.

Does Mark 9:44 Belong in the New Testament?

This verse is included by THE TEXTUS RECEPTUS, THE MAJORITY TEXT, THE KING JAMES VERSION, AND THE NEW KING JAMES VERSION, and omitted by THE WESTCOTT/HORT, NESTLE, UNITED BIBLE SOCIETY GREEK TEXTS, AND THE AMERICAN STANDARD VERSION, THE REVISED STANDARD VERSION, TODAY'S ENGLISH VERSION, THE LIVING BIBLE, THE NEW INTERNATIONAL VERSION, THE COMMON ENGLISH BIBLE, AND THE ENGLISH STANDARD VERSION.

Passage	TR	W/H	NT	BS	MT	KJV	ASV	RSV	TEV	LB	NAS	NIV	NKJ	CEB	ESV
Mark 9:44	--	o	o	o	--	--	o	O	o	o	o	O	--	o	o

The verse will be examined according to the method proposed by J.W. Burgon and Edward Miler.

Antiquity of witnesses

The second century sees the Diatessaron of Tatian and two Syriac versions (Peshitta and Harclean) including the verse, while one Syriac (the Sinaitic) omits it.

The third century sees a lone witness, Irenaeus, for the inclusion of the verse, while three Coptic versions (Sahidic, Bohairic, and Fayyumic) omit the verse.

The fourth century sees one Old Latin version (Vercellensis), the Vulgate and the Gothic version including the verse, while two uncials ({Aleph} Sinaiticus and {B} Vaticanus), one Old Latin version (Bobiensis) and the Armenian version omit it.

The verse has ancient evidence for its inclusion; but, the evidence of the first four centuries slightly favors omitting the verse.

FOR	AGAINST

2ND CENTURY

FOR	AGAINST
Diatessaron of Tatian	
Peshitta Syriac version (II-VII)	Sinaitic Syriac version (II-VII)
Harclean Syriac version (II-VII)	

3RD CENTURY

FOR	AGAINST
	Sahidic Coptic (III-VI)
Irenaeus	Bohairic Coptic (III-VI)
	Fayyumic Coptic (III-VI)

4TH CENTURY

FOR	AGAINST
Vercellensis Old Latin version	Aleph Sinaiticus uncial
Vulgate version	B Vaticanus uncial
Gothic version	Bobiensis Old Latin (IV/V)
	Armenian version (IV/V)

Number

There are thirty-two Greek manuscripts which include the verse, and sixteen which exclude it.

There are fifteen Versions which include the verse, and seven which exclude it.

There are three early writers which include the verse, and none who exclude it.

It is found in the Byzantine Manuscripts, which text type the vast majority of Greek manuscripts are placed in.

FOR   **AGAINST**

GREEK MSS	VERSIONS	EARLY WRITERS	BYZ MSS	TEXT	BYZ MSS	EARLY WRITERS	VERSIONS	GREEK MSS
32	15	3	+	Mk. 9:44	-	0	7	16

There is no doubt that the numbers are in favor of inclusion of the verse, over two to one in the UBS critical apparatus, and far more than that when the "Byzantine Manuscripts" are included.

Variety

The verse is testified by Greek manuscripts (both Uncial and Minuscule) from every area that they are extant. It is included in versions coming from various areas and influences. The early writers who testify to its inclusion are few, but they do not waver. It is not found just in the New Testaments in a particular area, but is found universally.

Weight

When you consider the character of the evidence, it favors the inclusion of the verses. All of the Syriac versions (possibly the first language the New Testament was translated into) include the verse. It is noted by the Coptic. It is included in most known old Latin version (regardless of location). It is included even in the less reliable Vulgate. The more reliable uncials include it (W, amongst others). The vast majority of minuscules include it. It is found in both versions of the lectionaries.

The exclusion is based upon mainly witnesses of Egyptian origin or influence: some Bohairic Coptic, the Sinaiticus and Vaticanus and Regius uncials (whose character rarely agrees with one another), etc.

The reliability and strength of the witnesses for the inclusion is weightier.

Continuity

In the 2ND Century, DIATESSARON OF TATIAN and two SYRIAC VERSIONS (PESHITTA, HARCLEAN dated between the 2ND and 7TH Centuries) include the verse. The SINAITIC SYRIAC VERSION omits it.

In the 3RD Century, IRENAEUS (in the Latin) includes the verse. Three COPTIC VERSIONS (SAHIDIC, BOHAIRIC, FAYYUMIC – dating from the 3RD to the 6TH Century) omit the verse.

In the 4TH Century, three versions (VERCELLENSIS OLD LATIN, VULGATE, GOTHIC) include the verse. Two uncials (SINAITICUS {ALEPH}, VATICANUS {B}) and two versions (BOBIENSIS OLD LATIN, ARMENIAN – dated either 4TH or 5TH Century) omit the verse.

In the 5TH Century, one uncial (ALEXANDRINUS), four Old LATIN VERSIONS (VERONENSIS, BEZAE CANTABRIGIENSIS, CORBEIENSIS II, VINDOBONENSIS) and AUGUSTINE include the verse. Two uncials (EPHRAEMI RESCRIPTUS {C}, FREER GOSPELS {W}) and the GEORGIAN VERSION omit the verse.

In the 6TH Century, one uncial (BEZAE CANTABRIGIENSIS {D}) and the ETHIOPIC VERSION include the verse.

In the 7TH Century, four OLD LATIN VERSIONS (AUREUS, MONACENSIS, USSERIANUS I, RHEDIGERANUS) include the verse.

In the 8TH Century, two uncials (REGIUS {L}, ψ) omit the verse.

In the 9TH Century, three uncials (□, KORIDETHI {Θ}, Π) include the verse. One uncial (D) and two minuscules (565, 892) omit it.

In the 10TH Century, one uncial (X) and one minuscule (1079) include the verse.

In the 11TH Century, four minuscules (124, 788, 700, 1216) include the verse. One minuscule (28) omits the verse.

In the 12TH Century, twelve minuscules (346, 543, 826, 828, 983, 1010, 1071, 1241, 1344, 1195, 1230, 1646) and THE COLBERTINUS OLD LATIN VERSION (dating either 12TH or 13TH Century) include the verse. Two minuscules (1, 1365) omit the verse.

In the 13TH Century, five minuscules (13, 1009, 1242, 1689, 1546) include the verse. One minuscule (118) omit the verse.

In the 14TH Century, two minuscules (2174, 2148) include the verse. Two minuscules (131, 209) omit the verse.

In the 15TH Century, two minuscules (69, 1253) include the verse.

The majority of the lectionaries in the SYNAXARION (the so-called "moveable year" beginning with Easter) and in the MENOLOGIAN (the "fixed year" beginning with September 1) include the verse.

The majority of the Byzantine manuscripts include the verse.

The majority of the lectionaries in the SYNAXARION (the so-called "moveable year" beginning with Easter) and in the MENOLOGIAN (the "fixed year" beginning with September 1) omit the verse.

The majority of the BYZANTINE MANUSCRIPTS include the verse.

The majority of the lectionaries in the SYNAXARION (the so-called "moveable year" beginning with Easter) and in the MENOLOGIAN (the "fixed year" beginning with September 1) include the verse.

THE EVIDENCE FOR MARK 9:44

FOR	AGAINST
2ND CENTURY	
Diatessaron of Tatian	
Peshitta Syriac version (II-VII)	Sinaitic Syriac version (II-VII)
Harclean Syriac version (II-VII)	
3RD CENTURY	
	Sahidic Coptic (III-VI)
Irenaeus	Bohairic Coptic (III-VI)
	Fayyumic Coptic (III-VI)

4TH CENTURY

Vercellensis Old Latin version

Vulgate version

Gothic version

Aleph Sinaiticus uncial

B Vaticanus uncial

Bobiensis Old Latin (IV/V)

Armenian version (IV/V)

5TH CENTURY

A Alexandrinus uncial

Veronensis Old Latin version

Bezae Cantabrigiensis Old Latin

Corbeiensis II Old Latin

Augustine

C Ephraemi Rescriptus uncial

W Freer Gospels uncial

Georgian version

6TH CENTURY

D Bezae Cantabrigiensis uncial

Ethiopic version

7TH CENTRY

Aureus Old Latin version

Monacensis Old Latin version

Usserianus I Old Latin version

Rhedigeranus Old Latin version

8TH CENTURY

L Regius uncial

Psi uncial (VIII/IX)

9TH CENTURY

K uncial

Koridethi Theta uncial

PI uncial

Delta uncial

565 minuscule

892 minuscule

10TH CENTURY

X uncial

1079 minuscule

11TH CENTURY

124 minuscule

788 minuscule

700 minuscule

1216 minuscule

28 minuscule

12TH CENTURY

346 minuscule

543 minuscule

826 minuscule

828 minuscule

983 minuscule

1010 minuscule

1071 minuscule

1241 minuscule

1344 minuscule

1195 minuscule

1230 minuscule

1646 minuscule

1 minuscule

1365 minuscule

13TH CENTURY

13 minuscule

1009 minuscule

1242 minuscule

1689 minuscule

1546 minuscule

118 minuscule

14TH CENTURY

2174 minuscule	131 minuscule
2148 minuscule	209 minuscule

15TH CENTURY

69 minuscule

1253 minuscule

The 8th century is the only century not to show evidence (according to the UBS apparatus) for the inclusion of the verse. Yet, the witness from this century is scant, including only two witnesses which omit the verse. On the other hand, the 6th, 7th, and 10th centuries fail to produce a single witness to omit the passage. In addition, the 11th and 13th produce only one witness to omit. There is a break in the continuity of the omission of the verse, which gives pause as to its authenticity.

The Context of Passage

"For whosoever shall give you a cup of water to drink in my name, because ye belong to Christ, verily I say unto you, he shall not lose his reward. And whosoever shall offend one of these little ones that believe in me, it is better for him that a millstone were hanged about his neck, and he were cast into the sea.

"And if thy hand offend thee, cut it off: it is better for thee to enter into life maimed, than having two hands to go into hell, into the fire that never shall be quenched: **Where their worm dieth not, and the fire is not quenched.** *And if thy foot offend thee, cut it off: it is better for thee to enter halt into life, than having two feet to be cast into hell, into the fire that never shall be quenched:* **Where their worm dieth not, and the fire is not quenched.** *And if thine eye offend thee, pluck it out: it is better for thee to enter into the kingdom of God with one eye, than having two eyes to be cast into hell fire: Where their worm dieth not, and the fire is not quenched.*

"For every one shall be salted with fire, and every sacrifice shall be salted with salt. Salt is good: but if the salt have lost his saltness, wherewith will ye season it? Have salt in yourselves, and have peace one with another." (MARK 9:40-50 KJV)

The highlighted verses above are verses 44 & 46, both of which are questioned. They are the same as verse 48.

The verses in question introduce a repetitive theme in the passage: "where their worm dieth not, and the fire is not quenched." It describes the hell fire that follows the punishment for those who offend. It is better to have only one hand, only one foot, or only one eye than to go "where their worm dieth not, and the fire is not quenched." It is a reference to the prophecy of Isaiah.

And they shall go forth, and look upon the carcasses of the men that have transgressed against me: **for their worm shall not die, neither shall their fire be quenched;** *and they shall be* *an abhorring unto all flesh.* (ISAIAH **66:24 KJV**)

The repetition of the statement provides poetic balance in the passage.

Internal Evidence.

There appears to be no objection internally to the verse.

The conclusion

Metzger says,

"The words, οπου ο σκωληζ ... ου σβεννυται, **which are lacking in important early witnesses** *(including Aleph B C W it*ᵏ *syr*ˢ *cop*ˢᵃ *), were added by copyists from ver. 48."* [p. 102]

The only reason for rejecting the verse is that it is repeated in the passage. Yet, the poetic beauty, the dramatic emphasis, the oratorical balance accomplished by this repetition seem to be ignored. It is a passage in which Jesus *waxes poetic*.

There is no reason to reject the verse, and every reason to accept it.

When the seven points of truth are examined, all seven (**1. Antiquity, 2. Number, 3. Variety, 4. Weight, 5. Continuity, 6. Context of the Passage,** and **7. Internal Considerations**) are in favor of the inclusion of the verse.

Does Mark 9:46 Belong In the New Testament?

This verse is included by THE TEXTUS RECEPTUS, THE MAJORITY TEXT, THE KING JAMES VERSION, AND THE NEW KING JAMES VERSION, and omitted by THE WESTCOTT/HORT, NESTLE, UNITED BIBLE SOCIETY GREEK TEXTS, AND THE AMERICAN STANDARD VERSION, THE REVISED STANDARD VERSION, TODAY'S ENGLISH VERSION, THE LIVING BIBLE, THE NEW INTERNATIONAL VERSION, THE COMMON ENGLISH BIBLE, AND THE ENGLISH STANDARD VERSION.

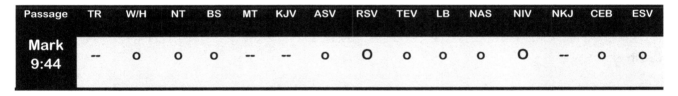

Passage	TR	W/H	NT	BS	MT	KJV	ASV	RSV	TEV	LB	NAS	NIV	NKJ	CEB	ESV
Mark 9:44	--	o	o	o	--	--	o	O	o	o	o	O	--	o	o

*The verse will be examine*d according to the method proposed by J.W. Burgon and Edward Miler.

Antiquity of witnesses

The second century sees the Diatessaron of Tatian and two Syriac versions (Peshitta and Harclean) including the verse, while one Syriac (the Sinaitic) omits it.

The third century sees a lone witness, Irenaeus, for the inclusion of the verse, while three Coptic versions (Sahidic, Bohairic, and Fayyumic) omit the verse.

The fourth century sees one Old Latin version (Vercellensis), the Vulgate and the Gothic version including the verse, while two uncials ({Aleph} Sinaiticus and {B} Vaticanus), one Old Latin version (Bobiensis) and the Armenian version omit it.

The verse has ancient evidence for its inclusion; but, the evidence of the first four centuries slightly favors omitting the verse.

FOR	AGAINST
2ND CENTURY	
Diatessaron of Tatian	
Peshitta Syriac version (II-VII)	Sinaitic Syriac version (II-VII)
Harclean Syriac version (II-VII)	
3RD CENTURY	
	Sahidic Coptic (III-VI)
Irenaeus	Bohairic Coptic (III-VI)
	Fayyumic Coptic (III-VI)
4TH CENTURY	
	Aleph Sinaiticus uncial
Vercellensis Old Latin version	B Vaticanus uncial
Vulgate version	Bobiensis Old Latin (IV/V)
Gothic version	Armenian version (IV/V)

Number

There are thirty-one Greek manuscripts which include the verse, and fifteen which exclude it.

There are seventeen Versions which include the verse, and six which exclude it.

There are two early writers which include the verse, and one who exclude it.

It is found in the Byzantine Manuscripts, which text type the vast majority of Greek manuscripts are placed in.

FOR   **AGAINST**

GREEK MSS	VERSIONS	EARLY WRITERS	BYZ MSS	TEXT	BYZ MSS	EARLY WRITERS	VERSIONS	GREEK MSS
31	17	2	+	Mk. 9:46	-	1	6	15

There is no doubt that the numbers are in favor of inclusion of the verse, over two to one in the UBS critical apparatus, and far more than that when the "Byzantine Manuscripts" are included.

Variety

The verse is testified by Greek manuscripts (both Uncial and Minuscule) from every area that they are extant. It is included in versions coming from various areas and influences. The early writers who testify to its inclusion are few, but they do not waver. It is not found just in the New Testaments in a particular area, but is found universally.

Weight

When you consider the character of the evidence, it favors the inclusion of the verses. All of the Syriac versions (possibly the first language the New Testament was translated into) include the verse. It is noted by the Coptic. It is included in most known old Latin version (regardless of location). It is included even in the less reliable Vulgate. The more reliable uncials include it (W, amongst others). The vast majority of minuscules include it. It is found in both versions of the lectionaries.

The exclusion is based upon mainly witnesses of Egyptian origin or influence: some Bohairic Coptic, the Sinaiticus and Vaticanus and Regius uncials (whose character rarely agrees with one another), etc.

The reliability and strength of the witnesses for the inclusion is weightier.

Continuity

The evidence favors the inclusion of the verse. Even when you only consider the evidence in the UBS critical apparatus it is still in favor of inclusion almost two to one.

In the 2ND Century, DIATESSARON OF TATIAN and two SYRIAC VERSIONS (PESHITTA, HARCLEAN dated between the 2ND and 7TH Centuries) include the verse. The SINAITIC SYRIAC VERSION and certain copies of DIATESSARON OF TATIAN omits it.

In the 3RD Century, three COPTIC VERSIONS (SAHIDIC, BOHAIRIC, FAYYUMIC – dating from the 3RD to the 6TH Century) omit the verse.

In the 4TH Century, three versions (VERCELLENSIS OLD LATIN, VULGATE, GOTHIC) include the verse. Two uncials (SINAITICUS {ALEPH}, VATICANUS {B}) and two versions (BOBIENSIS OLD LATIN, ARMENIAN – dated either 4TH or 5TH Century) omit the verse.

In the 5TH Century, one uncial (ALEXANDRINUS), four OLD LATIN VERSIONS (VERONENSIS, BEZAE CANTABRIGIENSIS, CORBEIENSIS II, VINDOBONENSIS), the GEORGIAN VERSION and AUGUSTINE include the verse. Two uncials (EPHRAEMI RESCRIPTUS {C}, FREER GOSPELS {W}) omit the verse.

In the 6TH Century, one uncial (BEZAE CANTABRIGIENSIS {D}), the BRIXIANUS OLD LATIN VERSION and the ETHIOPIC VERSION include the verse.

In the 7TH Century, four OLD LATIN VERSIONS (AUREUS, MONACENSIS, USSERIANUS I, RHEDIGERANUS) include the verse.

In the 8TH Century, two uncials (REGIUS {L}, □) omit the verse.

In the 9TH Century, three uncials (K, KORIDETHI {Θ}, Π) include the verse. Two minuscules

(565, 892) omit it.

In the 10TH Century, one uncial (X) and one minuscule (1079) include the verse.

In the 11TH Century, four minuscules (124, 788, 700, 1216) include the verse. One minuscule (28) omits the verse.

In the 12TH Century, twelve minuscules (346, 543, 826, 828, 983, 1010, 1071, 1241, 1344, 1195, 1230, 1646) and the COLBERTINUS OLD LATIN VERSION (dating either 12TH or 13TH Century) include the verse. Two minuscules (1, 1365) omit the verse.

In the 13TH Century, four minuscules (13, 1242, 1689, 1546) include the verse. Two lectionaries (L18, L19) omit the verse.

In the 14TH Century, two minuscules (2174, 2148) include the verse. Two minuscules (131, 209) omit the verse.

In the 15TH Century, two minuscules (69, 1253) include the verse.

The majority of the lectionaries in the SYNAXARION (the so-called "moveable year" beginning with Easter) and in the MENOLOGIAN (the "fixed year" beginning with September 1) include the verse.

The majority of the BYZANTINE MANUSCRIPTS include the verse.

THE EVIDENCE FOR Mark 9:46

FOR	AGAINST
2ND CENTURY	
Diatessaron of Tatian	Diatessaron of Tatian
Augustine	
3RD CENTURY	
	Sahidic Coptic version (III-VI)
4TH CENTURY	
	Aleph Sinaiticus uncial
Vulgate version	B Vaticanus uncial
Gothic version	Bobiensis Old Latin (IV/V)
Vercellensis Old Latin version	Armenian version (IV/V)

5TH CENTURY

A Alexandrinus uncial

Veronensis Old Latin version

Corbeiensis Old Latin version

Corbeiensis II Old Latin version

Vidobonensis Old Latin version

Georgian version

Augustine

C Ephraemi Rescriptus uncial

W Freer Gospels uncial

6TH CENTURY

D Bezae Cantabrigiensis uncial

Brixianus Old Latin version

Ethiopic version

7TH CENTURY

Aureus Old Latin version

Monacensis Old Latin version

Usserianus I Old Latin version

Rhedigeranus Old Latin (VII/VIII)

8TH CENTURY

L Regius uncial

Psi uncial (VII/VIII)

9TH CENTURY

K uncial

Koridethi Theta uncial

Psi uncial

565 minuscule

892 minuscule

10TH CENTURY

X uncial

1079 minuscule

11TH CENTURY

124 minuscule

788 minuscule

700 minuscule   28 minuscule

1216 minuscule

12TH CENTURY

346 minuscule

543 minuscule

826 minuscule

828 minuscule

983 minuscule

1010 minuscule

1071 minuscule   1 minuscule

1241 minuscule   1365 minuscule

1344 minuscule

1195 minuscule

1230 minuscule

1646 minuscule

Colbertinus Old Latin version (XII/XIII)

13TH CENTURY

13 minuscule

1242 minuscule   118 minuscule

1689 minuscule   L19 lectionary

1546 minuscule

14TH CENTURY

2174 minuscule   131 minuscule

2148 minuscule   209 minuscule

69 minuscule

1253 minuscule

The 3rd and 8th centuries are the only centuries not to show evidence (according to the UBS apparatus) for the inclusion of the verse. Yet, the witness from the 3rd century is limited to only one witness who omits the verse, and the witness from the 8th century is scant, including only two witnesses which omit the verse. On the other hand, the 6th, 7th, 10th and 15th centuries fail to produce a single witness to omit the passage. In addition, the 1st, 2nd, and 11th produce only one witness to omit. There is a break in the continuity of the omission of the verse, which gives pause as to its authenticity.

The Context of Passage

"For whosoever shall give you a cup of water to drink in my name, because ye belong to Christ, verily I say unto you, he shall not lose his reward. And whosoever shall offend one of these little ones that believe in me, it is better for him that a millstone were hanged about his neck, and he were cast into the sea.

"And if thy hand offend thee, cut it off: it is better for thee to enter into life maimed, than having two hands to go into hell, into the fire that never shall be quenched: **Where their worm dieth not, and the fire is not quenched.** *And if thy foot offend thee, cut it off: it is better for thee to enter halt into life, than having two feet to be cast into hell, into the fire that never shall be quenched:* **Where their worm dieth not, and the fire is not quenched.** *And if thine eye offend thee, pluck it out: it is better for thee to enter into the kingdom of God with one eye, than having two eyes to be cast into hell fire: Where their worm dieth not, and the fire is not quenched.*

"For every one shall be salted with fire, and every sacrifice shall be salted with salt. Salt is good: but if the salt have lost his saltness, wherewith will ye season it? Have salt in yourselves, and have peace one with another." (MARK 9:40-50 KJV)

The highlighted verses above are verses 44 & 46, both of which are questioned. They are the same as verse 48.

The verses in question introduce a repetitive theme in the passage: "where their worm dieth not, and the fire is not quenched." It describes the hell fire that follows the punishment for those who offend. It is better to have only one hand, only one foot, or only one eye than to go "where their worm dieth not, and the fire is not quenched." It is a reference to the prophecy of Isaiah.

And they shall go forth, and look upon the carcasses of the men that have transgressed against me: **for their worm shall not die, neither shall their fire be quenched;** *and they shall be an abhorring unto all flesh.* (ISAIAH 66:24 KJV)

The repetition of the statement provides poetic balance in the passage.

Internal Evidence.

There appears to be no objection internally to the verse.

The conclusion

Metzger says,

"The words, οπου ο σκωληζ ... ου σβεννυται, which are lacking in important early witnesses (including Aleph B C W it^k syr^s cop^{sa}), were added by copyists from ver. 48." [p. 102]

The only reason for rejecting the verse is that it is repeated in the passage. Yet, the poetic beauty, the dramatic emphasis, the oratorical balance accomplished by this repetition seem to be ignored. It is a passage in which Jesus *waxes poetic*.

There is no reason to reject the verse, and every reason to accept it.

When the seven points of truth are examined, all seven (**1. Antiquity, 2. Number, 3. Variety, 4. Weight, 5. Continuity, 6. Context of the Passage,** and **7. Internal Considerations**) are in favor of the inclusion of the verse.

Does Mark 11:26 Belong in the New Testament?

This verse is included by THE TEXTUS RECEPTUS, THE MAJORITY TEXT, THE KING JAMES VERSION, AND THE NEW KING JAMES VERSION, and omitted by THE WESTCOTT/HORT, NESTLE, UNITED BIBLE SOCIETY GREEK TEXTS, AND THE AMERICAN STANDARD VERSION, THE REVISED STANDARD VERSION, TODAY'S ENGLISH VERSION, THE LIVING BIBLE, THE NEW INTERNATIONAL VERSION, THE COMMON ENGLISH BIBLE, AND THE ENGLISH STANDARD VERSION.

Passage	TR	W/H	NT	BS	MT	KJV	ASV	RSV	TEV	LB	NAS	NIV	NKJ	CEB	ESV
Mark 11:26	--	o	o	o	--	--	o	O	o	o	o	O	--	o	o

The verse will be examined according to the method proposed by J.W. Burgon and Edward Miler.

Antiquity of witnesses

The second century sees the Diatessaron of Tatian and two Syriac versions (Peshitta and Harclean) including the verse, while two Syriac (the Sinaitic and Palestinian) omits it.

The third century sees two witnesses, one Coptic version (Bohairic in some manuscripts) and Syrian, for the inclusion of the verse, while two Coptic versions (Sahidic, and Bohairic) omit the verse.

The fourth century sees one Old Latin version (Vercellensis), the Vulgate and the Gothic version including the verse, while two uncials ({Aleph} Sinaiticus and {B} Vaticanus), one Old Latin version (Bobiensis) and the Armenian version omit it.

The verse has ancient evidence for its inclusion; but, the evidence of the first four centuries slightly favors omitting the verse.

	FOR			AGAINST	
	2ND CENTURY				
Peshitta Syriac version (II-VII)			Sinaitic Syriac version (II-VI)		
Harclean Syriac version (II-VI)			Palestinian Syriac (II-VII)		
Diatessaron of Tatian					
	3RD CENTURY				
Bohairic Coptic version (III-VI)			Sahidic Coptic version (III-VI)		
Syrian			Bohairic Coptic version (III-VI)		
	4TH CENTURY				
			Aleph Sinaiticus uncial		
Gothic version			B Vaticanus uncial		
Vulgate version			Vulgate		
Vercellensis Old Latin version			Bobiensis Old Latin (IV/V)		
			Armenian version (IV/V)		

Number

There are fifty Greek manuscripts which include the verse, and ten which exclude it.

There are fifteen Versions which include the verse, and nine which exclude it.

There are three early writers which include the verse, and none who exclude it.

It is found in the Byzantine Manuscripts, which text type the vast majority of Greek manuscripts are placed in.

FOR   **AGAINST**

GREEK MSS	VERSIONS	EARLY WRITERS	BYZ MSS	TEXT	BYZ MSS	EARLY WRITERS	VERSIONS	GREEK MSS
50	15	3	+	Mk. 11:26	-	0	9	10

There is no doubt that the numbers are in favor of inclusion of the verse, five to one manuscripts in the UBS critical apparatus, and far more than that when the "Byzantine Manuscripts" are included.

Variety

The verse is testified by Greek manuscripts (both Uncial and Minuscule) from every area that they are extant. It is included in versions coming from various areas and influences. The early writers who testify to its inclusion are few, but they do not waver. It is not found just in the New Testaments in a particular area, but is found universally.

Weight

When you consider the character of the evidence, it favors the inclusion of the verses. All of the Syriac versions (possibly the first language the New Testament was translated into) include the verse. It is noted by the Coptic. It is included in most known old Latin version (regardless of location). It is included even in the less reliable Vulgate. The more reliable uncials include it (W, amongst others). The vast majority of minuscules include it. It is found in both versions of the lectionaries.

The exclusion is based upon mainly witnesses of Egyptian origin or influence: some Bohairic Coptic, the Sinaiticus and Vaticanus and Regius uncials (whose character rarely agrees with one another), etc.

The reliability and strength of the witnesses for the inclusion is weightier.

Continuity

In the 2ND Century, the Diatessaron of Tatian and two Syriac versions (Peshitta, Harclean – dating from the 2ND to the 7TH Century) include the verse. Two Syriac versions (Sinaitic, Palestinian – dating from the 2ND to the 7TH Century) omit the verse.

In the 3RD Century, Cyprian and manuscripts according to the Bohairic Coptic version (dated from the 3RD to the 6th Century) includes the verse. The Sahidic Coptic version and the text of the Bohairic Coptic version (both dating from the 3RD to the 6TH Century) omit the verse.

In the 4TH Century, three versions (Gothic, Vulgate, Vercellensis Old Latin) include the verse. Two uncials (Sinaiticus {Aleph}, Vaticanus {B}), and three versions (manuscripts according to the Vulgate, Bobiensis Old Latin {dated 4TH or 5TH Century}, Armenian {dated 4TH or 5TH Century}) omit the verse.

In the 5TH Century, three uncials (Alexandrinus {A}, Bezae Cantabrigiensis {D}, Ephraemi Rescriptus {C}), four Old Latin versions (Veronensis, Bezae Cantabrigiensis, Corbeiensis II, Vindobonensis) and Augustine include the verse. One uncial (Freer Gospels {W}) and the Georgian version omit it.

In the 6TH Century, the Ethiopic version includes the verse.

In the 7TH Century, three Old Latin versions (Monacensis, Usserianus I, Aureus) include the verse. One Old Latin version (Rhedigeranus – dated 7TH or 8TH Century) omits the verse.

In the 8TH Century, two uncials (Regius {L}, Ψ) omit the verse.

In the 9TH Century, three uncials (K, Koridethi {Θ}, Π) and one minuscule (33) include the verse. One uncial (D) and two minuscules (565, 692) omit the verse.

In the 10TH Century, one uncial (X) and one minuscule (1079) include the verse. Two minuscules (700, 1216) omit the verse.

In the 11TH Century, three minuscules (124, 788, 28) and three lectionaries (L32 in the Synaxarion, L1627 in the Menologion, L374) include the verse.

In the 12TH Century, fourteen minuscules (1, 346, 543, 826, 828, 983, 1010, 1071, 1241, 1344, 1365, 1195, 1230, 1646), four lectionaries (L70, L80, L69, L203) and one Old Latin version (Colbertinus – dated either 12TH or 13TH Century) include the verse.

In the 13TH Century, five minuscules (118, 13, 1009, 1242, 1689, 1546) and three lectionaries (L10, L12 in part, L333) include the verse.

In the 14TH Century, four minuscules (131, 209, 2174, 2148) and two lectionaries (L313, L1579) include the verse.

In the 15TH Century, two minuscules (69, 1253) include the verse.

The majority of the lectionaries in the Synaxarion (the so-called "moveable year" beginning with Easter) and in the Menologian (the "fixed year" beginning with September 1) include the verse.

The majority of the Byzantine manuscripts include Mark 11:26.

THE EVIDENCE FOR MARK 11:26

FOR	AGAINST
2ND CENTURY	
Peshitta Syriac version (II-VII)	Sinaitic Syriac version (II-VI)
Harclean Syriac version (II-VI)	Palestinian Syriac (II-VII)
Diatessaron of Tatian	
3RD CENTURY	
Bohairic Coptic version (III-VI)	Sahidic Coptic version (III-VI)
Syrian	Bohairic Coptic version (III-VI)
4TH CENTURY	
	Aleph Sinaiticus uncial
Gothic version	B Vaticanus uncial
Vulgate version	Vulgate
Vercellensis Old Latin version	Bobiensis Old Latin version (IV/V)
	Armenian version (IV/V)
5TH CENTURY	
A Alexandrinus uncial	
D Bezae Cantabrigiensis uncial	
C Ephraemi Rescriptus uncial	
Veronensis Old Latin version	W Freer Gospels uncial
Bezae Cantabrigiensis Old Latin	Georgian version
Corbeiensis II Old Latin version	
Vindobonensis Old Latin version	
Augustine	
6TH CENTURY	
Ethiopic version	
7TH CENTURY	

Monacensis Old Latin version

Usserianus I Old Latin version   **Rhedigeranus Old Latin version**

Aureus Old Latin version

8TH CENTURY

L Regius uncial

Psi uncial

9TH CENTURY

K uncial

Koridethi Theta uncial   Delta uncial

Pi uncial   565 minuscule

33 minuscule   892 minuscule

10TH CENTURY

X uncial

1079 minuscule

11TH CENTURY

124 minuscule

788 minuscule

28 minuscule   700 minuscule

L32 (in the Synaxarion) lectionary   1216 minuscule

L1627 (in the Menologion) lectionary

L374 lectionary

12TH CENTURY

1 minuscule

346 minuscule

543 minuscule

826 minuscule

828 minuscule

983 minuscule

1010 minuscule

1071 minuscule

1241 minuscule

1344 minuscule

1365 minuscule

1195 minuscule

1230 minuscule

1646 minuscule

L69 lectionary

L70 lectionary

L80 lectionary

L303 lectionary

Colbertinus Old Latin version (XII/XIII)

13TH CENTURY

118 minuscule

13 minuscule

1009 minuscule

1242 minuscule

1689 minuscule

1546 minuscule

L10 lectionary

L12 (in part) lectionary

L333 lectionary

14TH CENTURY

131 minuscule

209 minuscule

2174 minuscule

2148 minuscule

L313 lectionary

L1579 lectionary

15TH CENTURY

69 minuscule

1253 minuscule

The 8th century is the only century not to show evidence (according to the UBS apparatus) for the inclusion of the verse. Yet, the witness from the 8th century is scant, including only two witnesses which omit the verse. On the other hand, the 6th, 10th, 12th, 13th, 14th and 15th centuries fail to produce a single witness to omit the passage. In addition, the 7th century produces only one witness to omit. There is a break in the continuity of the omission of the verse, which gives pause as to its authenticity.

The Context of Passage

"And when ye stand praying, forgive, if ye have ought against any: that your Father also which is in heaven may forgive you your trespasses. But if ye do not forgive, neither will your Father which is in heaven forgive your trespasses." **(MARK 11:24-26 KJV)**

Jesus is giving instruction on prayer following discussion of the withered fig tree. During that discussion of faith, He instructs His disciples when they prayer to forgive those who trespass against them that they also might be forgiven. The verse in question then provides the antithesis of this statement reinforcing His point: *But if ye do not forgive, neither will your Father which is in heaven forgive your trespasses.*

It parallels the statement of Jesus from **MATTHEW 6:15**. There is no question but that it fits into the flow of the context.

Internal Evidence.

There appears to be no objection internally to the verse.

The conclusion

Metzger says,

While it is possible that τι ειπωμεν *may have fallen out accidentally (*εαν ειπωμεν *follows immediately), the Committee was impressed by the antiquity and diversity of the evidence supporting the shorter text, and judged that the phrase was a colloquial addition that is often characteristic of the Western (and Caesarean) type of text.* [p. 110]

The verse is omitted because it is missing from their pet manuscripts, and it is a shorter reading. It fits the context, it fits the literary style, and the evidence is overwhelmingly in favor of its inclusion. Objectively the verse belongs as part of the inspired word of God.

There is no reason to reject the verse, and every reason to accept it.

When the seven points of truth are examined, all seven (**1. Antiquity, 2. Number, 3. Variety, 4. Weight, 5. Continuity, 6. Context of the Passage,** and **7. Internal Considerations**) are in favor of the inclusion of the verse.

Does Mark 15:28 Belong in the New Testament?

This verse is included by THE TEXTUS RECEPTUS, THE MAJORITY TEXT, THE KING JAMES VERSION, THE NEW KING JAMES VERSION, AND THE COMMON ENGLISH BIBLE and omitted by THE WESTCOTT/HORT, NESTLE, UNITED BIBLE SOCIETY GREEK TEXTS, AND THE AMERICAN STANDARD VERSION, THE REVISED STANDARD VERSION, TODAY'S ENGLISH VERSION, THE LIVING BIBLE, THE NEW INTERNATIONAL VERSION, , AND THE ENGLISH STANDARD VERSION.

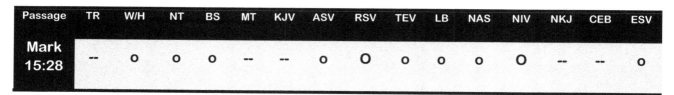

Passage	TR	W/H	NT	BS	MT	KJV	ASV	RSV	TEV	LB	NAS	NIV	NKJ	CEB	ESV
Mark 15:28	--	o	o	o	--	--	o	O	o	o	o	O	--	--	o

The verse will be examined according to the method proposed by Burgon and Miler.

Antiquity of witnesses

The second century sees the Diatessaron of Tatian and two Syriac versions (Peshitta and Harclean) including the verse, while two Syriac (the Sinaitic and Palestinian) omits it.

The third century sees two witnesses, one Coptic version (Bohairic in some manuscripts) and Cyprian, for the inclusion of the verse, while two Coptic versions (Sahidic, and Bohairic) omit the verse.

The fourth century sees one Old Latin version (Vercellensis), the Vulgate and the Gothic version including the verse, while two uncials ({Aleph} Sinaiticus and {B} Vaticanus), one Old Latin version (Bobiensis) and the Armenian version omit it.

The verse has ancient evidence for its inclusion; but, the evidence of the first four centuries slightly favors omitting the verse.

	FOR			AGAINST

	FOR			AGAINST
2ND CENTURY				
Peshitta Syriac (II-VII)				
Harclean Syriac (II-VII)			Sinaitic Syriac (II-VII)	
Palestinian Syriac (II-VII)				
3RD CENTURY				
			Ammonius	
Bohairic Coptic version (III-VI)			Sahidic Coptic (III-VI)	
Origen			Bohairic Coptic (III-VI)	
			Fayyumic Coptic version (apparent support) (III-VI)	
4TH CENTURY				
Gothic version			Aleph Sinaiticus uncial	
Vulgate version			B Vaticanus uncial	
Armenian version (IV/V)			Bobiensis Old Latin (IV/V)	
Eusebian Canons			Eusebian Canons	

Number

There are forty-six Greek manuscripts which include the verse, and seven which exclude it.

There are fifteen Versions which include the verse, and six which exclude it.

There are four early writers which include the verse, and two who exclude it.

It is found in the Byzantine Manuscripts, which text type the vast majority of Greek manuscripts are placed in.

FOR   **AGAINST**

GREEK MSS	VERSIONS	EARLY WRITERS	BYZ MSS	TEXT	BYZ MSS	EARLY WRITERS	VERSIONS	GREEK MSS
46	15	4	+	Mk. 15:28	-	2	6	7

There is no doubt that the numbers are in favor of inclusion of the verse, five to one manuscripts in the UBS critical apparatus, and far more than that when the "Byzantine Manuscripts" are included.

Variety

The verse is testified by Greek manuscripts (both Uncial and Minuscule) from every area that they are extant. It is included in versions coming from various areas and influences. The early writers who testify to its inclusion are few, but they do not waver. It is not found just in the New Testaments in a particular area, but is found universally.

Weight

When you consider the character of the evidence, it favors the inclusion of the verses. All of the Syriac versions (possibly the first language the New Testament was translated into) include the verse. It is noted by the Coptic. It is included in most known old Latin version (regardless of location). It is included even in the less reliable Vulgate. The more reliable uncials include it (W, amongst others). The vast majority of minuscules include it. It is found in both versions of the lectionaries.

The exclusion is based upon mainly witnesses of Egyptian origin or influence: some Bohairic Coptic, the Sinaiticus and Vaticanus and Regius uncials (whose character rarely agrees with one another), etc.

The reliability and strength of the witnesses for the inclusion is weightier.

Continuity

In the 2ND Century, three SYRIAC VERSIONS (PESHITTA, HARCLEAN, PALESTINIAN – dated from 2ND to 7TH Century) include the verse. One SYRIAC VERSION (SINAITIC – dated from 2ND to 7TH Century) omitted the verse.

In the 3RD Century, SOME MANUSCRIPTS ACCORDING TO THE BOHAIRIC COPTIC VERSION and Origen include the verse. AMMONIUS, the SAHIDIC COPTIC VERSION (dated from 3RD to 6TH Century), SOME MANUSCRIPTS ACCORDING TO THE BOHAIRIC COPTIC VERSION (dated from 3RD to 6TH Century), and APPARENT EVIDENCE FROM THE FAYYUMIC COPTIC VERSION (dated from 3RD to 6TH Century) omit the verse.

In the 4TH Century, three VERSIONS (GOTHIC, VULGATE, ARMENIAN dating from 4TH or 5TH Century) and SOME MANUSCRIPTS ACCORDING TO THE EUSEBIAN CANONS include the verse. Two uncials (SINAITICUS {ALEPH}, VATICANUS {B}), the BOBIENSIS OLD LATIN VERSION, and the TEXT OF THE EUSEBIAN CANONS omit the verse.

In the 5TH Century, the GEORGIAN VERSION, three OLD LATIN VERSIONS (COLBERTINUS, CORBEIENSIS II, SANGALLENSIS) and APPARENT SUPPORT FROM VIGILIUS include the verse. Two uncials (ALEXANDRINUS {A}, EPHRAEMI RESCRIPTUS {C}) and the BEZAE CANTABRIGIENSIS OLD LATIN VERSION omit the verse.

In the 6TH Century, two uncials (P, 0112 dating from the 6TH or 7TH Century) and the ETHIOPIC VERSION include the verse. One uncial (BEZAE CANTABRIGIENSIS {D}) omits the verse.

In the 7TH Century, three OLD LATIN VERSIONS (AUREUS, USSERIANUS I, RHEDIGERANUS dating from 7TH or 8TH Century) include the verse.

In the 8TH Century, two uncials (REGIUS {L}, 0250) include the verse. One uncial (☐) omits it.

In the 9TH Century, three uncials (KOREDETHI {Θ}, Π, K) and three minuscules (33, 565, 892) include the verse.

In the 10TH Century, one minuscule (1079) includes the verse, and one uncial (X) omits it.

In the 11TH Century, four minuscules (124, 788, 28, 700) and two lectionaries (L216, L883) include the verse.

In the 12TH Century, fourteen minuscules (1, 346, 543, 826, 828, 983, 1010, 1071, 1241, 1344, 1365, 1195, 1230, 1646) and one lectionary (L211) include the verse.

In the 13TH Century, six minuscules (118, 13, 1009, 1242, 1689, 1546) and two lectionaries (L10, L1642) include the verse.

In the 14TH Century, four minuscules (131, 209, 2174, 2148) include the verse.

In the 15TH Century, two minuscules (69, 1253) include the verse.

THE EVIDENCE FOR MARK 15:28

FOR	AGAINST
2ND CENTURY	
Peshitta Syriac (II-VII)	
Harclean Syriac (II-VII)	Sinaitic Syriac (II-VII)
Palestinian Syriac (II-VII)	
3RD CENTURY	
	Ammonius
	Sahidic Coptic (III-VI)
Bohairic Coptic version (III-VI)	Bohairic Coptic (III-VI)
Origen	Fayyumic Coptic version (apparent support) (III-VI)
4TH CENTURY	
Gothic version	Aleph Sinaiticus uncial
Vulgate version	B Vaticanus uncial

Armenian version (IV/V)	Bobiensis Old Latin (IV/V)
Eusebian Canons	Eusebian Canons

5TH CENTURY

Georgian version	
Colbertinus Old Latin version	A Alexandrinus uncial
Corbeiensis II Old Latin version	C Ephraemi Rescriptus uncial
Sangallensis Old Latin version	Bezae Cantabrigiensis Old Latin
Vigilius (apparent support?)	

6TH CENTURY

P uncial	
0112 uncial (V/VII)	D Bezae Cantabrigiensis uncial
Ethiopic version	

7TH CENTURY

Aureus Old Latin

Usserianus I Old Latin

Rhedigeranus Old Latin (VII/VIII)

8TH CENTURY

L Regius uncial	
0250 uncial	Psi uncial (VIII-IX)

9TH CENTURY

Koridethi Theta uncial

Pi uncial

K uncial

33 minuscule

565 minuscule

892 minuscule

10TH CENTURY

1079 minuscule	X uncial

11ᵀᴴ CENTRY

124 minuscule

788 minuscule

28 minuscule

700 minuscule

L216 lectionary

L883 lectionary

12ᵀᴴ CENTURY

1 minuscule

346 minuscule

543 minuscule

826 minuscule

828 minuscule

983 minuscule

1010 minuscule

1071 minuscule

1241 minuscule

1344 minuscule

1365 minuscule

1195 minuscule

1230 minuscule

L1646 lectionary

L211 lectionary

13ᵀᴴ CENTURY

118 minuscule

13 minuscule

1009 minuscule

1242 minuscule

1689 minuscule

1546 minuscule

L10 lectionary

L1642 lectionary

14TH CENTURY

131 minuscule

209 minuscule

2174 minuscule

2148 minuscule

15TH CENTURY

69 minuscule

1253 minuscule

The majority of lectionaries in the Synaxarion (the so-called "moveable year" beginning with Easter) and in the Menologian (the "fixed year" beginning with September 1) omit Mark 15:28.

The majority of the Byzantine manuscripts include Mark 15:28.

After the 6TH Century, there are only two manuscripts which omit the verse. Up to the 6TH Century, the evidence by Century is: 3-1, 2-4, 4-4, 5-3; at the worst even, at the best slightly in favor of Mark 15:28. After the 6TH Century the evidence is 47-2 in favor of inclusion. Again, this is not counting the BYZANTINE MANUSCRIPTS.

The Context of Passage

And they bring him unto the place Golgotha, which is, being interpreted, The place of a skull. And they gave him to drink wine mingled with myrrh: but he received it not. And when they had crucified him, they parted his garments, casting lots upon them, what every man should take. And it was the third hour, and they crucified him. And the superscription of his accusation was written over, THE KING OF THE JEWS. And with him they crucify two thieves; the one on his right hand, and the other on his left. **And the scripture was fulfilled, which saith, And he was numbered with the transgressors.** *And they that passed by railed on him, wagging their heads, and saying, Ah, thou that destroyest the temple, and buildest it in three days, Save thyself, and come down from the cross. Likewise also the chief priests mocking said among themselves with the scribes, He saved others; himself he cannot save. Let Christ* *the King of Israel descend now from the cross, that we may see and believe. And they that were crucified with him reviled him.* **(MARK 15:22-32 KJV)**

Jesus is about to be crucified. He is taken to Golgatha, better known as Mt. Calvary. He is nailed to the cross, and the guards gamble for his garments beneath him. Written over Him is the inscription, THE KING OF THE JEWS. He has been placed between two thieves. *"And the scripture was fulfilled, which saith, And he was numbered with the transgressors."* [see Isaiah 53:12]

The narrative continues with the railing of the people in fulfillment of the 22nd Psalm, including those who were crucified with Him.

The verse in question serves as a central point of focus, showing that the events of Jesus upon the cross were not a series of coincidences, but the fulfillment of God's plan from the beginning.

The verse fits into the flow of the context.

Internal Evidence.

There is a question concerning the use of the fulfillment of scripture by Mark.

Mark begins his Gospel with a reference to the prophets.

As it is written in the prophets, Behold, I send my messenger before thy face, which shall prepare thy way before thee. **[MARK 1:2 KJV]**

The reference in 15:28 would provide a bracketing effect of prophetic references to the Gospel.

The idea that what is to follow is a matter of prophecy is introduced in Jesus' statement from the prior chapter:

I was daily with you in the temple teaching, and ye took me not: but the scriptures must be fulfilled. **[MARK 14:49 KJV]**

The better known prophecies are left unmentioned, while the reference to being crucified with "the malefactors" is shown to show the minuteness of the fulfillment.

Mark uses a milder form of citing the Old Testament in the prior chapter, again from the mouth of Jesus:

The Son of man indeed goeth, as it is written of him: but woe to that man by whom the Son of man is betrayed! good were it for that man if he had never been born. **[MARK 14:21 KJV]**

Thus, although it is rare in Mark to refer to the fulfillment of prophecy, it is not unheard of. Therefore, it is stretching the argument to say it is non-Markan.

The following chart shows the prophecies that are fulfilled in common BY **MATTHEW**, **MARK**, **LUKE** and **JOHN**. Note that there are other instances where, if this is an interpolation, or had been injected into the text, the opportunity availed itself, but was not taken. To assume that it would only have been done in this one instance, is truly assuming the position taken.

PROPHECY	EVENT IN THE LIFE OF CHRIST	FULFILLMENT
Psalm 41:9	*Triumphal Entry into Jerusalem*	Matthew 21:15 Mark 14:10,21
Psalm 41: 9	*Betrayal by a friend*	Matthew 26:15 Mark 14:10, 21
Zechariah 11: 12, 13	*For 30 pieces of silver*	Matthew 26:15 Mark 14:10, 21
Isaiah 53:9-12	*Death with malefactors*	Matthew 26:15 Mark 15:28 Luke 23:40-43
Psalm 109:25 Psalm 22:6, 7	*Insults & Mocking*	Matthew 27:39 Mark 15:29
Psalm 22:18	*Lots cast for clothing*	Mark 15:24 John 19:24

The conclusion

Metzger says,

"The earliest and best witnesses of the Alexandrian and the Western types of text lack ver. 28. It is understandable that copyists could have added the sentence in the margin from Lk 22.37, whence it came into the text itself; there is no reason why, if the sentence were present originally, it should have been deleted. It is also significant that Mark very seldom expressly quotes the Old Testament." [p. 119]

"Could have, would have"... The truth of the matter is, the verse fits into the flow of the context, it fits the literary style of Mark, and the evidence is overwhelmingly in favor of the inclusion of the verse. Mark 15:28 belongs in the Gospel.

There is no reason to reject the verse, and every reason to accept it. When the seven points of truth are examined, all seven (**1. Antiquity, 2. Number, 3. Variety, 4. Weight, 5. Continuity, 6. Context of the Passage,** and **7. Internal Considerations**) are in favor of the inclusion of the verse.

Does Mark 16:9-20 Belong in the New Testament?

This verse is included by THE TEXTUS RECEPTUS, THE MAJORITY TEXT, THE KING JAMES VERSION, THE AMERICAN STANDARD VERSION, THE NEW INTERNATIONAL VERSION, AND THE NEW KING JAMES VERSION, single bracketed by the New American Standard, double-bracketed by THE WESTCOTT/HORT TEXT, THE NESTLE TEXT, AND THE UNITED BIBLE SOCIETIES TEXT, and omitted by THE REVISED STANDARD VERSION, TODAY'S ENGLISH VERSION, THE LIVING BIBLE, THE COMMON ENGLISH BIBLE, AND THE ENGLISH STANDARD VERSION.

Passage	TR	W/H	NT	BS	MT	KJV	ASV	RSV	TEV	LB	NAS	NIV	NKJ	CEB	ESV
Mark 16:9-20	--	DB	DB	DB	--	--	--	O	O	O	SB	--	--	O	O

Antiquity of witnesses

The second century sees the Diatessaron of Tatian and two Syriac versions (Peshitta and Harclean) including the verse, while two Syriac (the Sinaitic and Palestinian) omits it.
The third century sees two witnesses, one Coptic version (Bohairic in some manuscripts) and Cyprian, for the inclusion of the verse, while two Coptic versions (Sahidic, and Bohairic) omit the verse

The fourth century sees one Old Latin version (Vercellensis), the Vulgate and the Gothic version including the verse, while two uncials ({Aleph} Sinaiticus and {B} Vaticanus), one Old Latin version (Bobiensis) and the Armenian version omit it.

The verse has ancient evidence for its inclusion.

The last two pages of the Gospel of Mark –
Sahidic MS K 9075, 9076.

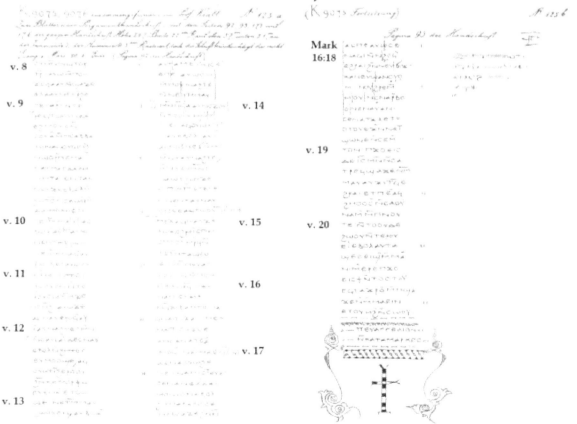

Transcription from pages 28 and 29 of Carl Wessely's
Griechische und Koptische Texte Theologischen Inhalts III (1912).

FOR	AGAINST
2ND CENTURY	
Diatessaron of Tatian	
Curetonian Syriac (II-VII)	
Peshitta Syriac (II-VII)	**Sinaitic Syriac version (II-VI)**
Harclean Syriac (II-VII)	
Palestinian Syriac (II-VII)	
Justin (?)	
3RD CENTURY	
Sahidic Coptic version (III-VI)	
Bohairic Coptic version (III-VI)	**Clement of Alexandria**
Fayyumic Coptic version (III-VI)	**Origen**
Irenaeus	**Ammonius**
Tertullian	
4TH CENTURY	
Vulgate version	**Aleph Sinaiticus uncial**
Armenian version (IV/V)	**B Vaticanus uncial**
Aphraates	**Bobiensis Old Latin (IV/V)**
Apostolic Constitutions	**Armenian (IV/V)**
Didymus	**Eusebius**

Number

There are sixty-four Greek manuscripts which include the verse, and three which exclude it.

There are eighteen Versions which include the verse, and five which exclude it.

There are seven early writers which include the verse, and five who exclude it.

It is found in the Byzantine Manuscripts, which text type the vast majority of Greek manuscripts are placed in.

The Truth Made
CLEAR™
*but not about the
ending of Mark*

In the 1996 edition of the New Living Translation, the following footnote accompanied Mark 16:8: "The most reliable early manuscripts conclude the Gospel of Mark at verse 8. Other manuscripts include various endings to the Gospel. Two of the more noteworthy endings are printed here."

In the current edition, the footnote says, "The most reliable early manuscripts of the Gospel of Mark end at verse 8. Other manuscripts include various endings to the Gospel. A few include both the "shorter ending" and the "longer ending." The majority of manuscripts include the "longer ending" immediately after verse 8."

The NLT's footnotes at the end of Mark should be redone. The number of early Greek manuscripts that end the text at 16:8 - TWO - should be stated. The misleading reference to "various endings" should be removed. The note should make it clear that all six Greek manuscripts that contain the Shorter Ending also contain at least part of verses 9-20. And the NLT should state that verses 9-20 follow verse 8 in over 99% of the Greek manuscripts of Mark 16. Why be vague when the truth can be made clear?

In addition, the NLT's new footnote about the Freer Logion (the additional material mentioned in the footnote that accompanies the end of 16:14) is incorrect. It should be removed or corrected. The claim that "Some early manuscripts" add this material is false. Only one manuscript (Codex W) in existence does so.

FOR   **AGAINST**

GREEK MSS	VERSIONS	EARLY WRITERS	BYZ MSS	TEXT	BYZ MSS	EARLY WRITERS	VERSIONS	GREEK MSS
68	18	7	+	Mk. 16: 9-20	-	5	5	3

There is no doubt that the numbers are in favor of inclusion of the verse, twenty-two to one manuscripts in the UBS critical apparatus, and far more than that when the "Byzantine Manuscripts" are included.

Variety

The verse is testified by Greek manuscripts (both Uncial and Minuscule) from every area that they are extant. It is included in versions coming from various areas and influences. The early writers who testify to its inclusion are few, but they do not waver. It is not found just in the New Testaments in a particular area, but is found universally.

Continuity

In the 2ND Century, Diatessaron of Tatian and possibly Justin and four Syriac versions (Curetonian, Peshitta, Harclean, Palestinian) include the verses. The Sinaitic Syriac version omits the verses.

In the 3RD Century, three Coptic versions (Sahidic, Bohairic, Fayyumic – dated from 3RD to 7TH Century) and two early writers (Irenaeus, Tertullian) include the verses. Three early writers (Clement of Alexandria, Origen, Ammonius) omit the verses.

In the 4TH Century, two versions (Vulgate, manuscripts according to Armenian – dated from 4TH or 5TH Century) and three early writers (Aphraates, Apostolic Constitutions, Didymus) include the verses. Two uncials (Sinaiticus {Aleph}, Vaticanus {B}), two versions (Bobiensis Old Latin, manuscripts according to Armenian – both date from either 4TH or 5TH Century) and Eusebius omit the verses.

In the 5TH Century, three uncials (Alexandrinus {A}, Ephraemi Rescriptus {C}, Freer Gospels {W}) and three versions (Georgian, Bezae Cantabrigiensis Old Latin, Corbeiensis II Old Latin) include the verses. The Georgian version and Jerome are cited as opposing the passage's inclusion.

In the 6TH Century, two uncials (D, 0112) include the verses. One version (manuscripts according to the Ethiopic) omit it.

In the 7TH Century, one uncial (099) and four Old Latin versions (Aureus, Sangallensis, Monacensis, Thedigeranus – dated either 7TH or 8TH Century) include the passage.

In the 8TH Century, two uncials (Regius {L}, Ψ) and the Sangallensis Old Latin version include the verses.

In the 9TH Century, four uncials (K, D, Θ, Π) and three minuscules (33, 565, 892) include the passage.

In the 10TH Century, one uncial (X) and three minuscules (274text , 1079, 1582) include the verses.

In the 11TH Century, nine minuscules (137, 1110, 1210, 1216, 1221, 124, 788, 28, 700) and three lectionaries (L185, L883, L60) include the passage.

In the 12TH Century, sixteen minuscules (1, 138, 1241?, 346, 543, 826, 828, 983, 1010, 1071, 1344, 1365, 1217, 1195, 1230, 1646), two lectionaries (L69, L70) and the Colbertinus Old Latin version (dated either 12TH or 13TH Century) include the verses.

In the 13TH Century, eight minuscules (118, 1215, 13, 1009, 1242, 579, 1689, 1546) and one lectionary (L547) include the passage.

In the 14TH Century, four minuscules (131, 209, 2174, 2148) include the verses.

In the 15TH Century, two minuscules (69, 1253) include the passage.

Codex Aleph
Mark 16
Notice the empty space left for the final verses (9-20)

All of the Byzantine manuscripts include the verses.

The majority of the lectionaries in the Synaxarion (the so-called "moveable year" beginning with Easter) and in the Menologian (the "fixed year" beginning with September 1) do not include the passage.? [see Chapter X, *"The Testimony of the Lectionaries shewn to be absolutely decisive as to the genuineness of these Verses,"* in J.W. Burgon's THE LAST TWELVE VERSES OF THE GOSPEL ACCORDING TO S. MARK; reprinted by Faith and Facts Press – 3910 Rankin Drive – Erlanger, KY 41018]

In reference to the writers who are quoted in support of omitting the passage, see *Chapter III, "The early Fathers appealed to, and observed to bear favourable witness to these Verses!,"* and *Chapter V, The alleged hostile witness of certain of the early Fathers proved to be an imagination of the Critics;"* in J.W. Burgon's THE LAST TWELVE VERSES OF THE GOSPEL ACCORDING TO S. MARK.

Uncial manuscripts are written in capital block letters, in a formal hand for libraries and collections. The Uncial manuscripts are divided into two categories, the lettered uncials and the numbered uncials.

Traditionally the lettered uncials are the older manuscripts. The lettered uncials are numerically in favor of the inclusion of the passage eleven (11) to two (2). The two manuscripts which argue against the inclusion of the passage are the Sinaiticus and the Vaticanus, both from the fourth century. They both have a reputation as two of the oldest and most complete manuscripts; but, it is a reputation that is overstated as is seen by their exclusion of this passage (among others).

The Vaticanus may give a backhanded witness to the inclusion of the passage. At Mark 16:8 it is true that verses nine through twenty are missing, but so is the beginning of the Gospel of Luke. The Vaticanus is not like modern bibles which begin the next book on the next page, the Vaticanus began the next book on the next line. Why then is there a blank space at the end of Gospel of Mark? Not only is there a blank space, but it corresponds with the size of the last twelve verses of the Gospel as it appears in our version. Therefore, the hand which produced the Vaticanus was familiar with these twelve verses and leaves a testimony that he believed that something was missing from the Gospel as it was produced in this manuscript.

This leaves the sole testimony among the uncials in Sinaiticus. This manuscript similarly has a blank space where these twelve verses would fit. Again, the copier of the Sinaiticus was familiar with the passage in question, and left room for it, presumably because he believed it belonged.

Other lettered uncials of renown, such as the Alexandrinus, the Ephraemi Rescriptus, the Freer Gospels, D, and the Regius as well as a number of others all include these verses.

The lettered uncials which include the passage date from the fifth to the tenth centuries, which indicate the existence of the passage in manuscripts back to the third century and beyond.

There are two numbered uncials which include the verses, which date from the sixth and seventh centuries. There are no numbered uncials which do not include the passage.

The minuscule or cursive manuscripts are those written in the smaller case running hand that would be the less formal, or ordinary communication of every day. These manuscripts would represent those Bibles used by individuals more than likely. There are forty-five (45) manuscripts which include the passage, ranging from the 9th through the 15th centuries. There is one (1) manuscript which stands alone in its testimony for exclusion from the 12th century.

Although the exact numbers of the Byzantine manuscripts which include the passage, and the numbers which exclude it (which I understand to be zero -0-) are not known, the reading of the majority of the Byzantine manuscripts overwhelmingly includes Mark 16:9-20.

The manuscript evidence, excluding the Byzantine texts (which comprise the vast majority -- up to 95% -- of manuscripts extant), is numerically sixty-eight (68) to three (3) in favor of the inclusion of the passage.

Once the testimony of the Byzantine texts is added, the result is more manuscripts, versions, lectionaries, and early writers favor of the passage. Therefore, unless one arbitrarily determines the Sinaiticus and Vaticanus texts to contain the purest text, the passage is overwhelmingly verified as part of the original text.

The evidence concerning the last twelve verses of Mark favors the inclusion of the verses overwhelmingly. In fact, it makes one wonder why the passage was ever questioned.

Lectionaries are books of selected readings for churches. They are by nature fragmentary. Therefore, their testimony is more important if the reading includes, rather than excludes a passage, unless the passage is in the middle of a reading. It is not surprising that a passage would be missing if it either proceeds a reading or follows a reading. From the 11th to the 13th centuries there are six (6) lectionaries which include the verses in question. The reading of the majority of lectionaries in the Synaxarion (the so-called "movable year" beginning with Easter) and in the Menologion (the fixed year "beginning with September 1) do not include Mark 16:9-20. The lections end with verse eight (8). [For a further discussion of the testimony of the lectionaries see CHAPTER X, *"The Testimony of the Lectionaries shown to be absolutely decisive as to the genuineness of these Verses."*, in J.W. Burgon's THE LAST TWELVE VERSES OF THE GOSPEL ACCORDING TO S. MARK; reprinted by Faith and Facts Press – 3910 Rankin Drive – Erlanger, KY 41018.]

The early versions (translations) present a preponderance of evidence in favor of the twelve verses in eighteen (18) different versions, from the 2nd to the 13th centuries. The Curetonian, Peshitta, Harclean and Palestinian Syriac; the Sahidic, Bohairic and Fayyumic Coptic; the Vulgate; the Armenian; the Georgian; and the old Latin versions known as Bezae Cantabrigiensis, Corbeiensis II, Aureus, Sangallensis, Monacensis, Rhedigeranus, Sangallensis, and Colbertinus all include Mark 16:9-20. There are five (5) early versions, dating from the 2nd to the 6th centuries, which are cited as excluding the passage: the Sinaitic Syriac, the old Latin Bobiensis, certain Armenian manuscripts, certain Georgian manuscripts and Ethiopic manuscripts.

Early writers give a numerical edge to the inclusion of the passage. The Diatessaron of Tatian from the 2nd century, Justin (165 AD), Irenaeus (202 AD) in the Greek and Latin, Tertullian (220 AD), Aphraates (367 AD), the Apostolic Constitutions (380 AD), and Didymus (398 AD) all cite the verses as belonging to the Gospel of Mark. Those which are given as testimony against the passage are: Clement of Alexandria (215 AD), Origen (254 AD), Eusebius (239 AD), certain manuscripts according to Eusebius, Jerome (420 AD), certain manuscripts according to Jerome, and Ammonius from the 3rd century. [For a fuller discussion about the testimony of early writers see J.W. Burgon's THE LAST TWELVE VERSES OF THE GOSPEL ACCORDING TO S. MARK; CHAPTER III, *"The early Fathers appealed to, and observed to bear favourable witness to these Verses."*, and CHAPTER V, *"The alleged hostile witness of certain of the early Fathers proved to be an imagination of the Critics."*]

When you line the evidence up by century, it becomes even more compelling. From the 2nd century the evidence is six (6) for and one (1) against. In the 3rd century, it is five (5) for and three (3) against. In the 4th century it is five (5) for and five (against). In the 5th century it is six (6) for and two (2) against. In the 6th century it is two (2) for and one (1) against. In the 7th century it is five (5) for and zero (0) against. In the 8th century it is three (3) for and none (0) against. In the 9th century it is seven (7) for and zero (0) against. In the 10th century it is four (4) for and none (0) against. In the 11th century it is twelve (12) for and none (0) against. In the 12th century it is nineteen (19) for and one (1) against. In the 13th century it is nine (9) for and zero (0) against. In the 14th century it is four (4) for and none (0) against. In the 15th century it is two (2) for and zero (0) against. In every century except the 4th century the evidence favors the inclusion of the passage. Considering the evidence of the Vaticanus and the Sinaiticus, the scale may be considered tipped in favor of the inclusion of the verses in the 4th century as well.

THE EVIDENCE FOR MARK 16:9-20

FOR	AGAINST
2ND CENTURY	
Diatessaron of Tatian	
Curetonian Syriac (II-VII)	
Peshitta Syriac (II-VII)	Sinaitic Syriac version (II-VI)
Harclean Syriac (II-VII)	
Palestinian Syriac (II-VII)	
Justin (?)	
3RD CENTURY	
Sahidic Coptic version (III-VI)	Clement of Alexandria
Bohairic Coptic version (III-VI)	Origen
Fayyumic Coptic version (III-VI)	Ammonius

Irenaeus

Tertullian

Vulgate version	Aleph Sinaiticus uncial
Armenian version (IV/V)	B Vaticanus uncial
Aphraates	Bobiensis Old Latin (IV/V)
Apostolic Constitutions	Armenian version (IV/V)
Didymus	Eusebius

A Alexandrinus uncial

C Ephraemi Rescriptus uncial

W Freer Gospels uncial — Georgian version

Georgian version — Jerome

Bezae Cantabrigiensis Old Latin

Corbeiensis II Old Latin

D Bezae Cantabrigiensis uncial

0112 uncial — Ethiopic version

099 uncial

Aureus Old Latin

Sangallensis Old Latin

Monacensis Old Latin

Rhedigeranus Old Latin (VII/VIII)

L Regius uncial

Psi uncial (VIII/IX)

9ᵀᴴ CENTURY

K uncial

Delta uncial

Theta uncial

Pi uncial

33 minuscule

565 minuscule

892 minuscule

10ᵀᴴ CENTURY

X uncial

274 minuscule

1079 minuscule

1582 minuscule

11ᵀᴴ CENTURY

137 minuscule

1110 minuscule

1210 minuscule

1216 minuscule

1221 minuscule

124 minuscule

788 minuscule

28 minuscule

700 minuscule

L185 lectionary

L883 lectionary

L60 lectionary

1 minuscule

138 minuscule

1241 (apparent support?) minuscule

346 minuscule

543 minuscule

826 minuscule

828 minuscule

983 minuscule

1010 minuscule

1071 minuscule   2386 minuscule

1344 minuscule

1365 minuscule

1217 minuscule

1195 minuscule

1230 minuscule

1646 minuscule

L69 lectionary

L70 lectionary

Colbertinus Old Latin (XII-XIII)

118 minuscule

1215 minuscule

13 minuscule

1009 minuscule

1242 minuscule

579 minuscule

1689 minuscule

1546 minuscule

L547 lectionary

14TH CENTURY

131 minuscule

209 minuscule

2174 minuscule

2148 minuscule

15TH CENTURY

69 minuscule

1253 minuscule

The majority of the lectionaries in the Synaxrion (the so-called "moveable year" beginning with Easter) and in the Menologion (the "fixed year" beginning September 1) do not include Mark 16:9-20.

The majority of the Byzantine manuscripts include Mark 16:9-20.

The Context of Passage

The passage before us has generated more heated discussion possibly than any other passage. The question is: Which ending of Mark is the true one? This traditional ending to the gospel? Or, a truncated ending found in a handful of manuscripts?

Now when Jesus was risen early the first day of the week, he appeared first to Mary Magdalene, out of whom he had cast seven devils. And she went and told them that had been with him, as they mourned and wept. And they, when they had heard that he was alive, and had been seen of her, believed not.

After that he appeared in another form unto two of them, as they walked, and went into the country. And they went and told it unto the residue: neither believed they them.

Afterward he appeared unto the eleven as they sat at meat, and upbraided them with their unbelief and hardness of heart, because they believed not them which had seen him after he was risen. And he said unto them, Go ye into all the world, and preach the gospel to every creature. He that believeth and is baptized shall be saved; but he that believeth not shall be damned. And these signs shall follow them that believe; In my name shall they cast out devils; they shall speak with new tongues; They shall take up serpents; and if they drink any deadly thing, it shall not hurt them; they shall lay hands on the sick, and they shall recover.

He that believes and is baptized shall be saved.

Mark 16:16

So then after the Lord had spoken unto them, he was received up into heaven, and sat on the right hand of God. And they went forth, and preached every where, the Lord working with them, and confirming the word with signs following. Amen. (Mark 16:9-20 KJV)

And when the sabbath was past, Mary Magdalene, and Mary the mother of James, and Salome, had bought sweet spices, that they might come and anoint him. And very early in the morning the first day of the week, they came unto the sepulchre at the rising of the sun. And they said among themselves, Who shall roll us away the stone from the door of the sepulchre? And when they looked, they saw that the stone was rolled away: for it was very great. And entering into the sepulchre, they saw a young man sitting on the right side, clothed in a long white garment; and they were affrighted. And he saith unto them, Be not affrighted: Ye seek Jesus of Nazareth, which was crucified: he is risen; he is not here: behold the place where they laid him. But go your way, tell his disciples and Peter that he goeth before you into Galilee: there shall ye see him, as he said unto you. And they went out quickly, and fled from the sepulchre; for they trembled and were amazed: neither said they any thing to any man; for they were afraid. (Mark 16:1-8 KJV)

The purpose of the Gospels is to build faith. (see John 20:30,31) To end an appeal for faith with the words *"for they trembled and were amazed: neither said they anything to any man; for they were afraid"* seems to be incredulous. The passage immediately preceding the verses in question calls for a further explanation to give meaning and completion to the Gospel account. If nothing was said, and they were afraid, how and why was the gospel spread throughout the world with such fervor and boldness?

The last twelve verses as they appear in the King James Version give the explanation that the first eight verses in the chapter call for. The reassurance of the appearance of Jesus to Mary Magdalene causes her to speak to the apostles, although they still do not believe. The appearance to the two disciples on the road causes them to believe, but the rest of the disciples still did not believe. It took the appearance of Jesus to them all to convince them of the truth of the resurrection. His further words of encouragement and command give them the impetus to proceed on the mission and commission which would take the rest of their lives. The continued presence of miracles bolstered their faith and courage.

Westcott and Hort give the alternative ending found in L: *"And they announced briefly to Peter and those around him all the things enjoined. And after these things Jesus himself also sent forth through them from the east even unto the west the holy and incorruptible proclamation of the eternal salvation."*

Read the two endings. Does the so-called alternative ending of L give the assurance that is given by the last twelve verses of our version? Does it provide the answers needed to complete the chapter? Does it explain the courage and faith of the disciples as they evangelized the world? Does it give reason for their willingness to give their lives for the story they were telling? In every way, and in every category the alternative ending is lacking.

If it is unreasonable to expect the chapter to end after verse eight, and the alternative ending is inadequate for the questions and explanations needed to complete the Gospel, we are left with the ending of the last twelve verses being the only rational answer.

Internal Evidence.

In the case of Mark 16:9-20, this means: Is the passage written in the same style as Mark wrote the rest of his Gospel? Those who reject the passage claim that the style (i.e., the choice of words and the use of grammar) of these verses is contrary to that found in the remainder of the book. Thus, they claim the passage not to be a part of the Gospel of Mark.

The claims for differences in vocabulary and phraseology for this passage, and other portions of scripture, both large and small, are similar. Words or phrases are pointed out as only being used in a particular place, and therefore indicative of being placed there by another author. Whether it is the JPED theory applied to the writings of Moses, or the writers of the Gospels, it limits the vocabulary and style of the writer when presenting different topics to the same choices. It assumes that the writer has a limited vocabulary, and a limited means of expressing himself.

J.W. Burgon notes twenty-seven instances which are noted by critics to attempt to exclude these verses as not genuinely Markan [p. 226 footnote; THE LAST TWELVE VERSES OF THE GOSPEL ACCORDING TO S. MARK]. He deals with these objections in detail in *Chapter IX. Internal Evidence demonstrated to be the very reverse of unfavourable to these Verses.*

The simple and easy answer to this seeming dilemma is seen by a comparison of Mark 1:9-20 which these same critics do not question, and Mark 16:9-20 which they seem to almost unanimously reject. The same uniqueness of vocabulary and style which they use to condemn the last twelve verses of the Gospel are equally applicable to the last twelve verses of the first chapter. *"The legs of the lame are unequal."*

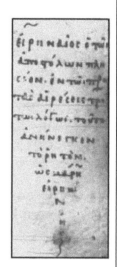
The conclusion

Westcott/Hort, in notice of this passage says,

387. The examination of individual readings in detail is reserved for the Appendix. In a few cases however a short explanation of the course adopted seems to be required here. First in importance is the very early supplement by which the mutilated or unfinished close of St. Mark's Gospel was completed. This remarkable passage on one hand may be classed among the interpolations mentioned at the end of L384 as deserving of preservation for their own sake in spite of their omission by Non-Western documents. On the other it is placed on a peculiar footing by the existence of a second ancient supplement, preserved in five languages, sometimes appearing as a substitute, sometimes as a duplicate. This less known alternative supplement, which is very short, contains no distinctive matter, and was doubtless composed merely to round off the abrupt ending of the Gospel as it stood with ⬜⬜⬜⬜⬜⬜⬜⬜⬜⬜⬜ for its last words. In style it is unlike the ordinary narratives of the Evangelists, but comparable to the four introductory verses of St. Luke's Gospel. The current supplement (xvi 9-20) was evidently an independently written succinct narrative beginning with the Resurrection and ending with the Ascension, probably forming part of some lost evangelic record, and appropriated entire, as supplying at once a needed close to St Mark's words and a striking addition to the history, although the first line started from the same point as the beginning of the sixteenth chapter. The two supplements are thus of very unequal interest; but as independent attempts to be of equal antiquity as regards introduction into copies of St Mark's Gospel; so that we have felt bound to print them both within [[]] in the same type. Moreover, as we cannot believe that, whatever may be the cause of the present abrupt termination of the Gospel at v. 8, it was intended by the Evangelist to end at this point, we have judged it right to mark the presumed defect by asterisks, and to suggest the probability that not the book and paragraph only but also the last sentence is incomplete. [THE NEW TESTAMENT IN THE ORIGINAL GREEK: THE TEXT REVISED BY BROOKE FOSS WESTCOTT D.D. AND FENTON JOHN ANTHONY HORT – INTRODUCTION – INDEX; London, MacMillan Co. LTD; 1896; p. 298, 299]

DTS

Where inerrancy is a peripheral essential.

The NET, a translation made mainly by Dallas Theological Seminary faculty-members, needs some work in its note about Mark 16:9-20.

● The NET's note lists manuscripts 083 and 0112 as if they are two distinct manuscripts, but they are the same manuscript.
● The NET's note misrepresents the testimonies of Eusebius and Jerome.
● The NET's note references manuscript 2427, even though 2427 has been demonstrated to be a forgery.
● The NET describes the Freer Logion as a "different shorter ending," which simply makes no sense.
● The NET mentions some relatively late evidence, but does not mention any of the second-century support for Mark 16:9-20, such as the testimony of Irenaeus in <u>Against Heresies</u>, Book 3.

W. Hall Harris,
Project Director

Daniel B. Wallace,
Senior NT Editor

● That's not all. But isn't that enough to require an update?

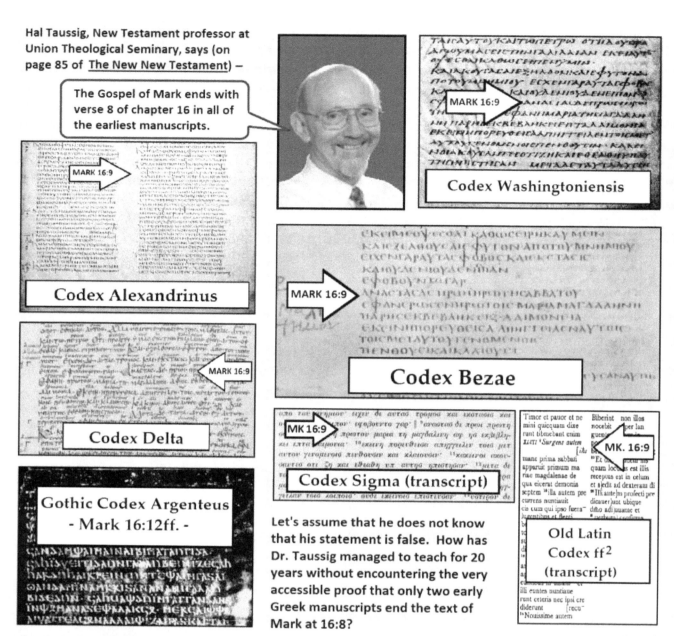

Hal Taussig, New Testament professor at Union Theological Seminary, says (on page 85 of The New New Testament) –

The Gospel of Mark ends with verse 8 of chapter 16 in all of the earliest manuscripts.

MARK 16:9

Codex Washingtoniensis

MARK 16:9

Codex Alexandrinus

MARK 16:9

Codex Bezae

MARK 16:9

Codex Delta

MK 16:9

Codex Sigma (transcript)

MK. 16:9

Old Latin Codex ff[2] (transcript)

Gothic Codex Argenteus - Mark 16:12ff. -

Let's assume that he does not know that his statement is false. How has Dr. Taussig managed to teach for 20 years without encountering the very accessible proof that only two early Greek manuscripts end the text of Mark at 16:8?

(And why does he also say, on the same page, "A number of second- and third-century early Christian commentators defend this"? There are no such statements from any writers in the second and third centuries. Distortions of this sort should be withdrawn and corrected. Fix your work, Dr. Taussig!)

The New New Testament is copyrighted ©2013 by Hal Taussig.

Metzger concludes,

"… Thus, on the basis of good external evidence and strong internal considerations it appears that the earliest ascertainable form of the Gospel of Mark ended with 16.8.[7] [7 Three possibilities are open: (a) the evangelist intended to close the Gospel at this place; or (b) the Gospel was never finished; or, as seems most probable, (c) the Gospel accidentally lost its last leaf before it was multiplied by transcription.] At the same time, however, out of deference to the evident antiquity of the longer ending and its importance in the textual tradition of the Gospel, the Committee decided to include verses 9-20 as part of the text, but to enclose *them within double square brackets to indicate that they are the work of an author other than the evangelist."* [p. 126]

What does Dr. John MacArthur Teach About Mark 16:9-20?

"Frankly, I think it's a bad ending."

It is crystal clear that whether you're reading a patristic writing, or the Vulgate, or a Syriac copy, they all agree with Sinaiticus and Vaticanus: Mark's text ends at 16:8.

In Vaticanus and Sinaiticus and the other ancient manuscripts, Mark's text stops at 16:8. 8,000 copies in Latin and over 350 copies in Syriac say the same thing.

Irenaeus knew about endings of Mark besides verses 9-20.

I've studied about the manuscripts of the New Testament. Sinaiticus is the whole New Testament, and Vaticanus is the whole Bible.

There's more. These are samples.

There are 5,600 or so Greek manuscripts; they go way back. We have all these ancient manuscripts, and they all say the same thing at the end of Mark. With so many accurate manuscripts, you can know with no hesitation that the Bible you hold in your hand is a true English translation of the original text.

What do the facts say about Mark 16:9-20?

● Those thousands of Vulgate copies and hundreds of Syriac copies INCLUDE Mark 16:9-20.
● Vaticanus and Sinaiticus are the ONLY ancient Greek manuscripts of Mark in which the text of chapter 16 clearly ends at verse 8.
● Irenaeus (in the 180's) specifically quoted Mark 16:19 as part of the text.
● Other patristic writers such as Ambrose, Augustine, and Macarius Magnes clearly cited the contents of Mark 16:9-20 as Scripture.
● About 1,600 Greek manuscripts include the book of Mark.
● The sixteenth chapter of Mark clearly stops at the end of verse 8 in two of them.

For details about Dr. MacArthur's false claims, see the transcript of his June 5, 2011 sermon at http://www.gty.org/resources/sermons/41-85/The-Fitting-End-to-Marks-Gospel

A three-part response to Dr. MacArthur's claims begins at https://www.youtube.com/watch?v=Bx2Q1X0_r5g .

"Ignoring the cancerous effects of false teaching is a serious dereliction of our duty as believers."
- John MacArthur, February 27, 2014

The three possibilities that are proposed by Metzger in his footnote, the third of which both the UBS committee and Westcott/Hort accepted as the most probable, are unacceptable. It is unbelievable that this Gospel would end with verse eight. It is an insult to inspiration that it would have been left incomplete. It is contrary to the preservation of the Word of God that the ending would have been lost.

Perhaps, Mark 16:9-20, as much as any other passage, shows the attitude of many textual critics toward the scripture. Inspiration is not considered a viable alternative when considering the history of the text from the beginning. The preservation of the Word of God is not considered a force in the history of the text. Yet, both are a reality in the origin and history of the text.

If Mark 16:9-20 are not a part of the New Testament, there is no reason to be assured of any portion of the New Testament.

EVIDENCE
OF SHALLOW RESEARCH

"In the case of the Mark 16 passage, the three most important early manuscripts, Codex Vaticanus, Alexandrinus and Sinaiticus all do not include this passage. Codex Bezae, from about the same time, does include this passage. None of the very early church fathers quoted from this section."

Dr. John Oakes

President of the Apologetics Research Society

Codex Alexandrinus contains Mark 16:9-20. Irenaeus quoted Mark 16:19 in the 180's, in *Against Heresies*, Book 3.

Please fix your article at www.evidenceforchristianity.org, Dr. Oakes.

Ben Witherington III, please fix your book.

Codex A lacks verses 9-20.

Eusebius tells us that all Greek copies known to him did not contain verses 9-20 - and that's a fact.

In 2001, Dr. Ben Witherington III, a professor at Asbury Theological Seminary, made some incorrect statements about Mark 16:9-20 on pages 412-413 of The Gospel of Mark - a Socio-Rhetorical Commentary.

Jerome tells us that all Greek copies known to him did not contain verses 9-20 - and that's a fact.

A few Old Latin, Syriac, Sahidic, and Ethiopic manuscripts simply have the Shorter Ending after verse 8.

All these statements are wrong.

Dr. Lawrence O. Richards -
- *graduate of Dallas Theological Seminary*
- *former professor at Wheaton College*
- *Promoter of the following false statements about Mark 16:9-20 (as a writer or editor) —*

"In many ancient Greek manuscripts, Mark's Gospel ends here." [That is, at the end of 16:8.] "But other manuscripts add 11 more verses." - <u>Bible Reader's Companion</u>, page 648.

> Vaticanus + Sinaiticus = 2. That is not many.
> And Mark 16:9-20 = 12 verses, not just 11.

"None of the early church fathers indicate awareness of these verses for the first few centuries of Christianity." - H. Walker Evans, in <u>The Smart Guide to the Bible</u>, page 308. Editor: Larry Richards.

> Some early writers and compositions that utilized Mark 16:9-20: Justin. Tatian. *Epistula Apostolorum*. Irenaeus. Hippolytus. Vincentius. Hierocles. Marinus. *Acts of Pilate*. Ambrose. *Apostolic Constitutions*. Jerome. Augustine. *De Trinitate*. Nestorius. Marcus Eremita. Prosper of Aquitaine. Patrick.

These verses "don't show up until over 200 years after Mark lived." - <u>The Smart Guide to the Bible</u>, page 308 again.

> Mark's death probably occurred in 67 or 68. Justin, Tatian, and Irenaeus wrote less than 150 years after that. Codex Vaticanus was produced c. 325, about 250 years after Mark's death.

A footnote in the <u>NASB Study Bible for Boys</u> (edited by Larry Richards) says, referring to the Shorter Ending, "A few late mss and versions contain this paragraph, usually after v. 8; a few have it at the end of ch. 2." Eh?? The end of chapter two??

There is no reason to reject the verses, and every reason to accept them.

When the seven points of truth are examined, all seven (**1. Antiquity, 2. Number, 3. Variety, 4. Weight, 5. Continuity, 6. Context of the Passage,** and **7. Internal Considerations**) are in favor of the inclusion of the verses.

VERITAS EVANGELICAL SEMINARY

Proclaiming the Gospel. Equipping the Saints. Defending the Faith.
Misinforming thousands of readers about Mark 16:9-20.

Norman Geisler, commenting on Mark 16:9-20 in <u>When Critics Ask</u>, page 378:
(Dr. Geisler's statements are in brown. Corrections are in black.)

"These verses are lacking in many of the oldest and most reliable Greek manuscripts."
Actual number of ancient Greek manuscripts in which the text of Mark ends at 16:8: 2.

"Many of the ancient church fathers reveal no knowledge of these verses, including Clement, Origen, and Eusebius."
Clement did not quote from 12 *chapters* of the Gospel of Mark.
Origen made no use of several much larger sections of the Gospel of Mark.
Eusebius wrote about the ending of Mark in his composition <u>Ad Marinum</u> and used Mark 16:9 repeatedly.
Over 40 early patristic writers utilize Mark 16:9-20, including Irenaeus, in <u>Against Heresies</u>, Book 3, which he composed around A.D. 184, over a century before the production-date of the earliest existing manuscript of Mark 16.

"Many manuscripts that do have this section place a mark by it indicating it is a spurious addition to the text."
Number of manuscripts of Mark: over 1,600.
Number of manuscripts of Mark with a special note accompanying Mark 16:9-20: 14.
Number of manuscripts without a note, but with a mark to indicate that the passage is spurious: zero.

"These verses are lacking . . . in important Old Latin, Syriac, Armenian, and Ethiopic manuscripts."
Number of Latin manuscripts of Mark: over 5,000.
Number of undamaged Latin manuscripts that do not include Mark 16:9-20: one.
Number of Syriac manuscripts of Mark: over 350.
Number of Syriac manuscripts that end Mark's text at 16:8: one.
Number of Armenian manuscripts of Mark 16 in existence that were produced before 700: zero.
Number of Ethiopic manuscripts of Mark: over 100.
Number of Ethiopic manuscripts that end Mark's text at 16:8: zero.

This is a true story.

One time a preacher was making his point on *Mark 16:16 – "He that believeth and is baptized shall be saved; but he that believeth not shall be damned."*

He forcefully cried out to the audience on hand: "If you don't believe me, I'll come and show it to you in your own Bible!"

"It's not in my Bible!" cried a woman in the back.

Immediately the preacher strode to the back, took the Bible from the lady's hand, turned to the sixteenth chapter of Mark, and, lo and behold, the passage was not there! She had taken a pair of scissors and cut it out!

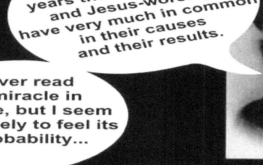

When I was a boy, I remember hearing this illustration used in a sermon to show the disrespect which some people had for the Bible, and how they removed certain unwanted passages from the Scriptures in one way or another.

What the woman did was unconscionable. But pray tell, what is the difference between a woman taking a pair of scissors and cutting passages she does like out of her personal Bible, and an editor taking an exacto knife and slicing the same verses out of a Bible he is preparing for publication?

Is it not of far greater import when the editor does it; because the Bible he so mutilates will not only be for his own private reading and study, but is prepared to be used by thousands, or even millions?

Friends and brethren, how far have we already drifted?

[My personal thanks to James M. Snapp for the usage of his memes throughout this chapter.]

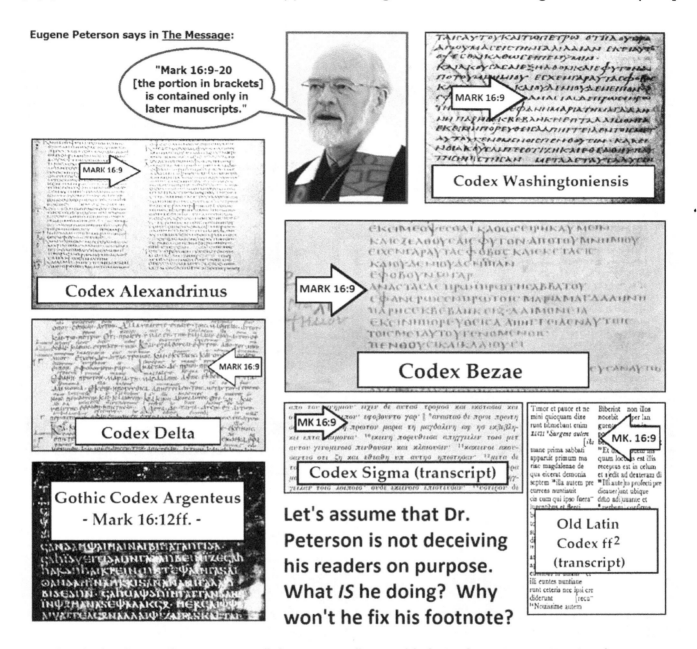

Eugene Peterson says in The Message:

"Mark 16:9-20 [the portion in brackets] is contained only in later manuscripts."

Codex Washingtoniensis

Codex Alexandrinus

MARK 16:9

Codex Bezae

Codex Delta

Gothic Codex Argenteus
- Mark 16:12ff. -

Codex Sigma (transcript)

Old Latin Codex ff² (transcript)

Let's assume that Dr. Peterson is not deceiving his readers on purpose. What *IS* he doing? Why won't he fix his footnote?

(And why does Colossians 2:9 in "The Message" resemble lyrics from George Harrison's song "Awaiting on You All"? Where did Paul get a telescope and a microscope?)

Does Luke 17:36 Belong in the New Testament?

This verse is included by THE TEXTUS RECEPTUS, THE KING JAMES VERSION, TODAY'S ENGLISH VERSION AND THE NEW KING JAMES VERSION, and omitted by THE WESTCOTT/HORT, THE NESTLE, THE UNITED BIBLE SOCIETY, AND THE MAJORITY GREEK TEXTS, THE AMERICAN STANDARD VERSION, THE REVISED STANDARD VERSION, THE LIVING BIBLE, THE NEW AMERICAN STANDARD BIBLE, THE NEW INTERNATIONAL VERSION, THE COMMON ENGLISH BIBLE, AND THE ENGLISH STANDARD VERSION.

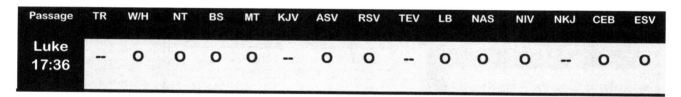

Passage	TR	W/H	NT	BS	MT	KJV	ASV	RSV	TEV	LB	NAS	NIV	NKJ	CEB	ESV
Luke 17:36	--	O	O	O	O	--	O	O	--	O	O	O	--	O	O

The verse will be examined according to the method proposed by J.W. Burgon and Edward Miler.

Antiquity of witnesses

The second century sees the Diatessaron of Tatian and four Syriac versions (Curetonian, Sinaitic, Peshitta and Harclean) including the verse, while none omits it.

The third century sees one papyrus (Bodmer {p75}) and two Coptic versions (Sahidic, and Bohairic) omit the verse.

The fourth century sees one Old Latin version (Vercellensis), the Vulgate, the Armenian version, and Ambrose including the verse, while two uncials ({Aleph} Sinaiticus and {B} Vaticanus), the Gothic version and Basil omit it.

The verse has ancient evidence for its inclusion.

FOR	AGAINST
2ND CENTURY	
Curetonian Syriac (II-VII)	
Sinaitic Syriac (II-VII)	
Peshitta Syriac (II-VII)	
Harclean Syriac (II-VII)	
Diatessaron of Tatian	
3RD CENTURY	
	P75 P. Bodmer XIV,XV
	Sahidic Coptic version (III-VI)
	Bohairic Coptic version (III-VI)
4TH CENTURY	
Vercellensis Old Latin version	Aleph Sinaiticus uncial
Vulgate version	B Vaticanus uncial
Armenian version (IV/V)	Gothic version
Ambrose	Basil

Number

There are twenty-four Greek manuscripts which include the verse, and thirty which exclude it.

There are nineteen Versions which include the verse, and four which exclude it.

There are three early writers which include the verse, and three who exclude it.

It is not found in the majority of Byzantine Manuscripts, which text type the vast majority of Greek manuscripts are placed in.

FOR   **AGAINST**

GREEK MSS	VERSIONS	EARLY WRITERS	BYZ MSS	TEXT	BYZ MSS	EARLY WRITERS	VERSIONS	GREEK MSS
24	19	3	-	Lk. 17:36	+	3	4	30

The numbers do not necessarily favor the inclusion of this verse. The versions, however, favor its inclusion by a ratio of six to one.

Variety

The verse is testified by Greek manuscripts (both Uncial and Minuscule). The versions who testify to its inclusion are six times those who exclude the verse. The early writers are equally divided as to the inclusion or exclusion of the verse. The Syriac version includes it, as well as various Latin versions, both Old Latin and Vulgate era. It is not found just in the New Testaments in a particular area, but is found universally.

Weight

When you consider the character of the evidence, it favors the inclusion of the verses. All of the Syriac versions (possibly the first language the New Testament was translated into) include the verse. It is included in most known old Latin version (regardless of location). It is included even in the less reliable Vulgate. It is only found in one uncial, Bezae Cantabrigiensis {B}. It is found in both versions of the lectionaries.

The exclusion is based upon mainly witnesses of Egyptian origin or influence: Bohairic Coptic, the Sinaiticus and Vaticanus and Regius uncials (whose character rarely agrees with one another), etc. The uncials of the 8th and 9th centuries omit the verse, as well as the majority of Byzantine manuscripts.

The reliability and strength of the witnesses, especially the versions in this case, tip the scales.

Continuity

In the 2ND Century, the Diatessaron of Tatian and four Syriac versions (Curetonian, Sinaitic, Peshitta, Harclean – all dating from the 2ND to the 7TH Century) include the verse.

In the 3RD Century, one papyrus (P. Bodmer XIV, XV {p75}) and two Coptic versions (Sahidic, Bohairic – dated 3RD to 6TH Century) omit the verse.

In the 4TH Century, three versions (Vercellensis Old Latin, Vulgate, Armenian dated 4TH or 5TH Century) and Ambrose include the verse. Two uncials (Sinaiticus {Aleph}, Vaticanus {B}), the Gothic version, and Basil omit the verse.

In the 5TH Century, six versions (Veronensis Old Latin, Bezae Cantabrigiensis Old Latin, Palatinus Old Latin, Corbeiensis II Old Latin, Vindobonensis Old Latin, Georgian) and Augustine include the verse. Two uncials (Freer Gospels {W}, Alexandrinus {A}) and Maximus II of Turin omit the verse.

In the 6TH Century, one uncial (Bezae Cantabrigiensis {D}) and the Brixianus Old Latin version include the verse. The Ethiopic version and Ps-Chysostom omit the verse.

In the 7TH Century, four versions (Aureus, Monacensis, Usserianus I, Rhedigeranus dated either 7TH or 8TH Century) include the verse.

In the 8TH Century, two uncials (Regius {L}, Ψ) omit the verse.

In the 9TH Century, five uncials (K, Δ, Koridethi {Θ}, Π, 063) and three minuscules omit the verse.

In the 10TH Century, one uncial (X) and one minuscule (1079) omit the verse.

In the 11TH Century, five minuscules (700, 174, 124, 230, 788) and one lectionary (L185) include the verse. Two minuscules (28, 1216) omit the verse.

In the 12TH Century, ten minuscules (1071, 1230, 1241, 1344, 1646, 346, 543, 826, 828, 983) and the Colbertinus Old Latin version (dated either 12TH or 13TH Century) include the verse. Four minuscules (1, 1010, 1365, 1195) omit the verse.

In the 13TH Century, two minuscules (13, 1689) include the verse. Three minuscules (118, 1009, 1242) and one lectionary (L950) omit the verse.

In the 14TH Century, two minuscules (2174, 2148) and one lectionary (L1579) include the verse. Two minuscules (131, 209) and one lectionary (L184) omit the verse.

In the 15TH Century, two minuscules (1253, 69) include the verse.

The majority of the lectionaries in the Synaxarion (the so-called "moveable year" beginning with Easter) and in the Menologian (the "fixed year" beginning with September 1) include Luke 17:36.

The majority of the Byzantine Manuscripts omit Luke 17:36.

THE EVIDENCE FOR LUKE 17:36

FOR	AGAINST
2ND CENTURY	
Curetonian Syriac (II-VII)	
Sinaitic Syriac (II-VII)	
Peshitta Syriac (II-VII)	
Harclean Syriac (II-VII)	
Diatessaron of Tatian	
3RD CENTURY	
	P75 P. Bodmer XIV,XV
	Sahidic Coptic (III-VI)
	Bohairic Coptic (III-VI)

4TH CENTURY

Vercellensis Old Latin	Aleph Sinaiticus uncial
Vulgate	B Vaticanus uncial
Armenian (IV/V)	Gothic
Ambrose	Basil

5TH CENTURY

Veronensis Old Latin	
Bezae Cantabrigiensis Old Latin	
Palatinus Old Latin	W Freer Gospels uncial
Corbeiensis II Old Latin	A Alexandrinus uncial
Vindobonensis Old Latin	Maximus II of Turin
Georgian	
Augustine	

6TH CENTURY

D Bezae Cantabrigiensis uncial	Ethiopic
Brixianus Old Latin	Ps-Chrysostom

7TH CENTURY

Aureus Old Latin	
Monacensis Old Latin	
Usserianus I Old Latin	
Rhedigeranus Old Latin (VII/VIII)	

8TH CENTURY

	L Regius uncial
	Psi uncial

9TH CENTURY

	K uncial
	Delta uncial

	Koridethi Theta uncial
	Pi uncial
	063 uncial
	33 minuscule
	565 minuscule
	892 minuscule

10TH CENTURY

| | 1079 minuscule |

11TH CENTURY

700 minuscule	
174 minuscule	
124 minuscule	28 minuscule
230 minuscule	1216 minuscule
788 minuscule	
L185 lectionary	

12TH CENTURY

1071 minuscule

1230 minuscule

1241 minuscule

1344 minuscule

1646 minuscule

346 minuscule

543 minuscule

826 minuscule

828 minuscule

983 minuscule

Colbertinus Old Latin (XII/XIII)

13TH CENTURY

	118 minuscule
13 minuscule	1009 minuscule
1689 minuscule	1242 minuscule
	L950 lectionary

14TH CENTURY

2174 minuscule	131 minuscule
2148 minuscule	209 minuscule
L1579 lectionary	L184 lectionary

15TH CENTURY

1253 minuscule
69 minuscule

The majority of the lectionaries in the Synaxarion (the so-called "moveable year" beginning with Easter) and in the Menologian (the "fixed year" beginning with September 1) include Luke 17:36.

The majority of the Byzantine manuscripts omit Luke 17:36.

The 2nd, 7th, 12th and 15th centuries have no evidence for the exclusion of the verse. The 3rd, 8th, 9th, and 10th centuries have no evidence for the inclusion of the verse. The 3rd century only has three witnesses, the 8th century only has two witnesses, and the 10th century only has one witness; thus, it is not surprising that the witnesses for these centuries go in one direction. The weight of evidence in the 9th century, however, is not so easily dismissed. However the evidence from the 2nd, 7th, and 12th centuries is overwhelmingly in favor of the verse's inclusion.

The Context of Passage

And when he was demanded of the Pharisees, when the kingdom of God should come, he answered them and said, The kingdom of God cometh not with observation: Neither shall they say, Lo here! or, lo there! for, behold, the kingdom of God is within you.

And he said unto the disciples, The days will come, when ye shall desire to see one of the days of the Son of man, and ye shall not see it. And they shall say to you, See here; or, see there: go not after them, nor follow them. For as the lightning, that lighteneth out of the one part under heaven, shineth unto the other part under heaven; so shall also the Son of man be in his day. But first must he suffer many things, and be rejected of this generation.

And as it was in the days of Noe, so shall it be also in the days of the Son of man. They did eat, they drank, they married wives, they were given in marriage, until the day that Noe entered into the ark, and the flood came, and destroyed them all. Likewise also as it was in the days of Lot; they did eat, they drank, they bought, they sold, they planted, they builded; But the same day that Lot went out of Sodom it rained fire and brimstone from heaven, and destroyed them all. Even thus shall it be in the day when the Son of man is revealed.

*In that day, he which shall be upon the housetop, and his stuff in the house, let him not come down to take it away: and he that is in the field, let him likewise not return back. Remember Lot's wife. Whosoever shall seek to save his life shall lose it; and whosoever shall lose his life shall preserve it. I tell you, in that night there shall be two men in one bed; the one shall be taken, and the other shall be left. Two women shall be grinding together; the one shall be taken, and the other left. **Two men shall be in the field; the one shall be taken, and the other left.***

And they answered and said unto him, Where, Lord?

And he said unto them, Wheresoever the body is, thither will the eagles be gathered together. [LUKE 17:20-37 KJV]

After answering the demand of the Pharisees, noting that "the kingdom of God is within you", Jesus then turns His attention to His disciples.

He speaks to them about "the coming of the Son of man," or rather, a second coming. It will not be a private showing, but a public event, even as the lighting shines from one end of the sky to the other. But, before this come to pass, first the Son of man must suffer many things, being rejected by His people, the Jews, and crucified.

In the days of Noah, they ate, drank and carried on as though nothing was going to happen. They were oblivious to what was to transpire. Lot, when he dwelt in the plains of Sodom and Gomorrah, had no indication of what was to transpire until the angel came to him. The people of those cities had no idea what was to transpire, but as soon as Lot left "fire and brimstone" rained from heaven upon them. The same will be true before this second coming.

When this second coming occurs, do not delay your escape. Do not even take the time to go inside the house to gather anything to take with you. Do not go back to your house to get your belongings. Remember what happened to Lot's wife, she turned to a pillar of salt when she looked back. Leave, and do not look back. If you seek to preserve what you have, you will die. If you give up what was your life, you will save your life.

At that time, of two men lying in the same bed, one shall live and one shall die. Of two men in the field, one shall live and one shall die.

The disciples asked, Where?

Jesus answered where the carcass is the vultures will gather. It is not difficult to see where the dead body is, the vultures are circling above.

Many have taken this passage to deal with the Rapture (a concept I do not find in the scripture). I believe this passage to be dealing with the destruction of Jerusalem by Rome in 70 A.D. The difficulties or delaying of flight would be a death sentence as Rome was ready to attack Jerusalem.

The verse in question fills the parallel of the statement of Jesus about being on the top of the house, or in the field. The results are discussed in verses thirty-five and thirty-six. Whether in the house, or away from it, the results would be the same for delaying the departure. Without verse 36, the explanation is left short – the parallel of result with prediction is missing.

Internal Evidence.

There is no argument made for the exclusion of the verse based upon internal evidence.

The conclusion

Metzger says,

Although it is possible that ver. 36, δυο εν αγρο εισ παραλημφθησεται και ο ετεροσ αφεθνσεται, *was accidently omitted through homoeoteleuton (an accident which happened to ver. 35 in Aleph* and a few other witnesses), in view of the weighty manuscript authority supporting the shorter text (p75 Aleph A B L W Δ Θ Ψ f¹ 28 33 565) it is more probable that copyists assimilated the passage to Mt 24.40.* [p. 168]

There is the possibility of omission, but it is considered "more probable" that the passage was added by copyists. Why? Both are possible. It is not possible to read the minds of so many people separated by time and geology. All that we can deal with is the fact that either occasion is possible. But, what of the evidence? What of the weight of the versions, and lectionaries? What of the universality of inclusion? Let the evidence make the decision. It belongs.

When the seven points of truth are examined, they (**1. Antiquity, 2. Number, 3. Variety, 4. Weight, 5. Continuity, 6. Context of the Passage,** and **7. Internal Considerations**) are in favor of the inclusion of the verse.

Does Luke 22:20 Belong in the New Testament?

This verse is included by THE TEXTUS RECEPTUS, THE MAJORITY TEXT, THE UNITED BIBLE SOCIETIES TEXT, THE KING JAMES VERSION, THE AMERICAN STANDARD VERSION, THE NEW AMERICAN STANDARD VERSION, THE NEW INTERNATIONAL VERSION, THE NEW KING JAMES VERSION, THE COMMON ENGLISH BIBLE, AND, AND THE ENGLISH STANDARD VERSION, double-bracketed by THE WESTCOTT/HORT TEXT AND THE NESTLE TEXT, single-bracketed by TODAY'S ENGLISH VERSION and omitted by THE REVISED STANDARD VERSION.

Passage	TR	W/H	NT	BS	MT	KJV	ASV	RSV	TEV	LB	NAS	NIV	NKJ	CEB	ESV
Luke 22:20	--	DB	DB	--	--	--	--	O	--	S	--	--	--	--	--

The verse will be examined according to the method proposed by J.W. Burgon and Edward Miler.

Antiquity of witnesses

The second century sees two Syriac versions (Palestinian and Harclean) including the verse, while none omits it.

The third century sees one papyrus (Bodmer {p75}) and two Coptic versions (Sahidic, and Bohairic) include the verse, while none omit it.

The fourth century sees, and Ambrose including the verse, while two uncials ({Aleph} Sinaiticus and {B} Vaticanus), the Vulgate, and the Armenian version include the verse, while one Old Latin version (Vercellensis) omit it.

The verse has ancient evidence for its inclusion.

FOR	AGAINST

2ND CENTURY

Harclean Syriac version (II-VII)

Palestinian Syriac (II-VII)

3RD CENTURY

P75 P Bodmer XIV,XV

Sahidic Coptic version III-VI

Bohairic Coptic version III-VI

4TH CENTURY

Aleph Sinaiticus uncial

B Vaticanus uncial

Vulgate version

Armenian version (IV/V)

Vercellensis Old Latin version

Number

There are fifty Greek manuscripts which include the verse, and one which excludes it.

There are twelve Versions which include the verse, and five which exclude it.

There are zero early writers which include the verse, and none who exclude it.

It is found in the majority of Byzantine Manuscripts, which text type the vast majority of Greek manuscripts are placed in.

FOR   AGAINST

GREEK MSS	VERSIONS	EARLY WRITERS	BYZ MSS	TEXT	BYZ MSS	EARLY WRITERS	VERSIONS	GREEK MSS
50	12	0	+	LK. 22:20	-	0	5	1

The numbers favor the inclusion of this verse at a ratio of fifty to one. The versions favor its inclusion by a ratio of better than two to one.

Variety

The verse is testified by Greek manuscripts (both Uncial and Minuscule). The versions who testify to its inclusion are more than twice those who exclude the verse. The early writers give no testimony as to the inclusion or exclusion of the verse. The Syriac version includes it, as well as various Latin versions, both Old Latin and Vulgate era. It is not found just in the New Testaments in a particular area, but is found universally.

Continuity

In the 2ND Century, two Syriac versions (HARCLEAN, PALESTINIAN – both dating from 2ND to 7TH Century) include the verse.

In the 3RD Century, one papyrus (P. BODMER XIV, XV) and two COPTIC VERSIONS (SAHIDIC, BOHAIRIC – both dating from the 3RD to the 6TH Century) include the verse.

In the 4TH Century, two uncials (SINAITICUS {ALEPH}, VATICANUS {B}) and two VERSIONS (VULGATE, ARMENIAN dating from the 4TH or 5TH Century) include the verse. The VERCELLENSIS OLD LATIN VERSION omits LUKE 22:20.

In the 5TH Century, four uncials (ALEXANDRINUS {A}, EPHRAEMI RESCRIPTUS {C}, T {apparent support}, FREER GOSPELS {W}) and the GEORGIAN VERSION include the verse. Three OLD LATIN VERSIONS (BEZAE CANTABRIGIENSIS, CORBEIENSIS II, VINDOBONENSIS) omit the verse.

In the 6TH Century, the BRIXIANUS OLD LATIN VERSION includes it, and one uncial (BEZAE CANTABRIGIENSIS {D}) omit LUKE 22:20.

In the 7TH Century, three OLD LATIN VERSIONS (AUREUS, MONACENSIS, USSERIANUS I) include Luke 22:20. The RHEDIGERANUS OLD LATIN VERSION (7TH or 8TH Century) omits it.

In the 8TH Century, two uncials (REGIUS {L}, Ψ dating from the 8TH or 9TH Century) include the verse.

In the 9TH Century, five uncials (K, Δ, KORIDETHI {Θ}, Π, 063) and two minuscules (565, 892) include the verse.

In the 10th Century, one uncial (X) and one minuscule (1079) include LUKE 22:20.

In the 11TH Century, six minuscules (124, 788, 700, 1216, 174, 230) include the verse.

In the 12TH Century, fourteen minuscules (1, 346, 543, 826, 828, 983, 1010, 1071, 1241, 1344, 1365, 1195, 1230, 1646) and the COLBERTINUS OLD LATIN VERSION (dated 11TH or 12TH Century) include the verse.

In the 13TH Century, six minuscules (118, 13, 1009, 1242, 1689, 1546) include Luke 22:20.

In the 14TH Century, four minuscules (131, 209, 2174, 2148) include the verse.

In the 15TH Century, two minuscules (69, 1253) include LUKE 22:20.

The majority of lectionaries in the SYNAXARION (the so-called "moveable year" beginning with Easter), and in the MENOLOGIAN (the "fixed year" beginning with September 1) include LUKE

22:20.

The majority of the BYZANTINE MANUSCRIPTS include LUKE 22:20.

THE EVIDENCE FOR LUKE 22:20

FOR	AGAINST
2ND CENTURY	
Harclean Syriac version (II-VII)	
Palestinian Syriac (II-VII)	
3RD CENTURY	
P75 P Bodmer XIV,XV	
Sahidic Coptic version III-VI	
Bohairic Coptic version III-VI	
4TH CENTURY	
Aleph Sinaiticus uncial	
B Vaticanus uncial	
Vulgate version	Vercellensis Old Latin version
Armenian version (IV/V)	
5TH CENTURY	
A Alexandrinus uncial	
C Ephraemi Rescriptus	Bezae Cantabrigiensis Old Latin
T (apparent support) uncial	Corbeiensis II Old Latin version
W Freer Gospels uncial	Vindobonensis Old Latin version
Georgian version	
6TH CENTURY	
Brixianus Old Latin version	D Bezae Cantabrigiensis uncial
7TH CENTURY	
Aureus Old Latin version	Rhedigeranus Old Latin (VII/VIII)
Monacensis Old Latin version	

8TH CENTURY

L Regius uncial

Psi uncial

9TH CENTURY

K uncial

Delta uncial

Koridethi Theta uncial

Pi uncial

063 uncial

565 minuscule

892 minuscule

10TH CENTURY

X uncial

1079 minuscule

11TH CENTURY

124 minuscule

788 minuscule

700 minuscule

1216 minuscule

174 minuscule

230 minuscule

12TH CENTURY

1 minuscule

346 minuscule

543 minuscule

826 minuscule

828 minuscule

983 minuscule

1010 minuscule

1071 minuscule

1241 minuscule

1344 minuscule

1365 minuscule

1195 minuscule

1230 minuscule

1646 minuscule

Colbertinus Old Latin version XII/XIII

13TH CENTURY

118 minuscule

13 minuscule

1009 minuscule

1242 minuscule

1689 minuscule

1546 minuscule

14TH CENTURY

131 minuscule

209 minuscule

2174 minuscule

2148 minuscule

15TH CENTURY

69 minuscule

1253 minuscule

The 2nd, 3rd, 8th, 9th, 10th 11th ,12th, 13th, 14th, and 15th centuries have no evidence for the exclusion of the verse. _Every century_ has evidence for the inclusion of the verse. The 4th, 5th, 6th, and 7th centuries are the only time periods were any evidence of omission is found. The 4th, 6th and 7th centuries only have one witness per century. One lone uncial {D} omits the verse.

There is no question but that the continuity of evidence favors inclusion strongly.

The Context of Passage

And when the hour was come, he sat down, and the twelve apostles with him. And he said unto them, With desire I have desired to eat this passover with you before I suffer: For I say unto you, I will not any more eat thereof, until it be fulfilled in the kingdom of God. And he took the cup, and gave thanks, and said, Take this, and divide it among yourselves: For I say unto you, I will not drink of the fruit of the vine, until the kingdom of God shall come.

And he took bread, and gave thanks, and brake it, and gave unto them, saying, This is my body which is given for you: this do in remembrance of me. **Likewise also the cup after supper, saying, This cup is the new testament in my blood, which is shed for you.** [LUKE 22:14-20 KJV]

The time had come for the observance of the Passover with His disciples, the twelve apostles. He wanted to eat this Passover with them before He was crucified, for He would not again eat it until the kingdom of God has come. He therefore, took the cup and gave it to them, telling them to "divide it among yourselves." The reason, He would not again drink of "the fruit of the vine" (a phrase that is always used of freshly pressed grapes, or new wine, or grape juice), "until the kingdom of God shall come." This was the observance of the Passover.

Following the Passover meal, Jesus instituted the memorial for His body and blood, the Lord's Supper. First, He took the bread representative of His body. Then He took the cup after "the supper," the Passover, and told them of the representation of His blood.

Without the verse, Jesus institutes the taking of the bread, but not the drinking of the cup. That would be an awkward construction. The verse is necessary to complete the action.

As Metzger points out in a footnote: _"The whole difficulty arose, in our opinion, from a misunderstanding of the longer version. The first cup given to the disciples to divide among themselves should be taken in connection with the previous verse (ver. 16) as referring to the eating of the Passover with them at the reunion in Heaven. This is followed by the institution of the Sacrament, to be repeated continually on earth in memory of Him. It is easy to see that it would occasion difficulties of interpretation, which would give rise to the attempts at revision that appear in various forms of the shorter version"_ [Sir Frederick G. Kenyon and S.C.E. Legg in THE MINISTRY AND THE SACRAMENTS, ed. By Roderic Dunkerley [London, 1937], pp. 285 f.).

Although I would disagree with Kenyon and Legg on the interpretation of "the kingdom of God;" their point on the division of the reading at verse 16 is well taken.

Internal Evidence.

"Verses 19b-20 contain several linguistic features that are non-Lukan." [Ibid., p. 176]

"The similarity between verses 19b-20 and 1 Cor 11.24b-25 arises from the familiarity of the evangelist with the liturgical practice among Pauline churches, a circumstance that accounts also for the presence of non-Lukan expressions in verses 19b-20." [Ibid.; pp. 176-7]

The questions are raised and answered by Metzger.

The conclusion

The manuscripts and early translations give a variety of readings for Luke 22:17-20. However, when it is realized that only one lone manuscript gives a different reading, and only a handful of early versions, the question is asked, "Why would anyone at anytime question the inclusion of this verse?" The answer is found in the predisposition of the critic. Those who question this verse believe the New Testament as it was originally given was corrupted. They believe the New Testament, and indeed the whole Bible, came about through naturalistic means. They believe Jesus sayings circulated by mouth until they were written down, with some expansion. They then believe these written accounts were combined, with more expansion. Therefore, because they reject inspiration and divine preservation, they take every sliver of evidence that the text at one time was shorter to be the truth. The person who does not have this predisposition and the person who believes in both inspiration and divine preservation sees the evidence, and has no problem with the inclusion of the verse.

What of the evidence? What of the weight of the versions, and lectionaries? What of the universality of inclusion? Let the evidence make the decision. It belongs.

When the seven points of truth are examined, they (**1. Antiquity, 2. Number, 3. Variety, 4. Weight, 5. Continuity, 6. Context of the Passage,** and **7. Internal Considerations**) are in favor of the inclusion of the verse.

Does Luke 22:43-44 Belong in the New Testament?

These verses are included by THE TEXTUS RECEPTUS, THE MAJORITY TEXT, THE KING JAMES VERSION, THE AMERICAN STANDARD VERSION, THE NEW AMERICAN STANDARD VERSION, THE REVISED STANDARD VERSION, THE LIVING BIBLE, THE NEW AMERICAN STANDARD, THE NEW INTERNATIONAL VERSION, THE NEW KING JAMES VERSION, THE COMMON ENGLISH BIBLE, AND, AND THE ENGLISH STANDARD VERSION, double-bracketed by THE WESTCOTT/HORT TEXT, THE NESTLE TEXT AND THE UNITED BIBLE SOCIETIES TEXT, and single-bracketed by TODAY'S ENGLISH VERSION.

Passage	TR	W/H	NT	BS	MT	KJV	ASV	RSV	TEV	LB	NAS	NIV	NKJ	CEB	ESV
Luke 22:43,44	--	DB	DB	DB	--	--	--	--	S	--	--	--	--	--	--

Antiquity of witnesses

The second century sees four Syriac versions (Curetorian, Peshitta, Palestinian and Harclean), the Diatessaron of Tatian, and Justin including the verse, while one Syriac (Siniatic) and Marcion omit it.

The third century sees one papyrus (Bodmer {p75}) and two Coptic versions (Sahidic, and Bohairic), along with Clement and Origen exclude the verses, while Irenaeus, Hippolytus and Dionysius include it.

The fourth century sees one uncial (Aleph Sinaiticus [original hand]), three versions (Vulgate, Vercellensis Old Latin, Armenian [IV/V]), and five early writers (Arius, Eusebius, Hilary, Caesarius – Nazianzus, Gregory – Nazianzus) and Didymus include the verse, while one Old Latin version (Vercellensis) omit it.

The verse has ancient evidence for its inclusion.

FOR	AGAINST
2ND CENTURY	
Curetorian Syriac (II-VII)	
Peshitta Syriac (II-VII)	
Harclean Syriac (II-VII)	Sinaitic Syriac (II-VII)
Palestinian Syriac (II-VII)	Marcion
Diatessaron of Tatian	
Justin	
3RD CENTURY	
	P75 P. Bodmer papyrus
Irenaeus	Sahidic Coptic (III-VI)
Hippolytus	Bohairic Coptic (III-VI)
Dionysius	Clement
	Origen
4TH CENTURY	
Aleph Sinaiticus uncial (original hand)	
Vulgate	
Vercellensis Old Latin	
Armenian (IV/V)	
Arius	Aleph Sinaiticus uncial (corrector)
Eusebius	B Vaticanus uncial
Hilary	
Caesarius – Nazianzus	
Gregory – Nazianzus	
Didymus	

Number

GREEK MSS	VERSIONS	EARLY WRITERS	BYZ MSS	TEXT	BYZ MSS	EARLY WRITERS	VERSIONS	GREEK MSS
32	18	20	+	LK 22:43	-	4	5	11
32	18	20	+	LK 22:44	-	4	5	11

The evidence for the inclusion of the verses is about three to one in favor.

Continuity

In the 2ND Century, four SYRIAC VERSIONS (CURETORIAN, PESHITTA, HARCLEAN, PALESTINIAN, PALESTINIAN – all dating from the 2ND to the 7TH Century), the DIATESSARON OF TATIAN and JUSTIN include the verses. The SINAITIC SYRIAC VERSION (dating from the 2ND to the 7TH Century) and MARCIAN omit the verses.

In the 3RD Century, IRENAEUS, HIPPOLYTUS and DIONYSIUS include verses 43 and 44. One papyrus (P. BODMER {P75}), two COPTIC VERSIONS (SAHIDIC, BOHAIRIC – both dating 3RD to the 6TH Century), CLEMENT and ORIGEN omit the verses.

In the 4TH Century, one uncial bears dual witness (SINAITICUS {ALEPH}, THE ORIGINAL HAND AND A SECONDARY CORRECTOR), three VERSIONS (VULGATE, VERCELLENSIS OLD LATIN, ARMENIAN dating from the 4TH or 5TH Century), ARIUS ACCORDING TO EPAPHANIUS, EUSEBIUS, HILARY, CAESARIUS – NAZIANZUS, GREGORY – NAZIANZUS, and DIDYMUS include the verses. One CORRECTOR TO THE SINAITICUS {ALEPH} and the VATICANUS {B} omit the verses.

In the 5TH Century, five OLD LATIN VERSIONS (VERONENSIS, BEZAE CANTABRIGIENSIS, PALATINUS, CORBEIENSIS II, VINDOBONENSIS), PS-DIONYSIUS, EPIPHANIUS, CHRYSOSTOM, JEROME, AUGUSTINE and THEODORET include LUKE 22:43-44. Three uncials (ALEXANDRINUS {A}, T, FREER GOSPELS {W}) and the GEORGIAN VERSION omit the verses.

In the 6TH Century, one uncial (BEZAE CANTABRIGIENSIS {D}), the ETHIOPIAN VERSION, LEONTIUS, COSMOS AND FACUNDUS include the verses.

In the 7TH Century, four OLD LATIN VERSIONS (AUREUS, MONACENSIS, USSERIANUS I, RHEDIGERANUS) include LUKE 22:43,44.

In the 8TH Century, one uncial (REGIUS {L}) includes the verses, and JOHN – DAMASCUS omits them.

In the 9TH Century, four uncials (Δ {ORIGINAL HAND}, KORIDETHI {Θ}, Π {ORIGINAL HAND}, K) and two minuscules (565, 892 {ORIGINAL HAND}) include verses 43 and 44. The AUGIENSIS OLD LATIN VERSION omits them.

In the 10TH Century, one uncial (**X**) includes the verses.

In the 11TH Century, one minuscule (**700**) includes the verses.

In the 12TH Century, seven minuscules (**1010, 1071 {MARGIN}, 1241, 1344, 1365, 1230, 1646**), one lectionary in part (**L211**) and the COLBERTINUS OLD LATIN VERSION include these verses. The original hand of one minuscule (**1071**) and four lectionaries in part (**L69, L70, L211, L1127**) omit verses 43 and 44.

In the 13TH Century, four minuscules (**118, 1009, 1242, 1546**) include the verses.

In the 14TH Century, four minuscules (**131, 209, 2174, 2148**) and one lectionary (**L184**) INCLUDE LUKE 22:43, 44.

In the 15TH Century, one minuscule (**1253**) includes the verses.

The majority of the SYNAXARION (the so-called "moveable year" beginning with Easter) and in the MENOLOGIAN (the "fixed year" beginning with September 1) omit verses 43 and 44.

The majority of the BYZANTINE MANUSCRIPTS include LUKE 22:43-44.

THE EVIDENCE FOR LUKE 22:43-44

FOR	AGAINST
2ND CENTURY	
Curetorian Syriac (II-VII)	
Peshitta Syriac (II-VII)	
Harclean Syriac (II-VII)	Sinaitic Syriac (II-VII)
Palestinian Syriac (II-VII)	Marcion
Diatessaron of Tatian	
Justin	
3RD CENTURY	
	P75 P. Bodmer papyrus
	Sahidic Coptic (III-VI)
Irenaeus	Bohairic Coptic (III-VI)
Hippolytus	Clement
Dionysius	Origen

4TH CENTURY

Aleph Sinaiticus uncial
(original hand)

Vulgate version

Vercellensis Old Latin

Armenian (IV/V)

Arius

Eusebius

Hilary

Caesarius – Nazianzus

Gregory – Nazianzus

Didymus

Aleph Sinaiticus uncial (corrector)

B Vaticanus uncial

5TH CENTURY

Veronensis Old Latin

Bezae Cantabrigiensis Old Latin

Palatinus Old Latin

Corbeiensis II Old Latin

Vindobonensis Old Latin

Ps-Dionysius

Epiphanius

Chrysostom

Jerome

Augustine

Theodoret

A Alexandrinus uncial

T uncial

W Freer Gospels uncial

Georgian

6TH CENTURY

D Bezae Cantabrigiensis uncial

Ethiopian

Leontius

Cosmos

Facundus

Aureus Old Latin

Monacensis Old Latin

Usserianus I Old Latin

Rhedigeranus Old Latin

L Regius uncial

Psi uncial

John – Damascus

Delta uncial (original hand)

Koridethi Theta uncial

Pi uncial (original hand)

K uncial

565 minuscule

892 minuscule (original hand)

Augiensis Old Latin

X uncial

700 minuscule

1 minuscule

1010 minuscule

1071 minuscule (margin)

1241 minuscule

1071 minuscule (original hand)

L69 lectionary (part)

L70 lectionary (part)

L211 lectionary (part)

1344 minuscule	L1127 lectionary (part)
1365 minuscule	
1230 minuscule	
1646 minuscule	
L211 lectionary (part)	
Colbertinus Old Latin	

13TH CENTURY

118 minuscule

1009 minuscule

1242 minuscule

1546 minuscule

14TH CENTURY

131 minuscule

209 minuscule

2174 minuscule

2148 minuscule

L184 lectionary

15TH CENTURY

1253 minuscule

The majority of the lectionaries in the Synaxarion (the so-called "moveable year" beginning with Easter) and in the Menologion (the "fixed year" beginning with September 1) omit Luke 22:43-44.

The majority of Byzantine manuscripts include Luke 22:43-44.

The 6th,7th, 10th,11th, 13th, 14th, and 15th centuries have no evidence for the exclusion of the verse. *Every century* has evidence for the inclusion of the verse. The 2nd, 3rd, 4th, 5th, 8th,9th, and 12th centuries are the only time periods were any evidence of omission is found. The 8th and 9th centuries only have one witness per century. The 6th,7th , 10th, 11th, 13th, 14th, and 15th centuries have no evidence for the exclusion.

There is no question but that the continuity of evidence favors inclusion.

The Context of Passage

And he came out, and went, as he was wont, to the mount of Olives; and his disciples also followed him. And when he was at the place, he said unto them, Pray that ye enter not into temptation.

And he was withdrawn from them about a stone's cast, and kneeled down, and prayed, Saying, Father, if thou be willing, remove this cup from me: nevertheless not my will, but thine, be done.

<u>And there appeared an angel unto him from heaven, strengthening him. And being in an agony he prayed more earnestly: and his sweat was as it were great drops of blood falling down to the ground.</u>

And when he rose up from prayer, and was come to his disciples, he found them sleeping for sorrow, And said unto them, Why sleep ye? rise and pray, lest ye enter into temptation. [LUKE 22:39-46 KJV]

Jesus went to the Mount of Olives, as was His custom, and "His disciples followed him." When they arrived, Jesus instructed His disciples to pray so they would "enter not into temptation." It was a simple request.

Withdrawing Himself about a stone's throw, He kneeled, humbling Himself before God, and prayed. His prayer was one of reverence and resignation. He addressed God as "Father," and asked that "this cup," the suffering and death of the trials and crucifixion, might be removed. He did not wish to perish, having the human trait of self-preservation. Yet there was within Him something greater than a need to survive; there was the need to do the will of His Father. He was willing to suppress His wants and wishes, for the will of God. Let that be done above all else. It was more important that the will of Father be done than to obey the instinct of self-preservation.

An angel descended from heaven to comfort and strengthen Him. God did not forget Him, nor leave Him comfortless. He provided Him an angel for comfort and strength.

But, this was not an easy decision to follow through on. He knew the torment that He was to face. As a man, it was agonizing to realize that He must go through this though He could escape. He could have called ten thousand angels ... but He died alone, for you and me. The anxiety of the situation broke Him out in a cold sweat. A sweat *as it were great drops of blood falling down to the ground.*

When Jesus was done, He returned to His disciples to find them asleep. The sorrow they felt in empathy and sympathy for Jesus, and for their own loss had deprived them of all energy. Yet Jesus asked them, Why do ye sleep? Yes, this was a time of sorrow and anxiety; but it is in such times that prayer is needed to comfort and strengthen the saint so that he will not fall to the snares, trials and temptations such circumstances bring upon them.

Without the verses in question, Jesus is not relieved by an angel, nor does He have sweat *as it were great drops of blood falling down to the ground.* These two images of Jesus in the garden are important. They give us a glimpse into the anxiety of Jesus, and the relief God supplies. They show that the same fatigue which overcame the disciples was present with Jesus, but He overcame it. He suffered as they did, but did not give in to it. It is an example that is worthy to note, and to imitate. Much is lost in their exclusion. The power, the pathos of the passage is weakened.

Internal Evidence.

There does not appear to be any question on the literary style of the passage.

The conclusion

Metzger says,

"Nevertheless, while acknowledging that the passage is a later addition to the text, in view of its evident antiquity and its importance in the textual tradition, a majority of the Committee decided to retain the words in the text but to enclose them within double square brackets." [IBID.; P. 177]

In other words, the committee lacked the courage of their convictions that the passage was not in the Bible, and included it anyway. This commentary shows that the purpose of the critics is not to restore the original hand, but to restore what is understood to be a changed text.

This is the basic question that confronts us as the subject of the text is considered: *Do we want a restoration of the original text? Or do we want a restoration of something else?*

When theories of inspiration and preservation are accepted which deny and set aside the scriptural concepts as they have been described, the result is a text which is questionable, or at least left in question by the critics.

When inspiration and preservation are accepted as they are taught in the scriptures, the text of the Bible is easy to ascertain and defend.

What of the evidence? What of the weight of the versions, and lectionaries? What of the universality of inclusion? Let the evidence make the decision. It belongs.

When the seven points of truth are examined, they (**1. Antiquity, 2. Number, 3. Variety, 4. Weight, 5. Continuity, 6. Context of the Passage,** and **7. Internal Considerations**) are in favor of the inclusion of the verse.

*All evidence is taken from the 3rd Edition of the UBS Greek Text.

Does Luke 23:17 Belong in the New Testament?

The verse is in **the Textus Receptus, the Majority Text, the King James Version** and **the New King James Version**. It is single bracketed [used to enclose words which are regarded as having dubious textual validity] by **Today's English Version**. The verse is omitted by the **Westcott/Hort Text, the Nestle Text** and **the United Bible Societies (III) Text, the American Standard Version, the Revised Standard Version, the Living Bible, the New American Standard Bible,** and **the New International Version**.

	T/R	W/H	NT	UBS	MT	KJV	ASV	RSV	TEV	LB	NAS	NIV	NKJ
LK 23:17	-	O	O	O	-	-	O	O	S	O	O	O	-

The evidence utilized will be that found in the critical apparatus of the UBSIII.

ANTIQUITY OF THE WITNESSES

In the 2nd century there are four Syriac Versions listed which include the verse [Peshitta II-VII, Harclean II-VII, Curetonian II-VII, Sinaitic II-VII], and one witness against it [Diatessaron of Tatian].

In the 3rd century there is one Coptic version [Bohairic mss III-VI] which includes the verse; and one papyrus [P75 Bodmer], and two Coptic versions [Sahidic III-VI, Bohairic III-VI] which omit it.

In the 4th century there is one uncial [Sinaiticus – Aleph], one version [Vulgate] and one writer [Eusebius] including the verse, and one uncial [Vaticanus – B] and one version [Vercellensis Old Latin] omitting it.

FOR	AGAINST

2ND CENTURY

FOR	AGAINST
Peshitta Syriac version (II-VII)	
Harclean Syriac version (II-VII)	Diatessaron of Tatian
Curetonian Syriac version (II-VII)	
Sinaitic Syriac version (II-VII)	

3RD CENTURY

FOR	AGAINST
	P75 P. Bodmer
Bohairic Coptic version (mss) (III-VI)	Sahidic Coptic version (III-VI)
	Bohairic Coptic version (III-VI)

4TH CENTURY

FOR	AGAINST
Aleph Sinaiticus uncial	
Vulgate version	B Vaticanus uncial
Eusebius	Vercellensis Old Latin version

NUMBER

Forty Greek manuscripts include the verse, while seventeen manuscripts omit it.

Seventeen versions include the verse, while three versions omit it.

It is included by one early writer, and excluded by one early writer.

It is included in the majority of Byzantine manuscripts.

FOR   **AGAINST**

GREEK MSS.	VERSIONS	EARLY WRITERS	BYZ. MSS.	TEXT	BYZ. MSS.	EARLY WRITERS	VERSIONS	GREEK MSS.
40	17	1	+	23:17	-	1	3	17

The numbers favor the inclusion of the verse. The Greek manuscripts favor its inclusion at forty to seventeen, or almost three to one. The versions favor its inclusion at seventeen to three, or about six to one. The early writers are even in their testimony. The majority of the Byzantine manuscripts (which make up approximately 95% of the extant manuscipts) include the passage.

Variety

The verse is testified by Greek manuscripts (both Uncial and Minuscule). The versions who testify to its inclusion are six times those who exclude the verse. The early writers are equally divided as to the inclusion or exclusion of the verse. The Syriac version includes it, as well as various Latin versions, both Old Latin and Vulgate era. It is not found just in the New Testaments in a particular area, but is found universally.

Continuity

In the 2nd century four Syriac versions [Peshitta, Harclean, Curetonian, Sinaitic – all II-VII] include the verse, while one witness [Diatessaron of Tatian].

In the 3rd century one Coptic version manuscript [Bohairic – III-VI] includes the verse, while one papyri [P75 Bodmer] and two Coptic versions [Sahidic, Bohairic – III-VI] omit it.

In the 4th century one uncial [Sinaiticus – Aleph], the Vulgate and Eusebius include the verse, while one uncial [Vaticanus – B], and one old Latin version [Vercellensis] testifies against it.

In the 5th century one uncial [Freer – W] and four old Latin versions [Veronensis, Palatinus, Corbeiensis II, Bezae Cantabrigiensis] include the verse, and two uncials [Alexandrinus – A, T] omit it.

In the 6th century one uncial [Beza Cantabrigiensis – D], one old Latin version [Brixianus] and the Ethiopic version include the verse, while one uncial [0124] omits it.

In the 7th century four old Latin versions [Aureus, Monacensis, Usserianus I, Rhedigeranus] include the verse, and no witnesses omit it.

In the 8th century one uncial [Ψ (VIII/IX)] includes it, and one uncial [L Regius] omits it.

In the 9th century three uncials [Koridethi θ, Δ, 063] and one minuscule [565] include it, while a second minuscule [892] includes it in the margin but omits it in the body of the manuscript, and two uncials [K, Π] do not include the verse.

In the 10th century one uncial [X] includes it, and one minuscule [1079] omits it.

In the 11th century six minuscules [124, 788, 700, 1216, 230, 174] include it, and one lectionary [L185] partially omits it.

In the 12th century thirteen minuscules [1, 346, 543, 826, 828, 983, 1010, 1365, 1071, 1344, 1195, 1230, 1646] and one Old Latin version [Colbertinus] include the verse, and no witnesses omit it.

In the 13th century five minuscules [118, 13, 1242, 1009, 1689] include it, and one minuscule [1546] omits it.

In the 14th century four minuscules [131, 209, 2174, 2148] include the verse, and no witnesses omit it.

In the 15th century two minuscules [69, 1253] include the verse, while again there are no witnesses against it.

There are six centuries (2nd, 6th, 8th, 10th, 11th, 13th) that only have a single witness to the exclusion of the verse, while only three centuries (3rd, 8th, 10th) have a single witness for its inclusion. Further, four centuries (7th, 12th, 14th, 15th) do not have a single witness which excludes the verse.

Unquestionably, there is a continuous witness for the inclusion of the verse, thus it passes the Continuity test.

THE EVIDENCE FOR LUKE 23:17

FOR	AGAINST
2ND CENTURY	
Peshitta Syriac version (II-VII)	
Harclean Syriac version (II-VII)	Diatessaron of Tatian
Curetonian Syriac version (II-VII)	
Sinaitic Syriac version (II-VII)	
3RD CENTURY	
	P75 P. Bodmer
Bohairic Coptic version (mss) (III-VI)	Sahidic Coptic version (III-VI)
	Bohairic Coptic version (III-VI)
4TH CENTURY	
Aleph Sinaiticus uncial	B Vaticanus uncial
Vulgate version	Vercellensis Old Latin version
Eusebius	
5TH CENTURY	
W Freer Gospels uncial	
Veronensis Old Latin version	
Palatinus Old Latin version	A Alexandrinus uncial
Corbeiensis II Old Latin version	T uncial
Bezae Cantabrigiensis Old Latin version	

6TH CENTURY

D Bezae Cantabrigiensis uncial

Brixianus Old Latin version   0124 uncial

Ethiopic version

7TH CENTURY

Aureus Old Latin version

Monacensis Old Latin version

Usserianus I Old Latin version

Rhedigeranus Old Latin version

8TH CENTURY

Psi uncial (VIII/IX)   L Regius uncial

9TH CENTURY

Koridethi Theta uncial

Delta uncial   K uncial

063 uncial   Pi uncial

565 minuscule   892 minuscule

892 minuscule (margin)

10TH CENTURY

X uncial   1079 minuscule

11TH CENTURY

124 minuscule

788 minuscule

700 minuscule

1216 minuscule   L185 lectionary (part)

230 minuscule

174 minuscule

12TH CENTURY

1 minuscule

346 minuscule

543 minuscule

826 minuscule

828 minuscule

983 minuscule

1010 minuscule

1365 minuscule

1071 minuscule

1344 minuscule

1195 minuscule

1230 minusucle

1646 minusucle

Colbertinus Old Latin version

13TH CENTURY

118 minuscule

13 minuscule

1242 minuscule   1546 minuscule

1009 minuscule

1689 minuscule

14TH CENTURY

131 minuscule

209 minuscule

2174 minuscule

2148 minuscule

69 minuscule

1253 minuscule

The majority of the lectionaries in the Synaxarion (the so-called "moveable year" beginning with Easter) and in the Menologion (the "fixed year" beginning with September 1) include Luke 23:17.

The majority of the Byzantine manuscripts include Luke 23:17.

CONTEXT

And Pilate, when he had called together the chief priests and the rulers and the people, Said unto them, Ye have brought this man unto me, as one that perverteth the people: and, behold, I, having examined him before you, have found no fault in this man touching those things whereof ye accuse him: No, nor yet Herod: for I sent you to him; and, lo, nothing worthy of death is done unto him. I will therefore chastise him, and release him.

(For of necessity he must release one unto them at the feast.)

And they cried out all at once, saying, Away with this man, and release unto us Barabbas: (Who for a certain sedition made in the city, and for murder, was cast into prison.)

Pilate therefore, willing to release Jesus, spake again to them.

But they cried, saying, Crucify him, crucify him.

And he said unto them the third time, Why, what evil hath he done? I have found no cause of death in him: I will therefore chastise him, and let him go.

And they were instant with loud voices, requiring that he might be crucified. And the voices of them and of the chief priests prevailed. And Pilate gave sentence that it should be as they required. And he released unto them him that for sedition and murder was cast into prison, whom they had desired; but he delivered Jesus to their will. [LUKE 23:13-25 KJV]

Jesus was brought before Pilate, who sent the chief priests, rulers and people to Herod to bring their charges against Jesus. Now they have returned to Pilate. Having tried to get rid of the problem by refusing to rule, he now rules that Jesus is innocent of the charges they have brought. Not only has he found him innocent, so had Herod. If it will appease them, he will "chastise him" and release him.

It was the tradition that at the Passover, Pilate would release one prisoner. He hoped Jesus would appease the people.

He calculated wrong. They cried for the release of Barabbas: one who had committed murder, rebelling against the power of the empire, and was now in jail.

Pilate tried to convince them to accept Jesus; but, it was to no avail.

They cried out, "Crucify him!" Rather than release the One who was innocent of all charges, and punish the one who was guilty of murder, they wanted the Innocent to be put to death.

Pilate protested. Jesus had done no wrong. He would "chastise" Him and release Him to them.

The protests seemed to fuel the fire. The people and the priests called for the death of Jesus. Pilate, not having the moral fortitude to stand against the mob, released Barabbas and delivered Jesus to die as they requested.

Why was Pilate going to release anyone? It was the custom. Without the verse in question, the question is left to the imagination. Without it, no one knows why Pilate is so determined to release a prisoner; and, why the crowd was offering an alternative that Pilate finally capitulates to.

The verse completes the story.

INTERNAL EVIDENCE

There does not appear to be any question on the literary style of the passage.

CONCLUSION

Metzger says,

The secondary character of the verse is disclosed not only by its omission from such early witnesses as p⁷⁵ A B itª copˢª al, but also by its insertion, in slightly different forms, either here or after ver. 19 (where codex Bezae agrees in wording with the reading of Θ Ψ). Although homoeoarcton (ΑΝΑΓΚΗΝ … ΑΝΕΚΡΑΓΟΝ) might account for the omission in one family of witnesses, such a theory is unable to explain its widespread omission and its presence at two different places. The verse is a gloss, apparently based on Mt 27.15 and Mk 15.6. [ID-ID., PP. 179-80]

The verse is attested to by the Greek manuscripts at a rate of four to one. It is attested to by the versions at almost six to one. It is found in the majority of the Byzantine Manuscripts. What part of this makes this verse questionable? Only if the evidence is considered to be secondary. Only if the presuppositions of what the text should be override all other considerations.

Does Luke 24:12 Belong in the New Testament?

LUKE 24:12 is double-bracketed by WESTCOTT/HORT GREEK TEXT, omtted by NESTLE'S GREEK TEXT, single bracketed BY THE NEW AMERICAN STANDARD, AND OMITTED BY THE REVISED STANDARD VERSION and THE NEW ENGLISH BIBLE.

	WH	N	BS	ASV	NAS	NIV	RSV	NKJV	CEB	ESV
Lk. 24:12*	DB	O	--	--	SB	--	O	--	--	--

The evidence utilized will be that found in the critical apparatus of the UBSIII.

ANTIQUITY OF THE WITNESSES

The second century lists five Syriac versions (Curetonian, Sinaitic, Peshitta, Harclean, Palestinian) which include the verse, and no witnesses to the contrary.

The third century lists one papyrus (P75 – P. Bodmer) and two Coptic versions (Sahidic, Bohairic) which include the verse, and not a single witness which omits the verse.

The fourth century lists two uncials (A – Vaticanus, Aleph – Sinaiticus), two versions (Vulgate, Armenian and half of Eusebius's references including the verse, and half of Eusebius' references omitting the verse.

FOR	AGAINST
2ND CENTURY	
Curetonian Syriac version (II-VII)	

Sinaitic Syriac version (II-VII)

Peshitta Syriac version (II-VII)

Harclean Syriac version (II-VII)

Palestinian Syriac version (II-VII)

3RD CENTURY

P75 P. Bodmer papyrus

Sahidic Coptic version (III-VI)

Bohairic Coptic version (III-VI)

4TH CENTURY

Aleph Sinaiticus uncial

B Vaticanus uncial

Vulgate version

Armenian version (IV/V)

Eusebius ½

Vercellensis Old Latin version

Eusebius ½

NUMBER

Fifty-two Greek manuscripts include the verse, while one manuscript omits it.

Fourteen versions include the verse, and seven versions omit it.

Two early writers quote the verse, while three early writers omit it.

The majority of the BYZANTINE MANUSCRIPTS include LUKE 24:12.

GREEK MSS	VERSIONS	EARLY WRITERS	BYZ MSS	TEXT	BYZ MSS	EARLY WRITERS	VERSIONS	GREEK MSS
52	14	2	+	Luke 24:12	-	3	7	1

The Greek manuscripts include the verse at a rate of over fifty to one. The versions include it at a rate of two to one. The evidence is overwhelming in favor of Luke 24:12.

Variety

Whether you look at the manuscripts which include the verse by number, by age, by family, or by type, they all favor the inclusion of the verse. The versions from every location include the verse. There is no doubt that the inclusion of the verse passes the Variety test.

Continuity

In the 2ND Century, five SYRIAC VERSIONS (CURETONIAN, SINAITIC, PESHITTA, HARCLEAN, SOME MANUSCRIPTS OF THE PALESTINIAN – all dating from 2ND to the 7TH Century) include the verse. SOME MANUSCRIPTS OF THE PALESTINIAN SYRIAC VERSION omit verse 12.

In the 3RD Century, one papyrus (P. BODMER {P75}), and two COPTIC VERSIONS (SAHIDIC, BOHAIRIC – both dated 3RD to 6TH Century) include the verse.

In the 4TH Century, two uncials (SINAITICUS {ALEPH}, VANTICANUS {B}), two versions (VULGATE, ARMENIAN from the 4TH or 5TH Century) and EUSEBIUS (AT LEAST HALF) include the verse. The VERCELLENSIS OLD LATIN VERSION and AT LEAST HALF OF EUSEBIUS omit the verse.

In the 5TH Century, two uncials (ALEXANDRINUS {A}, FREER GOSPELS {W}), two versions (GEORGIAN, CORBEIENSIS II OLD LATIN) and CYRIL include the verse. Three OLD LATIN VERSIONS (VERONENSIS, BEZAE CANTABRIGIENSIS, PALATINUS) omit verse 12.

In the 6TH Century, two uncials (079, 0124) and the BRIXIANUS OLD LATIN VERSION include verse 12. The sole manuscript to include it is the uncial BEZAE CANTABRIGIENSIS {D} from the 5TH Century.

In the 7TH Century, the AUREUS OLD LATIN VERSION includes the verse. Two OLD LATIN VERSIONS (USSERIANUS I, RHEDIGERANUS dated 7TH or 8TH Century) omit the verse.

In the 8TH Century, one uncial (Ψ) includes the verse.

In the 9TH Century, six uncials (K, REGIUS {L}, D, KORIDETHI {Θ}, Π, 063) and three minuscules (33, 365, 892) include the verse.

In the 10TH Century, one uncial (X) and one minuscule (1079) include the verse.

In the 11TH Century, seven minuscules (124, 788, 28, 700, 230, 1216, 174) and one marginal reading in the lectionary (L185) include the verse.

In the 12TH Century, fourteen minuscules (1, 346, 543, 826, 828, 983, 1010, 1071, 1241, 1344, 1365, 1195, 1230, 1646) and the COLBERTINUS OLD LATIN VERSION (12TH or 13TH Century) include the verse.

In the 13TH Century, five minuscules (118, 13, 1009, 1689, 1546) include the verse.

In the 14TH Century, four minuscules (131, 209, 2174, 2148) include the verse.

In the 15TH Century, two minuscules (69, 1253) include the verse.

The majority of the lectionaries in the SYNAXARION (the so-called "moveable year" beginning with Easter) and in the MENOLOGIAN (the "fixed year" beginning with September 1) include LUKE 24:12.

THE EVIDENCE FOR LUKE 24:12

FOR	AGAINST
2ND CENTURY	
Curetonian Syriac version (II-VII)	
Sinaitic Syriac version (II-VII)	
Peshitta Syriac version (II-VII)	
Harclean Syriac version (II-VII)	
Palestinian Syriac version (II-VII)	
3RD CENTURY	
P75 P. Bodmer papyrus	
Sahidic Coptic version (III-VI)	
Bohairic Coptic version (III-VI)	
4TH CENTURY	
Aleph Sinaiticus uncial	
B Vaticanus uncial	Vercellensis Old Latin version
Vulgate version	Eusebius ½
Armenian version (IV/V)	
Eusebius ½	
5TH CENTURY	
A Alexandrinus uncial	
W Freer Gospels uncial	Veronensis Old Latin version
Georgian version	Bezae Cantabrigiensis Old Latin version
Corbeiensis II Old Latin version	Palatinus Old Latin version
Cyril	
6TH CENTURY	
079 uncial	D Bezae Cantabrigiensis uncial
0124 uncial	

Brixianus Old Latin version

Aureus Old Latin version

Usserianus I Old Latin version

Rhedigeranus Old Latin version (VII/VIII)

8ᵀᴴ CENTURY

Psi uncial

9ᵀᴴ CENTURY

K uncial

L Regius uncial

Delta uncial

Koridethi Theta uncial

Pi uncial

063 uncial

33 minuscule

565 minuscule

892 minuscule

10ᵀᴴ CENTURY

X uncial

1079 uncial

11ᵀᴴ CENTURY

124 minuscule

788 minuscule

28 minuscule

700 minuscule

230 minuscule

1216 minuscule

174 minuscule

12TH CENTURY

1 minuscule

346 minuscule

543 minuscule

826 minuscule

828 minuscule

983 minuscule

1010 minuscule

1071 minuscule

1241 minuscule

1344 minuscule

1365 minuscule

1195 minuscule

1230 minuscule

1646 minuscule

13TH CENTURY

118 minuscule

13 minuscule

1009 minuscule

1689 minuscule

1546 minuscule

14TH CENTURY

131 minuscule

209 minuscule

2174 minuscule

2148 minuscule

69 minuscule

1253 minuscule

The majority of the lectionaries in the Synaxarion (the so-called "moveable year" beginning with Easter) and in the Menologion (the "fixed year" beginning with September 1) include Luke 24:12.

The majority of Byzantine manuscripts include Luke 24:12.

CONTEXT

Now upon the first day of the week, very early in the morning, they came unto the sepulchre, bringing the spices which they had prepared, and certain others with them. And they found the stone rolled away from the sepulchre. And they entered in, and found not the body of the Lord Jesus.

And it came to pass, as they were much perplexed thereabout, behold, two men stood by them in shining garments: And as they were afraid, and bowed down their faces to the earth, they said unto them, Why seek ye the living among the dead? He is not here, but is risen: remember how he spake unto you when he was yet in Galilee, Saying, The Son of man must be delivered into the hands of sinful men, and be crucified, and the third day rise again.

And they remembered his words, And returned from the sepulchre, and told all these things unto the eleven, and to all the rest. It was Mary Magdalene, and Joanna, and Mary the mother of James, and other women that were with them, which told these things unto the apostles.

And their words seemed to them as idle tales, and they believed them not. Then arose Peter, and ran unto the sepulchre; and stooping down, he beheld the linen clothes laid by themselves, and departed, wondering in himself at that which was come to pass. **[LUKE 24:1-12 KJV]**

The women who had followed Jesus from Galilee, having seen where He was buried, returned early upon the first day of the week (Sunday) along with some others. When they came to the grave (a sepulcher), the stone which had been rolled into place over the door was moved and Jesus' body was missing.

They are confused, but two men in shining clothing appear to them, scaring them. They hang their heads in fear. And the men ask them, *Why seek ye the living among the dead?* Jesus was not here, He is rinsen from the dead. Didn't they remember what Jesus had told them in Galilee? *The Son of man must be delivered into the hands of sinful men, and be crucified, and the third day rise again.*

When reminded of the words of Jesus, they remembered. So they told the remaining apostles (the eleven) and others what they saw at the sepulcher; but, no one believed them. Mary Magdelene, Joanna, Mary the mother of James, and others told the apostles these things;

but, they did not believe.

Peter then ran to the selpulcher, and bending down, looked inside. He saw the burial clothes laying by themselves, and left wandering what that meant.

The verse in question is the account of Peter running to the sepulcher and looking in. The women had told them, and they did not believe. In addition, Peter, even though he ran to the grave and saw for himself, still did not believe. The apostles, Peter included, did not think of the words of Jesus in Galilee. Were they too dense to remember what Jesus said? Were they too grief stricken? Were they too practical to believe that one rose from the dead? That we do not know. Peter's personal refusal to believe, is just one more step to show that the proofs of the resurrection were both needed, and convincing.

INTERNAL EVIDENCE

There does not appear to be any question on the literary style of the passage.

CONCLUSION

Metzger rating the verse with a {D} says,

Although ver. 12 is sometimes thought to be an interpolation ... derived from Jn 20.3, 5, 6, 10, a majority of the Committee regarded the passage as a natural antecedent to ver. 24, and was inclined to explain the similarity with the verses in John as due to the likelihood that both evangelists had drawn upon a common tradition. [IBID., P. 184]

The common tradition that both evangelists drew on is inspiration. Why the passage would rate a "D" grade is puzzling. The evidence, with the lone exception of one uncial manuscript and a handful of translations, is in favor of the verse. The only reason it would rate a poor grade is that the critic made up their mind before looking at the evidence.

Does Luke 24:40 Belong in the New Testament?

LUKE 24:40 is double-bracketed by WESTCOTT/HORT GREEK TEXT, omtted by NESTLE'S GREEK TEXT, AND OMITTED BY THE NEW AMERICAN STANDARD, THE REVISED STANDARD VERSION and THE COMMON ENGLISH BIBLE.

	WH	N	BS	ASV	NAS	NIV	RSV	NKJV	CEB	ESV
24:40*	DB	O	--	--	O	--	O	--	O	--

The evidence utilized will be that found in the critical apparatus of the UBSIII.

ANTIQUITY OF THE WITNESSES

In the 2ND Century, three Syriac versions (Peshitta, Harclean, Palestinian – all dated 2ND to 7TH Century) include the verse. Marcion and two Syriac versions (Curetorian, Sinaitic – dating from 2ND to 7TH Century) omit the verse.

In the 3RD Century, one papyrus (P. Bodmer {p75}) and two Coptic versions (Sahidic, Bohairic – dating from 2ND to 6TH Century) include the verse.

In the 4TH Century, two uncials (Sinaiticus {Aleph}, Vaticanus {B}), two versions (Vulgate, Armenian dating from 4TH or 5TH Century), Eusebius and Athanasius include the verse. The Vercellensis Old Latin version omits it.

FOR	AGAINST
2ND CENTURY	
Peshitta Syriac version (II-VII)	Marcion

Harclean Syriac version (II-VII)	Curetorian Syriac version (II-VII)
Palestinian Syriac version (II-VII)	Sinaitic Syriac version (II-VII)

3RD CENTURY

P75 P. Bodmer papyrus

Sahidic Coptic version (III-VI)

Bohairic Coptic version (III-VI)

4TH CENTURY

Aleph Sinaiticus uncial	
B Vaticanus uncial	
Vulgate version	**Vercellensis Old Latin version**
Armenian version (IV/V)	
Eusebius	
Athanasius	

NUMBER

Fifty Greek manuscripts include the verse, while one manuscript omits it.

Twelve versions include the verse, and seven versions omit it.

Five early writers quote the verse, while one early writer omits it.

The majority of the BYZANTINE MANUSCRIPTS include LUKE 24:40.

GREEK MSS	VERSIONS	EARLY WRITERS	BYZ MSS	TEXT	BYZ MSS	EARLY WRITERS	VERSIONS	GREEK MSS
50	12	5	+	LK 24:40	-	1	9	1

The Greek manuscripts include the verse at a rate of fifty to one. The versions include it at a rate of four to three. The evidence is overwhelming in favor of Luke 24:40.

Variety

Whether you look at the manuscripts which include the verse by number, by age, by family, or by type, they all favor the inclusion of the verse. The versions from every location include the verse. There is no doubt that the inclusion of the verse passes the Variety test.

Continuity

In the 2ND Century, three Syriac versions (Peshitta, Harclean, Palestinian – all dated 2ND to 7TH Century) include the verse. Marcion and two Syriac versions (Curetorian, Sinaitic – dating from 2ND to 7TH Century) omit the verse.

In the 3RD Century, one papyrus (P. Bodmer {p75}) and two Coptic versions (Sahidic, Bohairic – dating from 2ND to 6TH Century) include the verse.

In the 4TH Century, two uncials (Sinaiticus {Aleph}, Vaticanus {B}), two versions (Vulgate, Armenian dating from 4TH or 5TH Century), Eusebius and Athanasius include the verse. The Vercellensis Old Latin version omits it.

In the 5TH Century, two uncials (Alexandrinus {A}, Freer Gospels {W}), Chrysostom and Cyril include the verse. Four Old Latin versions (Veronensis, Bezae Cantabrigiensis, Palatinus, Corbeiensis II) omit Luke 24:40.

In the 6TH Century, the Brixianus Old Latin version includes the verse, and one uncial (Bezae Cantabrigiensis {D}) omits it.

In the 7TH Century, two Old Latin versions (Aureus, Monacensis) include the verse and two Old Latin versions (Usserianus I, Rhedigeranus dating from 7TH or 8TH Century) omit it.

In the 8TH Century, two uncials (Regius {L}, Y dated either 8TH or 9TH Century) and John – Damascus include the verse.

In the 9TH Century, four uncials (K, Δ, Koridethhi {Θ}, Π) and three minuscules (33, 565, 892) include the verse.

In the 10TH Century, one uncial (X) and one minuscule (1079) include the verse.

In the 11TH Century, seven minuscules (124, 788, 28, 700, 1216, 230 174) and the margin of one lectionary (L185) include the verse.

In the 12TH Century, fourteen minuscules 1, 346, 543, 826, 828, 983, 1010, 1071, 1241, 1344, 1365, 1195, 1230, 1646) and the Colvertinus Old Latin version include the verse.

In the 13TH Century, six minuscules (18, 13, 1009, 1242, 1689, 1546) include the verse.

In the 14TH Century, four minuscules (131, 209, 2174, 2148) include the verse.

In the 15TH Century, two minuscules (69, 1253) include the verse.

The majority of the lectionaries in the Synaxarion (the so-called "moveable year" beginning with Easter) and in the Menologian (the "fixed year" beginning with September 1) include Luke 24:40.

The majority of the Byzantine Manuscripts include Luke 24:40.

THE EVIDENCE FOR LUKE 24:40

FOR	AGAINST
2ND CENTURY	
Peshitta Syriac version (II-VII)	Marcion
Harclean Syriac version (II-VII)	Curetorian Syriac version (II-VII)
Palestinian Syriac version (II-VII)	Sinaitic Syriac version (II-VII)
3RD CENTURY	
P75 P. Bodmer papyrus	
Sahidic Coptic version (III-VI)	
Bohairic Coptic version (III-VI)	
4TH CENTURY	
Aleph Sinaiticus uncial	
B Vaticanus uncial	
Vulgate version	
Armenian version (IV/V)	Vercellensis Old Latin version
Eusebius	
Athanasius	
5TH CENTURY	
A Alexandrinus uncial	Veronensis Old Latin version
W Freer Gospels uncial	Bezae Cantabrigiensis Old Latin version
Chrysostom	Palatinus Old Latin version
Cyril	Corbeiensis II Old Latin version
6TH CENTURY	
Brixianus Old Latin version	D Bezae Cantabrigiensis uncial
7TH CENTURY	
Aureus Old Latin version	Usserianus I Old Latin version
Monacensis Old Latin version	Rhedigeranus Old Latin version (VII/VIII)

8TH CENTURY

L Regius uncial

Psi uncial (VIII/IX)

John – Damascus

9TH CENTURY

K uncial

Delta uncial

Koridethi Theta uncial

Pi uncial

33 minuscule

565 minuscule

892 minuscule

10TH CENTURY

X uncial

1079 minuscule

11TH CENTURY

124 minusucle

788 minuscule

28 minuscule

700 minuscule

1216 minuscule

230 minuscule

174 minuscule

L185 lectionary

12TH CENTURY

1 minuscule

246 minuscule

543 minuscule

826 minuscule

828 minuscule

983 minuscule

1010 minuscule

1071 minuscule

1241 minuscule

1344 minuscule

1365 minuscule

1195 minuscule

1230 minuscule

1646 minuscule

Colbertinus Old Latin version

13TH CENTURY

118 minuscule

13 minuscule

1009 minuscule

1242 minuscule

1689 minuscule

1546 minuscule

14TH CENTURY

131 minuscule

209 minuscule

2174 minuscule

2148 minuscule

15TH CENTURY

69 minuscule

The majority of the lectionaries in the Synaxarion (the so-called "moveable year" beginning with Easter) and in the Menologian (the "fixed year" beginning with September 1) include Luke 24:40.

The majority of the Byzantine manuscripts include Luke 24:40.

CONTEXT

And as they thus spake, Jesus himself stood in the midst of them, and saith unto them, Peace be unto you. But they were terrified and affrighted, and supposed that they had seen a spirit.

And he said unto them, Why are ye troubled? and why do thoughts arise in your hearts? Behold my hands and my feet, that it is I myself: handle me, and see; for a spirit hath not flesh and bones, as ye see me have. And when he had thus spoken, he shewed them his hands and his feet.

And while they yet believed not for joy, and wondered, he said unto them, Have ye here any meat? And they gave him a piece of a broiled fish, and of an honeycomb. And he took it, and did eat before them. **[LUKE 24:36-43 KJV]**

While the apostles were discussing the possibility of the resurrection, since they were told of the appearance to Simon Peter, Jesus appeared in the middle of them. As He addressed them, they were scared to death. They thought that they were seeing a ghost.

Jesus asks them why they were so frightened. Why would they think that He was a ghost? He tells them to look at His hands and His feet that had been scarred by the nails when hung upon the cross. Touch Him, and realize that He is not a ghost; but, He is flesh and bones. So He showed them His hands and His feet.

Still they had problems believing that Jesus had come forth from the grave, because the news was just too good to be believed. So then He asks them for something to eat, to prove that He is not an apparition. They gave him *a piece of a broiled fish, and a honeycomb,* which He ate.

In verse forty, Jesus shows them His hands and His feet after talking about it in verse thirty-nine. He has asked them to look, and he now offers the evidence. To those who are so unbelieving, who think that He is a ghost, not only would the statement, but the gesture be necessary.

INTERNAL EVIDENCE

There does not appear to be any question on the literary style of the passage.

CONCLUSION

Metger gives the verse a {D} rating, and says:

Was ver. 40 omitted by certain Western witnesses (D it[a,b,d,e,ff2,l,r1] *syr*[c,s] *Marcion) because it seemed superfluous after ver. 39? Or is it a gloss introduced by copyists in all other witnesses from Jn 20.20, with a necessary adaption (the passage in John refers to Christ's hands and side; this passage refers to his hands and feet)? A minority of the Committee preferred to omit the verse as an interpolation ...; the majority, however, was of the opinion that, had the passage been interpolated from the Johannine account, copyists would probably have left some trace of its origin by retaining* την πλευραν *in place of* τουσ ποδασ *(either here only, or in ver. 39 also).* [IBID.; P. **187**]

The idea of Western Non-Interpolations is dealt with elsewhere.

What difference does it make why? Curiosity might like to know; but, it does not determine the judgment. The judgment is determined by the evidence when it is so overwhelming.

Does John 5:4 Belong in the New Testament?

John 5:4 is omitted by THE WESTCOTT/HORT, UNITED BIBLE SOCIETIES, AND NESTLE GREEK TEXTS, BY THE AMERICAN STANDARD VERSION, THE NEW AMERICAN STANDARD, THE NEW INTERNATIONAL VERSION, THE REVISED STANDARD VERSION, THE COMMON ENGLISH BIBLE, AND THE ENGLISH STANDARD VERSION. It is single-bracketed [of doubtful origin] in TODAY'S ENGLISH VERSION. It is included in THE TEXTUS RECEPTUS, AND THE MAJORITY GREEK TEXTS, AND IN THE KING JAMES VERSION, THE LIVING BIBLE AND THE NEW KING JAMES VERSION.

Passage	TR	W/H	NT	UBS	MT	KJV	ASV	RSV	TEV	LB	NAS	NIV	NKJ	CEB	ESV
John 5:4	-	O	O	O	-	-	O	O	S	-	O	O	-	O	O

The evidence utilized will be that found in the critical apparatus of the UBSIII.

ANTIQUITY OF THE WITNESSES

In the 2ND Century, three Syriac versions (Peshitta, Harclean, Palestinian – all dated 2ND to 7TH Century) and the Diatessaron include the verse. One Syriac versions (Curetorian – dating from 2ND to 7TH Century) omits the verse.

In the 3RD Century, one Coptic versions (Bohairic – dating from 3RD to 6TH Century) and Tertullian include the verse. Two papyri (P66 – P. Bodmer II, P75 – P. Bodmer XIV, XV) and three Coptic versions (Sahidic, Bohairic, Sub-Achmnic – dating from 3RD to 6TH century) omit the verse.

In the 4TH Century three versions (Vercellensis Old Latin, Clementine Vulgate, Armenian – dating from the 4TH or 5TH century) and two writers (Ambrose, Didymus) include the verse. Two uncials (Aleph – Sinaiticus, B – Vaticanus) and the Wordworth-White Vulgate omit it.

	FOR		AGAINST	

2ND CENTURY

FOR	AGAINST
Peshitta Syriac version (II-VII)	
Palestinian Syriac version (II-VII)	**Curetonian Syriac version (II-VII)**
Harclean Syriac version (II-VII)	
Diatessaron	

3RD CENTURY

FOR	AGAINST
	P66 P. Bodmer II papyrus
	P75 P. Bodmer XIV,XV papyrus
Bohairic Coptic version (III-VI)	**Sahidic Coptic version (III-VI)**
Tertullian	**Bohairic Coptic version (mss) (III-VI)**
	Sub-Achminic Coptic (III-VI)

4TH CENTURY

FOR	AGAINST
Vercellensis Old Latin version	
Clementine Vulgate version	**Aleph Sinaiticus uncial**
Armenian version (IV/V)	**B Vaticanus uncial**
Ambrose	**Wordworth-White Vulgate version**
Didymus	

NUMBER

Forty-eight Greek manuscripts include the verse, while ten manuscripts omits it.

Twelve versions include the verse, and ten versions omit it.

Six early writers quote the verse, while one early writer omits it.

The majority of the BYZANTINE MANUSCRIPTS include JOHN 5:4.

GREEK MSS	VERSIONS	EARLY WRITERS	BYZ MSS	TEXT	BYZ MSS	EARLY WRITERS	VERSIONS	GREEK MSS
48	12	6	+	Jn 5:4	-	1	10	10

The Greek manuscripts favor the passage at a ratio of almost 5 to 1. Every category of evidence favors the inclusion of JOHN 5:4. The evidence shows JOHN 5:4 is a part of the New Testament.

Variety

Whether you look at the manuscripts which include the verse by number, by age, by family, or by type, they all favor the inclusion of the verse. The versions from every location include the verse. There is no doubt that the inclusion of the verse passes the Variety test.

Continuity

In the 2ND Century, three SYRIAC VERSIONS (PESHITTA, PALESTINIAN, HARCLEAN – all dating from 2ND to 7TH Century) and the certain copies of the DIATESSARON OF TATIAN (A, EARM, ι, N) include the verse. The CURETONIAN SYRIAC VERSION omits the verse.

In the 3RD Century, TERTULLIAN and CERTAIN MANUSCRIPTS OF THE BOHAIRIC COPTIC VERSION (3RD or 4TH Century) include the verse. Two papyri (P. BODMER II {P66}, P. BODMER XIV, XV {P75}) and three COPTIC VERSIONS (SAHIDIC, SUB-ACHMINIC, CERTAIN MANUSCRIPTS OF THE BOHAIR – dated 3RD to 6TH Century) omit the verse.

In the 4TH Century, the VERCELLENSIS OLD LATIN VERSION, THE CLEMENTINE VULGATE, THE ARMENIAN VERSION (4TH or 5TH Century), AMBROSE and DIDYMUS include the verse. Two uncials (SINAITICUS {ALEPH}, VATICANUS {B}) and the WORDSWORTH-WHITE VULGATE omit JOHN 5:4.

In the 5TH Century, two uncials (ALEXANDRINUS {A}, CORRECTOR OF THE EPHRAEMI RESCRIPTUS {C3}), three OLD LATIN VERSIONS (VERONENSIS, PALATINUS, CORBEIENSIS II), CHRYSOSTOM and CYRIL include the verses. Three uncials (THE ORIGINAL HAND OF EPHRAEMI RESCRIPTUS {C*}, SUPPLEMENTS TO THE FREER GOSPELS {W}, 0125), two versions (GEORGIAN, BEZAE CANTABRIGIENSIS OLD LATIN) and NONNUS omit the verse.

In the 6TH Century, one uncial (078) includes the verse. One uncial (BEZAE CANTABRIGIENSIS {D}) and the BRIXIANUS OLD LATIN VERSION omit the verse.

In the 7TH Century, the AUREUS OLD LATIN VERSION includes the verse, and two OLD LATIN VERSIONS (MONACENSIS, RHEDIGERANUS dated 7TH or 8TH Century) omit the verse.

In the 8TH Century, three uncials (REGIUS {L}, Ψ, 047) include the verse.

In the 9TH Century, five uncials (K, Δ, KORIDETHI {Θ}, Π, 063) and two minuscules (565,892) include the verse. One minuscule (33) omit the verse.

In the 10TH Century, commentary in one uncial (X) and one minuscule (1079) include the verse, while one uncial (0141) omits the verse.

In the 11TH Century, seven minuscules (124, 788, 28, 700, 1216, 230, 174) include the verse.

In the 12TH Century, fourteen uncials (1, 346, 543, 826, 828, 983, 1010, 1071, 1241, 1344, 1365, 1195, 1230, 1646) and the COLBERTINUS OLD LATIN VERSION include the verse.

In the 13TH Century, six minuscules (**118, 123, 1009, 1242, 1689, 1546**) include the verse.

In the 14TH Century, four minuscules (**131, 209, 2174, 2148**) include the verse.

In the 15TH Century, two minuscules (**69, 1253**) include the verse.

THE EVIDENCE FOR JOHN 5:4

FOR	AGAINST
2ND CENTURY	
Peshitta Syriac version (II-VII)	
Palestinian Syriac version (II-VII)	Curetonian Syriac version (II-VII)
Harclean Syriac version (II-VII)	
Diatessaron	
3RD CENTURY	
	P66 P. Bodmer II papyrus
	P75 P. Bodmer XIV,XV papyrus
Bohairic Coptic version (III-VI)	Sahidic Coptic version (III-VI)
Tertullian	Bohairic Coptic version (mss) (III-VI)
	Sub-Achminic Coptic (III-VI)
4TH CENTURY	
Vercellensis Old Latin version	
Clementine Vulgate version	
Armenian version (IV/V)	Aleph Sinaiticus uncial
Ambrose	B Vaticanus uncial
Didymus	Wordworth-White Vulgate version
5TH CENTURY	
A Alexandrinus uncial	C Ephraemi Rescriptus uncial (original hand)
C Ephraemi Rescriptus uncial (correction)	
Veronensis Old Latin version	W Freer Gospels uncial (supp)

Palatinus Old Latin version	0125 uncial
Corbeiensis II Old Latin version	Georgian version
Chrysostom	Bezae Cantabrigiensis Old Latin version
Cyril	Nomus

6TH CENTURY

078 uncial	D Bezae Cantabrigiensis uncial
	Brixianus Old Latin version

7TH CENTURY

Aureus Old Latin version	Monacensis Old Latin version
	Rhedigeranus Old Latin version (VII/VIII)

8TH CENTURY

L Regius uncial

Psi uncial

047 uncial

9TH CENTURY

K uncial

Delta uncial

Koridethi Theta uncial

Pi uncial

063 uncial

565 minuscule

892 minuscule

10TH CENTURY

X uncial (commentary)	0141 uncial
1079 minuscule	

11TH CENTURY

124 minuscule

788 minuscule

28 minuscule

700 minuscule

1216 minuscule

230 minuscule

174 minuscule

12TH CENTURY

1 minuscule

346 minuscule

543 minuscule

826 minuscule

828 minuscule

983 minuscule

1010 minuscule

1071 minuscule

1241 minuscule

1344 minuscule

1365 minuscule

1195 minuscule

1230 minuscule

1646 minuscule

13TH CENTURY

118 minuscule

13 minusucle

1009 minuscule

1242 minuscule

1689 minuscule

1546 minuscule

131 minuscule

209 minuscule

2174 minuscule

2148 minusucle

69 minusucle

1253 minusucle

The majority of the lectionaries in the Synaxarion (the s-called "moveable year" beginning with Easter) and in the Menologian (the "fixed year" beginning with September 1) include John 5:4.

The majority of the Byzantine manuscripts include John 5:4.

A single voice omits the verse in the 2ND century.

The 6TH and 7TH centuries are the only time a single voice includes the verse. The 3RD, 6TH, and 7TH centuries are the only time that omission outnumbers inclusion. The 6TH and 7TH centuries are 2 to 1.

The 8TH, 9TH, 11TH, 12TH, 13TH, 14TH, and 15TH centuries have no voice for the omission of the verse.

The continuity of the voice of witnesses includes the verse.

CONTEXT

After this there was a feast of the Jews; and Jesus went up to Jerusalem.

Now there is at Jerusalem by the sheep market a pool, which is called in the Hebrew tongue Bethesda, having five porches. In these lay a great multitude of impotent folk, of blind, halt, withered, waiting for the moving of the water. For an angel went down at a certain season into the pool, and troubled the water: whosoever then first after the troubling of the water stepped in was made whole of whatsoever disease he had.

And a certain man was there, which had an infirmity thirty and eight years. When Jesus saw him lie, and knew that he had been now a long time in that case, he saith unto him, Wilt thou be made whole?

The impotent man answered him, Sir, I have no man, when the water is troubled, to put me into the pool: but while I am coming, another steppeth down before me.

Jesus saith unto him, Rise, take up thy bed, and walk. And immediately the man was made whole, and took up his bed, and walked: and on the same day was the sabbath.

The Jews therefore said unto him that was cured, It is the sabbath day: it is not lawful for thee to carry thy bed.

He answered them, He that made me whole, the same said unto me, Take up thy bed, and walk.

Then asked they him, What man is that which said unto thee, Take up thy bed, and walk? And he that was healed wist not who it was: for Jesus had conveyed himself away, a multitude being in that place.

Afterward Jesus findeth him in the temple, and said unto him, Behold, thou art made whole: sin no more, lest a worse thing come unto thee.

The man departed, and told the Jews that it was Jesus, which had made him whole. And therefore did the Jews persecute Jesus, and sought to slay him, because he had done these things on the sabbath day. [JOHN 5:1-16 KJV]

Jesus goes up to Jerusalem to celebrate the Passover.

At Jerusalem, Jesus comes to the pool of Bethesda, where many sick, injured and lame people are to be found in shelters built to accommodate them.

Now enters the verse in controversy. An angel comes down and stirs the waters, at which time there is a healing property to those springs. Those who are able to enter the waters at that time are made whole. The Fountain of the Virgin in the area of the Temple was rumored to have such qualities in later times.

There was a man whom Jesus saw that had been lame for thirty-eight years. He asks him a question, "Do you want to be whole?"

The man answers in the affirmative; but, he cannot get to the water in time, and does not have someone else to lower him into the water.

Jesus told him, "Rise, take up your bed, and walk." The man got up, picked up his pallet, and walked. Now, all this happened on a Sabbath day.

The Jews seeing the man carrying his bed, told him that it was unlawful for him to carry his bed on the Sabbath.

The man answered, the man who healed me told me to.

They asked him who that was, but he did not know. There was a crowd there and Jesus had disappeared into it.

Later, Jesus sees him in the Temple, and says, now that you have been healed *sin no more, lest a worse thing come unto thee.*

Leaving Jesus, the man told the Jews who had healed him. That is why the Jews sought to persecute and kill Jesus, because He did this on the Sabbath.

If you take away verse four, why did the man want to get in the water? What difference did it make whether he went himself, or had someone else to help him? What were all these people doing at the Pool of Bethesda anyway?

Some object the verse as being out of character. God would not heal in this manner. The verse in its position could be an expression of what those who were their thought, without pronouncing upon the truth of the matter one way or another. Or, it could be a statement of fact that is a different way that God helped these people. It is not neccessary to explain the exact meaning of the verse when discussing whether it belongs in the New Testament, only that it fits the flow of the narrative. There is too much missing if this verse is not there. The flow of the passage is interrupted if John 5:4 is omitted.

INTERNAL EVIDENCE

(3) the presence of non-Johannine words or expressions (κατα καιρον, εμβαινω [of going into the water], εκδεχομαι, κατεχομαι, κινησισ, ταραχη, and νοσημα – the last three words only here in the New Testament), [Metzger, Ibid., p. 209]

Examine the following scriptures, and you will find the words referred to. Καιρον is used by John seven times.

Εμβαινω is used by John three times.

Εκδεχομαι is not found in verse 4, it is in verse 3; as is κινησισ.

Καταχομαι is used in Matthew 21:38, but this is the only instance in John. How many times does a word need to be used in a short piece like the Gospel of John? Do the circumstances of verse 4 occur elsewhere? Or, is this a unique situation?

Ταραχη is used only once in Mark (13:28), yet it is not rejected. Again, by what criteria must a word be used multiple times in order to be acceptable?

Νοσημα is only used this once in the New Testament; but, again why does that discredit the verse when the situation is so unique. It is not uncommon to use a word to describe a singular event that would not be appropriate under different circumstances.

καιρον

John 7:6, 8; Revelation 1:3; 11:18; 12:12, 14; 22:10

εμβαινω

John 6:17, 22, 24

εκδεχομαι

This word is in verse 3 which is not under consideration.

κατεχομαι

This word is also used only once in Matthew (21:38).

κινησις

This word is in verse 3 which is not under consideration.

ταραχη

This word is used in Mark 13:8 as well.

νοσημα

This is the only use of this word in the New Testament.

The uniqueness of the passage calls for a different vocabulary. This explains the literary difference, it is a different story.

CONCLUSION

Metzger says,

Ver. 4 is a gloss, whose secondary character is clear from (1) Its absence from the earliest and best witnesses (p⁶⁶,⁷⁵ {Aleph} B C* I) Wˢᵘᵖᵖ 33 itᵈ, ˡ, ᑫ the true text of the Latin Vulgate syrᶜ copˢᵃ, ᵇᵒᵐˢˢˢᶜʰ² geo Nonnus), (2) the presence of asterisks or obeli to mark the words as spurious in more than twenty Greek witnesses (including S Δ Π 047 1079 2174), (3) the presence of non-Johannine words or expressions (κατα εχομαι, εμβαινω [of going into the water], εκδεχομαι, κατεχομαι, κινησισ, ταραχη, and νοσημα – the last three words only here in the New Testament), and (4) the rather wide diversity of variant forms in which the verse was transmitted (see footnotes 6 to 10 on p. 338 of the text-volume for variant readings within ver. 4). Since the passage is lacking in the earlier and better witnesses, which normally assist in identifying types of text, it is sometimes difficult to make decisions among alternative readings. On the whole, however, the Committee gave preference to the readings that are supported by what was regarded as the preponderant weight of attestation, or that seemed best to account for the origin of the other reading(s). [IBID.; P. 209]

(1) Indeed, there are several early witnesses against this verse, but there are also some in favor of the verse. By the 8ᵀᴴ Century, the witnesses omitting the verse all but disappear. Although the continuity of the witnesses which include the verse continues, its opposition disappears. The variety of the witnesses and their universality stand in favor of the verse being included in the New Testament.
(2) Although the asterisks and obeli are present, the verse was still included. It may mark some doubt, but not serious enough to exclude the verse from these manuscripts. Therefore, their presence cannot be used for exclusion.
(3) This objection we dealt with above.
(4) The fact that there may be variants available within the verse, does not determine whether it is part of the scripture or not. The variants can be dealt with, but first one needs to honestly deal with the evidence which favors the inclusion of the verse.

There may be some reasons some people do not like the verse. It may seem a little different than some may think ought to be there. However, can the mind of man match the mind of God? It appears that is what some critics want to do, second guess God.

Does John 7:53-8:11 Belong in the New Testament?

John 7:53-8:11 is omitted by THE WESTCOTT/HORT, UNITED BIBLE SOCIETIES, AND NESTLE GREEK TEXTS, BY THE AMERICAN STANDARD VERSION, THE NEW AMERICAN STANDARD, THE NEW INTERNATIONAL VERSION, AND THE REVISED STANDARD VERSION. It is single-bracketed [of doubtful origin] in TODAY'S ENGLISH VERSION. It is double-bracketed [extremely dubious inclusion] in the Common English Bible and the English Standard Version. It is included in THE TEXTUS RECEPTUS, AND THE MAJORITY GREEK TEXTS, AND IN THE KING JAMES VERSION, THE LIVING BIBLE AND THE NEW KING JAMES VERSION.

Passage	TR	W/H	NT	UBS	MT	KJV	ASV	RSV	TEV	LB	NAS	NIV	NKJ	CEB	ESV
John 7:53-8:11	-	O	O	O	-	-	O	O	S	-	O	O	-	DB	SB/DB

The evidence utilized will be that found in the critical apparatus of the UBSIII.

ANTIQUITY OF THE WITNESSES

In the 2ND Century, ttwo Syriac versions (Harclean, Palestinian – all dated 2ND to 7TH Century) include the verse.e. Three Syriac versions (Curetorian, Sinaitic, and Peshitta – dating from 2ND to 7TH Century) omits the verse.

In the 3RD Century, one Coptic versions (Bohairic – dating from 3RD to 6TH Century) and Didascalia include the verse. Two papyri (P66 – P. Bodmer II, P75 – P. Bodmer XIV, XV) and two Coptic versions (Bohairic, Sub-Achmnic – dating from 3RD to 6TH century) omit the verse.

In the 4TH Century three versions (Armenian – dating from the 4TH or 5TH century) and three writers (Ambrosiaster, Apostolic Constitutions, and Ambrose) include the verse. Two uncials (Aleph – Sinaiticus, B – Vaticanus) and three versions (Gothic, Vercellensis Old Latin, and Armenian --- IV/V) omit it.

	FOR			AGAINST	

2ND CENTURY

FOR	AGAINST
Harclean Syriac version (II-VII)	Curetonian Syriac version (II-VII)
Palestinian Syriac version (II-VII)	Sinaitic Syriac version (II-VII)
	Peshitta Syriac version (II-VII)

3RD CENTURY

FOR	AGAINST
	P66 P. Bodmer II papyrus
Bohairic Coptic (III-VI)	P75 P. Bodmer XIV, XV (III-VI)
Didascalia	Bohairic Coptic version (III-VI)
	Sub-Achmimic Copitc version (III-VI)

4TH CENTURY

FOR	AGAINST
Armenian version (mss) (IV/V)	Aleph Sinaiticus uncial
Ambrosiaster	B Vaticanus uncial
Apostolic Constitutions	Gothic version
Ambrose	Vercellensis Old Latin version
	Armenian version (IV/V)

NUMBER

Fifty-three Greek manuscripts include the verse, while twenty-seven manuscripts omits it.

Fourteen versions include the verse, and tthirteen versions omit it.

Sevem early writers quote the verse, while ten early writers omits it.

The majority of the BYZANTINE MANUSCRIPTS include JOHN 7:54-8:11.

GREEK MSS	VERSIONS	EARLY WRITERS	BYZ MSS	TEXT	BYZ MSS	EARLY WRITERS	VERSIONS	GREEK MSS
53	14	7	+	7:53-8:11	-	10	13	27

The Greek manuscripts favor the passage at a ratio of almost 2 to 1. Every category of evidence favors the inclusion of JOHN 5:4. The evidence shows JOHN 5:4 is a part of the New Testament.

Variety

Whether you look at the manuscripts which include the verse by number, by age, by family, or by type, they all favor the inclusion of the verse. The versions from every location include the verse. There is no doubt that the inclusion of the verse passes the Variety test.

Continuity

In the 2ND Century, the PALESTINIAN SYRIAC VERSION and SOME MANUSCRIPTS OF THE HARCLEAN SYRIAC VERSION (both dating 2ND to 7TH Century) include the passage. THE DIATESSARON OF TATIAN and three SYRIAC VERSIONS (CURETONIAN, SINAITIC, PESHITTA – all dating from 2ND to 7TH Century) omit the passage.

In the 3RD Century, CERTAIN MANUSCRIPTS OF THE COPTIC BOHAIRIC VERSION and DIDASCALIA include the passage. Two papyri (P. BODMER II {P66}, P. BODMER XIV,XV {P75}), three COPTIC VERSIONS (SAHIDIC, CERTAIN MANUSCRIPTS OF THE BOHAIRIC, SUB ACHMIMIC – dating 3RD to 6TH Century), possibly CLEMENT, TERTULLIAN, ORIGEN and CYPRIAN omit the passage.

In the 4TH Century, certain manuscripts of the ARMENIAN VERSION (dated 4TH or 5TH Century) include it at its present location and some have it at the conclusion of John, while AMBROSIASTER, THE APOSTOLIC CONSTITUTIONS and AMBROSE include JOHN 7:53-8:11. Two uncials (SINAITICUS {ALEPH}, VATICANUS {B}), the GOTHIC VERSION, the Vercellensis Old Latin version, and the ARMENIAN VERSION omit the passage.

In the 5TH Century, three OLD LATIN VERSIONS (BEZAE CANTABRIGIENSIS, PALATINUS, CORBEIENSIS II), JEROME, BOTH GREEK AND LATIN MANUSCRIPTS ACCORDING TO JEROME, and AUGUSTINE include the passage. Two uncials (T, FREER GOSPELS {W}) and possibly two others (ALEXANDRINUS {A}, EPHRAEMI RESCRIPTUS {C} – there is doubt as to the reading they contain), the GEORGIAN VERSION, CHRYSOSTOM, NONNUS and CYRIL omit the passage.

In the 6TH Century, one uncial (BEZAE CANTABRIGIENSIS {D}), the SARZANENSIS OLD LATIN VERSION, and the ETHIOPIC VERSION include the passage. One uncial (N), the BRIXIANUS OLD LATIN VERSION, and COSMOS omit the passage.

In the 7TH Century, three OLD LATIN VERSIONS (AUREUS, USSERIANUS I, THE MARGIN OF RHEDIGERANUS dating either 7TH or 8TH Century) include the passage. Two OLD LATIN VERSIONS (MONACENSIS, THE TEXT OF RHEDIGERANUS dating either 7TH or 8TH Century) omit the passage.

In the 8TH Century, one uncial (E) includes 8:2-11. Two uncials (REGIUS{L}, □) omit the passage.

In the 9TH Century, eight uncials (Φ, Γ, H, K, M, Y, Λ {8:3-11}, Π {8:3-11}) and one minuscule (892) include the passage. Three uncials (Y, □, 053) and two minuscules (33, 565) omit the passage.

In the 10TH Century, two uncials (□, S) and two minuscules (1079, 1077) include the passage. Two uncials (X, 0141) and one minuscule (2193) omit the passage.

In the 11TH Century, four minuscules (**1216, 28, 700, 1433**) put it in the traditional place, three minuscules place it after Luke (**124, 788, 230**) and two lectionaries in the margin (**L185** {8:1-11}, **L833** {8:3-11}) include the passage. THEOPLYLACT omits the passage.

In the 12TH Century, seven minuscules (**1010, 1071, 1344, 1365, 1195, 1646, 225**) put it in the tradition place, one minuscules places it after John (**1**), and five minuscules place it after Luke (**346, 543, 826, 828, 983**), and it is included in the COLBERTINUS OLD LATIN VERSION (dated either 12TH or 13TH Century). Four minuscules (**22, 157, 1241, 1230**) omit the passage.

In the 13TH Century, two minuscules place the passage in its traditional place (**1109, 1546**), one minuscule places it after John (**118**), and two minuscules place it after Luke (**13, 1689**). One minuscule (**1242**) omits the passage.

In the 14TH Century, three minuscules place the passage in its traditional place (**2174, 2148, 1445**), two minuscules place it after John (**131, 209**) and it is in the margin of one lectionary (**L1579** {8:3-11}). It is omitted by one minuscule (**209**).

In the 15TH Century, one minuscule places it after Luke (**69**), and one minuscule (**1253**) omits it.

The majority of the lectionaries in the SYNAXARION (the so-called "moveable year" beginning at Easter) and in the MENOLOGIAN (the "fixed year" beginning at September 1) omit JOHN **7:53-8:11**.

The majority of the BYZANTINE MANUSCRIPTS include JOHN **7:53-8:11**.

THE EVIDENCE FOR JOHN 7:53-8:11

FOR	AGAINST
2ND CENTURY	
Harclean Syriac version (II-VII) Palestinian Syriac version (II-VII)	Curetonian Syriac version (II-VII) Sinaitic Syriac version (II-VII) Peshitta Syriac version (II-VII)
3RD CENTURY	
Bohairic Coptic (III-VI) Didascalia	P66 P. Bodmer II papyrus P75 P. Bodmer XIV, XV (III-VI) Bohairic Coptic version (III-VI) Sub-Achmimic Copitc version (III-VI)
4TH CENTURY	

Armenian version (mss) (IV/V)	Aleph Sinaiticus uncial
Ambrosiaster	B Vaticanus uncial
Apostolic Constitutions	Gothic version
Ambrose	Vercellensis Old Latin version
	Armenian version (IV/V)

5TH CENTURY

	A Alexandrinus uncial ?
Bezae Cantabrigiensis Old Latin version	C Ephraemi Rescriptus uncial ?
Palatinus Old Latin version	T uncial
Corbeiensis II Old Latin version	W Freer Gospels uncial
Jerome	Georgian version
Greek & Latin mss acc. To Jerome	Chrysostom
Augustine	Nonnus
	Cyril

6TH CENTURY

D Bezae Cantabrigiensis uncial	N uncial
Sarzanensis Old Latin version	Brixianus Old Latin version
Ethiopic version	Cosmos

7TH CENTURY

Aureus Old Latin version	
Usserianus I Old Latin version	Monacensis Old Latin version
Rhedigeranus Old Latin version (VII/VIII)	Rhedigeranus Old Latin version (VII/VIII)

8TH CENTURY

	L Regius uncial
E (8.2-11) uncial	Psi uncial

9TH CENTURY

F uncial	Y uncial

G uncial	Delta uncial
H uncial	053 uncial
K uncial	33 minuscule
M uncial	565 minuscule
U uncial	
Lamda (8.3-11) uncial	
Pi (8.3-11) uncial	
892 minuscule	

10TH CENTURY

Gamma uncial	
S uncial	X uncial
1079 minuscle	0141 uncial
1077 minuscule	2193 minuscule

11TH CENTURY

1216 minuscule	
28 minuscule	
700 minuscle	
1433 minuscule	
124 minuscule	Theophylact (commentary)
788 minuscule	
230 minusucle	
L185 (8.1-11) lectionary	
L833 (8.3-11) lectionary	

12TH CENTURY

1010 minuscule	22 minuscule
1071 minuscule	157 minuscule
1344 minuscule	1241 minuscule

1365 minuscule	1230 minuscule
1195 minuscule	
1646 minuscule	
1 minuscule	
346 minuscule	
543 minusucle	
826 minusucle	
828 minuscule	
983 minuscule	
225 minuscule	
L69 (8.3-11) lectionary	
L70 (8.3-11) lectionary	
L211 (8.3-11) lectionary	
Colbertinus Old Latin version	

13TH CENTURY

1009 minuscule	
1246 minuscule	
118 minuscule	
13 minuscule	1242 minuscule
1689 minuscule	

14TH CENTURY

2174 minuscule	
2148 minuscule	
1445 minuscule	209 minuscule
131 minuscule	
209 minuscule	

15TH CENTURY

69 minuscule   1253 minuscule

The passage is found in twelve (12) uncial manuscripts [dating from the 6th through the 9th centuries] and thirty-five (35) minuscules [dating from the 9th through the 15th centuries], plus the majority of the Byzantine manuscripts, which are not included in the above count. This brings the count of manuscripts to more than nine hundred (900) which include the passage. The majority of the passage (8:1-11 in one, and 8:3-11 in the others) is found in six (6) lectionaries, though it is missing in the majority of lectionaries. However, this is not surprising since lectionaries only include select readings.

The passage is found in fourteen (14) ancient versions [Syriac, Coptic, Old Latin, Armenian and Ethiopic -- dating from the 2nd century to the 13th century]. Seven (7) early writers quote the passage [from the 3rd century to 430 a.d.].

It is interesting to note that from the 9th century on, the passage is firmly accepted on the evidence available. It waits until the 19th century to say the passage is fraudulent.

The manuscript evidence, excluding the Byzantine texts (which comprise the vast majority -- up to 95% -- of manuscripts extant), is numerically seventy-five (75) to fifty (50) in favor of the inclusion of the passage. Once the testimony of the Byzantine texts is added, the result is more than nine hundred (900) manuscripts, plus versions, lectionaries, and early writers in favor of the passage.

CONTEXT

And every man went unto his own house.

Jesus went unto the mount of Olives.

And early in the morning he came again into the temple, and all the people came unto him; and he sat down, and taught them.

And the scribes and Pharisees brought unto him a woman taken in adultery; and when they had set her in the midst, They say unto him, Master, this woman was taken in adultery, in the very act. Now Moses in the law commanded us, that such should be stoned: but what sayest thou? This they said, tempting him, that they might have to accuse him.

But Jesus stooped down, and with his finger wrote on the ground, as though he heard them not. So when they continued asking him, he lifted up himself, and said unto them, He that is without sin among you, let him first cast a stone at her. And again he stooped down, and wrote on the ground.

And they which heard it, being convicted by their own conscience, went out one by one, beginning at the eldest, even unto the last: and Jesus was left alone, and the woman standing in

the midst. When Jesus had lifted up himself, and saw none but the woman, he said unto her, Woman, where are those thine accusers? hath no man condemned thee?

She said, No man, Lord. And Jesus said unto her, Neither do I condemn thee: go, and sin no more. [JOHN 7:53 - 8:11 KJV]

Those who reject this passage as being authentic rely heavily upon the alleged incongruity of this story with the context. They feel the story of the woman taken in adultery interrupts the "flow of Jesus" sojourn in Jerusalem. However, a careful reading of the passage where it is found shows it to be perfectly compatible to the context which surrounds it, and even helpful in completing the picture.

In verse 32 of the 7th chapter, we read: "The Pharisees heard that the people murmured such things concerning Him [i.e., indicating He was the Christ] and the Pharisees and chief priests sent officers to take Him."

Beginning with verse 45, these officers report back to the Pharisees. This meeting between the chief priests and the Pharisees and the officers is still in progress in verse 52.

Without the passage in question (7:53-8:11), the next verse (8:12) would begin: *"Then spake Jesus again unto them,..."*

There is no end to the conspiracy meeting of the chief priests, Pharisees and officers. There is no context for the place of Jesus' words beginning at 8:12. There is no contrast between the light which Jesus is, and the darkness which the scribes and the Pharisees have shown themselves to be by their sinful conduct.

"Nor is the narrative improperly suited to the place where it is found in the overwhelming majority of the nine hundred copies which contain it. On the contrary, a setting at the Feast of Tabernacles (cf. 7:2,14) is ideal for the story. It was on just such an occasion, when Jerusalem was crowded with pilgrims, that strangers might be thrown together with the resulting sin around which the story centers. An interview with a woman in a court of the temple would likely have been in the Court of the Women. And this evidently where Jesus was, as the reference to the 'treasury' in 8:20 indicates. Moreover, the way in which the woman's accusers are driven to cover by the moral exposure which Jesus brings upon them furnishes a suggestive introduction to the initial Johannine reference to the Lord as the Light of the World (8:12). The setting of the incident at daybreak is likewise suitable (cf. 8:2) since the rising sun furnishes the natural backdrop for the same title. It is in fact to the sun (not the temple candelabra, as Hort thought) that the title Light of the World refers (cf. 9:4,5; 11:9). Finally, as the Qumran find have shown (cf. 1QS iii 6-7), the thought of forgiveness of sin experienced here by the woman is properly linked to the phrase 'light of life' (8:12)."[THE GREEK NEW TESTAMENT ACCORDING TO THE MAJORITY TEXT; edited by Zane C. Hodges and Arthur L. Farstad; Thomas Nelson Publishers; 1982; p. xxiv].

The context suffers not by the addition of the passage (7:53-8:11), but by its omission.

There is no justification for the rejection of the passage upon the grounds of interrupting the flow of thought. In fact, contextual considerations favor its inclusion.

By the way, upon what basis is the assumption made that contextual considerations made by men would be superior to the contextual selection of the Holy Spirit? The idea that men, upon the basis of literary context, can determine where a passage belongs in the Bible is rather presumptuous. That would mean we can determine what and how the Holy Spirit would say something. That is not in the natural man (1 Corinthians 2:14).

INTERNAL EVIDENCE

In the case of John 7:53-8:11, this means: Is the passage written in the same style as John wrote the rest of his Gospel? Those who reject the passage claim that the style (i.e., the choice of words and the use of grammar) of these verses is contrary to that found in the remainder of the book. Thus, they claim the passage not to be a part of the Gospel of John.

"There is no compelling reason to doubt that the story is originally Johannine, despite the prevailing contrary opinion. Among the marks of Johannine style which it exhibits, none is clearer than the phrase in 8:6: τουτο δε ελεγον πειραζοντεσ αυτον. This is a pure and simple Johannism, which is evident by comparison with 6:6; 7:39; 11:51; 12:6,33; and 21:19. Likewise the use of the vocative γυναι (8:10) by Jesus to address a woman is a Johannine characteristic (cf. 2:4; 4:21; 19:26; CF. ALSO 20:13,15). The phrase υακετι αμαρτανε (8:11) occurs nowhere else in the New Testament, except John 5:14, and the historic present of αγουσι (8:3) is consonant with John's frequent use of this idiom." [IBID.; PP. XXIII-XXIV].

"In view of the features of Johannine style that have been noted and the narrative's almost unique suitability to this context, the idea that the passage is not authentically Johannine must finally be dismissed. If it is not an original part of the Fourth Gospel, its writer would have to be viewed as a skilled Johannine imitator, and its placement in this context as the shrewdest piece of interpolation in literary history!" [IBID.; P. XXIV].

CONCLUSION

Metzger says,

The evidence for the non-Johannine origin of the pericope of the adulteress is overwhelming. ...

When one adds to this impressive and diversified list of external evidence the consideration that the style and vocabulary of the pericope differ noticeably from the rest of the Fourth Gospel (see any critical commentary), and that it interrupts the sequence of 7.52 and 8.12ff., the case against its being Johannine authorship appears to be conclusive.

At the same time the account has all the earmarks of historical veracity. It is obviously a piece of oral tradition which circulated in certain parts of the Western church and which was subsequently incorporated into various manuscripts at various places. ...

Sometimes it is stated that the pericope was deliberately expunged from the Fourth Gospel because it was liable to be understood in a sense too indulgent to adultery. But, apart from the absence of any instance elsewhere of scribal excision of an extensive passage because of moral prudence, this theory fails "to explain why the three preliminary verses (vii 63; viii 1-2), so important as apparently descriptive of the time and place at which all the discourses of c. viii were spoken, should have been omitted with the rest" (Hort, *"Notes on Select Readings,"* p. 86f.).

Although the Committee was unanimous that the pericope was originally no part of the Fourth Gospel, in deference to the evident antiquity of the passage a majority decided to print it, enclosed within double brackets, at its traditional place following Jn 7.52. [IBID., PP. **219-221**]

This is another occasion in which the UBS, along with other texts, failed to have the courage to follow through with their convictions. Their failure, however, was the correct move. Consider all the tests to which the text should be placed – and the answer is clear: the passage belongs in the New Testament. It is a part of the Gospel of John.

Does Acts 8:37 Belong in the New Testament?

ACTS 8:37 is in the KING JAMES VERSION and the NEW KING JAMES VERSION., being found in THE TEXTUS RECEPTUS. The verse is omitted in the Greek texts of WESTCOTT/HORT, NESTLE'S, UNITED BIBLE SOCIEITIES and the MAJORITY TEXT; and it is omitted by the AMERICAN STANDARD VERSION, NEW AMERICAN STANDARD, NEW INTERNATIONAL VERSION, REVISED STANDARD VERSION, and NEW ENGLISH BIBLE, as well as others.

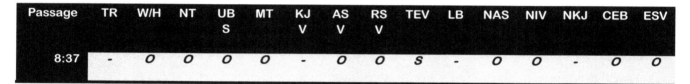

Passage	TR	W/H	NT	UBS	MT	KJV	ASV	RSV	TEV	LB	NAS	NIV	NKJ	CEB	ESV
8:37	-	O	O	O	O	-	O	O	S	-	O	O	-	O	O

The evidence utilized will be that found in the critical apparatus of the UBSIII.

ANTIQUITY OF THE WITNESSES

In the 2nd century (and possibly as late the the 7th century), THE SYRIAC HARCLEAN includes and omits in copies, and THE SYRIAC PESHITTA omits the passage.

In the 3rd century, IRENAEUS, TERTULLIAN AND CYPRIAN all include the passage (and by inference the manuscripts which they used), while THE CHESTER BEATTY P45 PAPYRUS AND THE COPTIC VERSIONS (BOTH SAHIDIC AND BOHAIRIC) which may date as late as the 6th century omit it.

In the 4th century the tide turns, with THE CLEMENTINE VULGATE VERSION, PS-AUGUSTINE OLD LATIN VERSION, ARMENIAN VERSION, AMBROSIASTER, PACIAN AND AMBROSE including the passage, WHILE ALEPH THE SINAITICUS UNCIAL, B THE VATICANUS UNCIAL, AND THE WORDSWORTH-WHITE VULGATE VERSION omit the passage.

	FOR				AGAINST	

2ND CENTURY

	FOR	AGAINST
	Harclean Syriac version	Harclean Syriac version
		Peshitta Syriac version

3RD CENTURY

	FOR	AGAINST
	Irenaeus	P45 Chester Beatty papyrus
	Tertullian	Sahidic Coptic version
	Cyrian	Bohairic Coptic version

4TH CENTURY

	FOR	AGAINST
	Clementine Vulgate version	
	Ps-Augustine Old Latin version	
	Armenian version	Aleph Sinaiticus uncial
	Ambrosiaster	B Vatincanus uncial
	Pacian	Wordsworth-White Vulgate version
	Ambrose	

NUMBER

Nine Greek manuscripts include the verse, while twenty-six manuscripts omit it.

Twelve versions include the verse, and six versions omit it.

Nine early writers quote the verse, while two early writers omit it.

The majority of the BYZANTINE MANUSCRIPTS omit ACTS 8:37.

GREEK MSS	VERSIONS	EARLY WRITERS	BYZ MSS	TEXT	BYZ MSS	EARLY WRITERS	VERSIONS	GREEK MSS
9	12	9	-	Ac. 8:37	+	2	6	26

The Greek manuscripts omit the passage at a ratio of almost 3 to 1. The versions include ACTS 8:37 at a ratio of approximately 2 to 1. The early writers include the passage at a ratio of over 4 to 1. The majority of the Byzantine manuscripts omit the passage. When you purely count numbers, the passage does not pass this test. However, when you break it down to categories, the evidence is fairly even.

Variety

Whether you look at the manuscripts which include the verse by number, by age, by family, or by type, they all have evidence in favor of the inclusion of the verse. The versions from every location include the verse. There is no doubt that the inclusion of the verse passes the Variety test.

Continuity

In the 2nd century (and possibly as late the the 7th century), THE SYRIAC HARCLEAN includes and omits in copies, and THE SYRIAC PESHITTA omits the passage.

In the 3rd century, IRENAEUS, TERTULLIAN AND CYPRIAN all include the passage (and by inference the manuscripts which they used), while THE CHESTER BEATTY P45 PAPYRUS AND THE COPTIC VERSIONS (BOTH SAHIDIC AND BOHAIRIC) which may date as late as the 6th century omit it.

In the 4th century the tide turns, with THE CLEMENTINE VULGATE VERSION, PS-AUGUSTINE OLD LATIN VERSION, ARMENIAN VERSION, AMBROSIASTER, PACIAN AND AMBROSE including the passage, WHILE ALEPH THE SINAITICUS UNCIAL, B THE VATICANUS UNCIAL, AND THE WORDSWORTH-WHITE VULGATE VERSION omit the passage.

In the 5th century, THE GEORGIAN VERSION AND AUGUSTINE include the passage, while A THE ALEXANDRINUS, C THE EPHRAEMI RESCRIPTUS along with CHRYSOSTOM omit it.

In the 6th century, E LAUDIANUS AND LAUDINUS OLD LATIN VERSION includes the verse, and THE ETHIOPIC VERSION omits it.

In the 7th century, THE SCHLETTSTANDTENSIS OLD LATIN VERSION AND LOGIONENSIS OLD LATIN VERSION include the passage, while P74 P BODMER XVII PAPYRUS omits it.

In the 8th century, GREEK MANUSCRIPTS ACCORDING TO BEDE include the passage, and PSI UNCIAL omits it.

In the 9th century, ARMACHANUS OLD LATIN VERSION includes the passage while 049 UNCIAL AND 33? UNCIAL include it. There is some question as to whether the passage is omitted by 33 UNCIAL.

In the 10th century, 1739 MINUSCULE includes the passage, and 056 UNCIAL AND 0142 UNCIAL omit it.

In the 11th century, MINUSCULES 945 AND 104? and some copies of THEOPHLACT include the passage, while the passage is omitted by MINUSCULES 181, 436, 451, 81, 1505, AND 104? and some copies of THEOPHYLACT.

In the 12th century, THE MINUSCULE 88 questionably includes the passage, as does THE LECTIONARY L59, PHILADELPHIENSIS OLD LATIN VERSION AND COLBERTINUS OLD LATIN VERSION, while possibly THE MINUSCULE 88, along with 326, 330, 1241, AND 2127.

In the 13th century, THE OLD LATIN VERSION GIGAS includes the verse, while THE MINUSCULES 614 AND 2492 exclude it.

In the 14th century, THE MINUSCULE 1877 AND 629 have the verse, while THE MINUSCULE 2495 excluded it.

THE EVIDENCE BY CENTURY

FOR	AGAINST
2ND CENTURY	
Harclean Syriac version	Harclean Syriac version
	Peshitta Syriac version
3RD CENTURY	
Irenaeus	P45 Chester Beatty papyrus
Tertullian	Sahidic Coptic version
Cyrian	Bohairic Coptic version
4TH CENTURY	
Clementine Vulgate version	
Ps-Augustine Old Latin version	
Armenian version	Aleph Sinaiticus uncial
Ambrosiaster	B Vatincanus uncial
Pacian	Wordsworth-White Vulgate version
Ambrose	
5TH CENTURY	
	A Alexandrinus uncial
Georgian version	C Ephraemi Rescriptus uncial
Augustine	Chrysostom
6TH CENTURY	
E Laudianus uncial	
	Ethiopic version
Laudinua Old Latin version	

7TH CENTURY

Schlettstadtensis Old Latin version

Legionensis Old Latin version

P74 P. Bodmer XVII papyrus

8TH CENTURY

Greek Manuscripts according to Bede

PSI

9TH CENTURY

P uncial

Armachanus Old Latin version

049 uncial

33? minuscule

10TH CENTURY

056 uncial

1739 minuscule

0142 uncial

11TH CENTURY

181 minuscule

436 minuscule

945 minuscule

451 minuscule

104? Minuscule

81 minuscule

Theophylact?

1505 minuscule

104? Minuscule

Theophlact?

12TH CENTURY

88? minuscule

88? minuscule

326 minuscule

L59 lectionary

330 minuscule

Philadelphrensis Old Latin version

1241 minuscule

Colbertinus Old Latin version

2127 minuscule

13TH CENTURY

Gigas Old Latin version

614 minuscule

2492 minuscule

14TH CENTURY

1877 minuscule

629 minuscule

2495 minuscule

The earliest manuscript that contains the passage in question is E (LAUDIANUS) from the 6th century. A (SINAITICUS), B (VATICANUS) FROM THE 4TH CENTIURY, A (ALEXANDRINUS) AND C (EPHRAEMI RESCRIPTUS) from the 5th century, as well as PSI from the 8th or 9th century, P AND 049 from the 9th century, 056 AND 0142 from the 10th century omit the verse. In addition P45 (CHESTER BEATTY) from the 3rd century and P74 (P. BODMER XVII) from the 7th century.

When this evidence is first glanced at, it is wondered why the passage was ever included in the New Testament. After all, it isn't until the 10th century that the passage is regularly found in Greek manuscripts, although it must be admitted that the number of manuscripts from earlier times is scant.

However, when you see that the majority of early versions or translations into other languages include the passage, starting with certain copies OF THE HARCLEAN SYRIAC, THE CLEMENTINE VULGATE, PS-AUGUTINE, ARMENIAN, GEORGIAN, LAUDINUS, SCHLETTSTADTENSIS, LEGIONENSIS, ARDMACHANUS, PHILADELPHIENSIS, COLBERTINUS, AND GIGAS, an eyebrow is raised. Opposing it are THE PESHITTA SYRIAC, certain copies of THE HARCLEAN SYRIAC, THE SAHIDIC COPTIC, THE BOHAIRIC COPTIC, THE WORDSWORTH-WHITE VULGATE AND THE ETHIOPIC. Why did these translations include it if there was no manuscript evidence?

In addition, the early writers unanimously include the passage: IRENAEUS, TERTULLIAN, CYPRIAN, AMBROSIASTER, PACIAN, AMBROSE, AUGUSTINE, BEDE (says it is in the Greek manuscripts), AND THEOPHLACT. Why did they include the passage if there was no manuscript evidence?

The majority of the Lectionaries from both schools (THE SYNAXARION, the so-called "movable year" beginning with easter; and THE MENOLOGIAN, "the fixed year" beginning September 1) do not include the passage. Only one lectionary is listed by THE UBS 3RD EDITION, L59. But, this is not surprising since these are a collection of partial passages.

When you look at the evidence over all, it is comparatively even.

"And the angel of the Lord spake unto Philip, saying, Arise, and go toward the south unto the way that goeth down from Jerusalem unto Gaza, which is desert. And he arose and went: and, behold, a man of Ethiopia, an eunuch of great authority under Candace queen of the Ethiopians, who had the charge of all her treasure, and had come to Jerusalem for to worship, Was returning, and sitting in his chariot read Esaias the prophet. Then the Spirit said unto Philip, Go near, and join thyself to this chariot. And Philip ran thither to him, and heard him read the prophet Esaias, and said, Understandest thou what thou readest? And he said, How can I, except some man should guide me? And he desired Philip that he would come up and sit with him. The place of the scripture which he read was this, He was led as a sheep to the slaughter; and like a lamb dumb before his shearer, so opened he not his mouth: In his humiliation his judgment was taken away: and who shall declare his generation? for his life is taken from the earth. And the eunuch answered Philip, and said, I pray thee, of whom speaketh the prophet this? of himself, or of some other man? Then Philip opened his mouth, and began at the same scripture, and preached unto him Jesus. And as they went on their way, they came unto a certain water: and the eunuch said, See, here is water; what doth hinder me to be baptized? And Philip said, If thou believest with all thine heart, thou mayest. And he answered and said, I believe that Jesus Christ is the Son of God. And he commanded the chariot to stand still: and they went down both into the water, both Philip and the eunuch; and he baptized him. And when they were come up out of the water, the Spirit of the Lord caught away Philip, that the eunuch saw him no more: and he went on his way rejoicing. But Philip was found at Azotus: and passing through he preached in all the cities, till he came to Caesarea." (ACTS 8:26-40 KJV)

The passage discusses the occasion of Phillip the evangelist teaching the Ethiopian Eunuch/Treasurer at the urging of the Holy Spirit. The Ethiopian had been to Jerusalem to worship. He was reading from the prophet Isaiah as he rode along on the return trip. The passage was a prophecy of the coming Messiah (Christ).

"He was oppressed, and he was afflicted, yet he opened not his mouth: he is brought as a lamb to the slaughter, and as a sheep before her shearers is dumb, so he openeth not his mouth. He was taken from prison and from judgment: and who shall declare his generation? for he was cut off out of the land of the living: for the transgression of my people was he stricken." (ISAIAH 53:7-8 KJV)

It would have been difficult to find a better verse to start preaching Jesus to the Ethiopian.

Phillip's question is one that every reader of scripture needs to ask, "Do you understand what you read?" Reading would not impart a blessing without understanding.

The Ethiopian's answer needs to be understood by any who would look at prophecy, "How can I understand it, unless someone guides me?" The guide to understanding the Old Testament prophecies is the New Testament, written under inspiration of the Holy Spirit [ROMANS 10:10-17]. Phillip here answers by inspiration of the Holy Spirit. Beginning with this scripture, he describes the fulfillment of this prophecy in Jesus of Nazareth, the Christ, the Messiah, the Son of the living God.

Phillip had come to the chariot of the Ethiopian and entered as it continued to travel. When they came to a certain body of water, in response to Phillip's teaching, the Ethiopian asked, "What keeps me from being baptized [immersed]?"

Jesus had taught *"Go ye into all the world, and preach the gospel to every creature. He that believeth and is baptized shall be saved; but he that believeth not shall be damned."* (MARK 16:15-16 KJV) Belief is necessary to be baptized, rather than dunked. The only means, that is available for determining whether someone believes or not, is their own statement. Thus, *"That if thou shalt confess with thy mouth the Lord Jesus, and shalt believe in thine heart that God hath raised him from the dead, thou shalt be saved. For with the heart man believeth unto righteousness; and with the mouth confession is made unto salvation."* (ROMANS 10:9-10 KJV)

The first part of verse 37 has Phillip answering the Ethiopian's question. Without verse 37, the question is asked, but no answer given. In the latter part of the verse, the Ethiopian responses to Phillip's answer.

Following the confession of faith, Phillip baptized the Ethiopian. He could not have scripturally baptized the Ethiopian, if he did not believe; and, he could not know whether he believed, unless he told him. Verse 37 fits into the flow of the context.

INTERNAL EVIDENCE

Bruce Metzger, in his textual commentary [A TEXTUAL COMMENTARY ON THE GREEK NEW TESTAMENT: A COMPANION VOLUME TO THE UNITED BIBLE SOCIETIES' GREEK NEW TESTAMENT (THIRD EDITION); United Bible Societies, London, New York; copyright 1971], states: *"Ver. 37 is a Western addtion, not found in P45, P74, ALEPH, A, B, C, 33, 81, 614, VG, SYR P, SYR H, COP SA, COP BO, ETH, but read, with many minor variations, by E, many minuscules, IT GIG, IT H, VG MSS, SYR H, SYR WITH, COP G67, ARM. There is no reason why scribes would have omitted the material, if it had originally stood in the text. It should be noted too that* τον Ιησουν Χριστον *is not a Lukan expression.*

"The formula πιστευω ... Ξριστον *was doubtless used by the early church in baptismal ceremonies, and may have been written in the margin of a copy of* ACTS. *Its insertion into the text seems to have been due to the feeling that Philip could not have baptized the Ethiopian without securing a confession of faith, which need to be expressed in the narrative. Although the earliest known New Testament manuscript which contains the words dates from the sixth century (ms. E), the tradition of the Ethiopian's confession of faith in Christ was current as early as the latter part of the second century, for Irenaeus quotes part of it (AGAINST HERESIES, III.XII.8).*

"Although the passage does not appear in the late medieval manuscript on which Erasmus chiefly depended for his edition (ms. 2), it stands in the margin of another (ms. 4), from which he inserted it into his text because 'he judged that it had been omitted by the carelessness of scribes (arbiter omissum librariorum incuria).'" (pp. 359-360).

The only objection to the literary style of this passage is *"... that* τον Ιησουν Χριστον *is not a Lukan expression."* Consider the usage of the following verses:

Acts 5:42 -- *"... Ιησουν τον Χριστον."*

Acts 11:17 – *"... τον Κυριον Ιησουν Χριστον."*

Acts 18:5 -- *"... τον Χριστον Ιησουν."*

Acts 18:28 – *"... τον Χριστον Ιησουν."*

Acts 20:21 – *"... τον Κυριον ημων Ιησουν Χριστον."*

Acts 28:31 – *"... του Κυριου Ιησου Χριστου ..."*

It is noted that Luke uses Christ Jesus more often than Jesus Christ; but, it must also be noted that he does use the formula Jesus Christ, along with the article (even if it includes Lord). Therefore, there is nothing in this usage to cause one to doubt the passage, unless they doubt it to begin with.

Does an author always use the same word order? Does a preacher or teacher always say Jesus Christ? Does he not also say Christ Jesus? Does the fact that he uses the one more often than the other mean that he never uses the other? The same latitude which is used in language today ought to be allowed in the scripture as well.

CONCLUSION

What tips the scales in this instance is the context. Something is definitely missing without the verse in question. The flow of the passage is interrupted without the question of Phillip and the response of the Ethiopian.

We could go further into the details of the evidence and the character of their readings, but this should suffice for the time.

Does Acts 15:34 Belong in the New Testament?

Acts 15:34 is omitted by the WESTCOTT/HORT, NESTLE'S, and UNITED BIBLE SOCIETIES GREEK TEXTS, THE AMERICAN STANDARD VERSION, THE NEW AMERICAN STANDARD, THE NEW INTERNATIONAL VERSION, THE REVISED STANDARD VERSION, THE LIVING BIBLE and THE NEW ENGLISH BIBLE, and single-bracketed by TODAY'S ENGLISH VERSION.

Passage	TR	W/H	NT	UBS	MT	KJV	ASV	RSV	TEV	LB	NAS	NIV	NKJ	CEB	ESV
Acts 15:34	-	O	O	O	O	O	O	O	--	O	O	O	O	O	O

The evidence utilized will be that found in the critical apparatus of the UBSIII.

ANTIQUITY OF THE WITNESSES

In the 2ND Century, the HARCLEAN SYRIAC VERSION WITH AN ASTERISK (dated 2ND to 7TH Century) included the verse. The PESHITTA SYRIAC VERSION (dated 2ND to 7TH Century) omitted the verse and the HARCLEAN SYRIAC VERSION is included in the witnesses against the verse.

In the 3RD Century, the SAHIDIC COPTIC VERSION and CERTAIN MANUSCRIPTS OF THE BOHAIRIC COPTIC VERSION (both dating from the 3RD to 6TH Century) include the verse, while OTHER MANUSCRIPTS OF THE BOHAIRIC COPTIC VERSION omit the verse.

In the 4TH Century, the CLEMENTINE VULGATE and the ARMENIAN VERSION (either 4TH or 5TH Century) include the verse, while two uncials (SINAITICUS {ALEPH}, VATICANUS {B}) and the WORDSWORTH-WHITE VULGATE omit the verse.

FOR	AGAINST
2ND CENTURY	
Harclean Syriac version (II-VII)	Peshitta Syriac version (II-VII)
	Harclean Syriac version (II-VII)
3RD CENTURY	
Sahidic Coptic version (III-VI)	
Bohairic Coptic version (III-VI)	Bohairic Coptic version (III-VI)
4TH CENTURY	
Clementine Vulgate version	Aleph Sinaiticus uncial
Armenian (IV/V)	B Vaticanus uncial
	Wordsworth-White Vulgate version

The evidence from the first four centuries shows that the verse has testimony as to its antiquity.

NUMBER

Twelve Greek manuscripts include the verse, while twenty-one manuscripts omit it.

Thirteen versions include the verse, and six versions omit it.

Two early writers quote the verse, while two early writers omit it.

The BYZANTINE MANUSCRIPTS are about evenly divided on ACTS 8:37.

GREEK MSS	VERSIONS	EARLY WRITERS	BYZ MSS	TEXT	BYZ MSS	EARLY WRITERS	VERSIONS	GREEK MSS
12	13	2	*	Ac 15:34	*	2	6	21

Although the Greek manuscripts omit the verse at a ratio of almost 2 to 1, the versions include the verse at a ratio of better than 2 to 1. The early writers and the Byzantine Manuscripts are about evenly divided. Thus, this is one instance where the flow of the context determines the fate of the verse.

Variety

Whether you look at the manuscripts which include the verse by number, by age, by family, or by type, they all have evidence in favor of the inclusion of the verse. The versions from every location include the verse. There is no doubt that the inclusion of the verse passes the Variety test.

Continuity

In the 2ND Century, the HARCLEAN SYRIAC VERSION WITH AN ASTERISK (dated 2ND to 7TH Century) included the verse. The PESHITTA SYRIAC VERSION (dated 2ND to 7TH Century) omitted the verse and the HARCLEAN SYRIAC VERSION is included in the witnesses against the verse.

In the 3RD Century, the SAHIDIC COPTIC VERSION and CERTAIN MANUSCRIPTS OF THE BOHAIRIC COPTIC VERSION (both dating from the 3RD to 6TH Century) include the verse, while OTHER MANUSCRIPTS OF THE BOHAIRIC COPTIC VERSION omit the verse.

In the 4TH Century, the CLEMENTINE VULGATE and the ARMENIAN VERSION (either 4TH or 5TH Century) include the verse, while two uncials (SINAITICUS {ALEPH}, VATICANUS {B}) and the WORDSWORTH-WHITE VULGATE omit the verse.

In the 5TH Century, one uncial (EPHRAEMI RESCRIPTUS {C}), the GEORGIAN VERSION, and the BEZAE CANTABRIGIENSIS OLD LATIN VERSION include the verse. One uncial (ALEXANDRINUS {A}) and CHRYSOSTOM omit the verse.

In the 6TH Century, one uncial (BEZAE CANTABRIGIENSIS {D}, WITH A CORRECTOR'S HAND PLACING AN ASTERISK WITH IT), the ETHIOPIAN VERSION, and CASSIODORUS include the verse. One uncial (LAUDIANUS {E}) and the LAUDIANUS OLD LATIN VERSION omit it.

In the 7TH Century, the LEGIONENSIS OLD LATIN VERSION includes the verse, and one papyrus (P. BODMER XVII {P75}) omit it.

In the 8TH Century, one uncial (□ – dating from the 8TH or 9TH Century) omits the verse.

In the 9TH Century, one minuscule (33) and the ARDMACHANUS OLD LATIN VERSION include the verse, and two uncials (Π, 049) omit it.

In the 10TH Century, one minuscule (1739) includes it, and two uncials (056, 0142) omit it.

In the 11th Century, three minuscules (181, 436, 945) and certain copies of THEOPHYLACT include the verse, while four minuscules (451, 81, 1505, 104) and CERTAIN COPIES OF THEOPHYLACT omit it.

In the 12TH Century, three minuscules (88, 326, 2412) and two OLD LATIN VERSIONS (PHILADELPHIENSIS, COLBERTINUS dating either 12TH or 13TH Century) include the verse. Three minuscules (330, 1241, 2127) omit the verse.

In the 13TH Century, one minuscule (614) and the GIGAS OLD LATIN VERSION include the verse, and one minuscule (2492) and the PERPINIANENSIS OLD LATIN VERSION omit it.

In the 14TH Century, one minuscule (630) includes the verse, and three minuscules (629,

1877, 2495 dating either 14TH or 15TH Century) omit it.

THE EVIDENCE FOR ACTS 15:34

FOR	AGAINST
2ND CENTURY	
Harclean Syriac version (II-VII)	Peshitta Syriac version (II-VII)
	Harclean Syriac version (II-VII)
3RD CENTURY	
Sahidic Coptic version (III-VI)	Bohairic Coptic version (III-VI)
Bohairic Coptic version (III-VI)	
4TH CENTURY	
Clementine Vulgate version	Aleph Sinaiticus uncial
Armenian (IV/V)	B Vaticanus uncial
	Wordsworth-White Vulgate version
5TH CENTURY	
C Ephraemi Rescriptus uncial	A Alexandrinus uncial
Georgian version	Chrysostom
Bezae Cantabrigiensis Old Latin version	
6TH CENTURY	
D Bezae Cantabrigiensis uncial	E Laudianus uncial
Ethiopian version	Laudianus Old Latin version
Cassiodorus	
7TH CENTURY	
Legionensis Old Latin version	P74 P. Bodmer XVII
8TH CENTURY	
	Psi uncial (VIII/IX)
9TH CENTURY	
33 minusucle	P uncial

Ardmachanus Old Latin version	049 uncial

10TH CENTURY

1739 minusucle	056 uncial
	0142 uncial

11TH CENTURY

181 minuscule	451 minuscule
436 minuscule	81 minuscule
945 minuscule	1505 minuscule
Theophylact	104 minuscule
	Theophylact

12TH CENTURY

88 minuscule	
326 minuscule	330 minuscule
2412 minuscule	1241 minuscule
Philadelphiensis Old Latin version	2127 minuscule
Colbertinus Old Latin version (XII/XIII)	

13TH CENTURY

614 minuscule	2492 minuscule
Gigas Old Latin version	Perpinianensis Old Latin version

14TH CENTURY

	629 minuscule
630 minuscule	1877 minuscule
	2495 minuscule XIV/XV)

Part of the Byzantine manuscripts include Acts 15:34.

Part of the Byzantine manuscripts omit Acts 15:34.

The verse has evidence showing its continuity, with the exception of the 8th century.

CONTEXT

Then pleased it the apostles and elders, with the whole church, to send chosen men of their own company to Antioch with Paul and Barnabas; namely, Judas surnamed Barsabas, and Silas, chief men among the brethren: And they wrote letters by them after this manner;

> *The apostles and elders and brethren send greeting unto the brethren which are of the Gentiles in Antioch and Syria and Cilicia: Forasmuch as we have heard, that certain which went out from us have troubled you with words, subverting your souls, saying, Ye must be circumcised, and keep the law: to whom we gave no such commandment: It seemed good unto us, being assembled with one accord, to send chosen men unto you with our beloved Barnabas and Paul, Men that have hazarded their lives for the name of our Lord Jesus Christ. We have sent therefore Judas and Silas, who shall also tell you the same things by mouth. For it seemed good to the Holy Ghost, and to us, to lay upon you no greater burden than these necessary things; That ye abstain from meats offered to idols, and from blood, and from things strangled, and from fornication: from which if ye keep yourselves, ye shall do well. Fare ye well.*

So when they were dismissed, they came to Antioch: and when they had gathered the multitude together, they delivered the epistle: Which when they had read, they rejoiced for the consolation. And Judas and Silas, being prophets also themselves, exhorted the brethren with many words, and confirmed them. And after they had tarried there a space, they were let go in peace from the brethren unto the apostles. <u>Notwithstanding it pleased Silas to abide there still</u>. Paul also and Barnabas continued in Antioch, teaching and preaching the word of the Lord, with many others also.

And some days after Paul said unto Barnabas, Let us go again and visit our brethren in every city where we have preached the word of the Lord, and see how they do. [ACTS 15:22-36 KJV]

Three brethren are talked about in the passage: Paul, Barnabas and Silas. Silas went with them to Antioch. For it to then speak of Paul and Barnabas remaining in Antioch, but to fail to mention what Silas did would make the dialogue incomplete.

INTERNAL EVIDENCE

There is nothing about the internal evidence which indicates the verse does not fit.

CONCLUSION

Metzger says,

The later Greek text, followed by the Textus Receptus, reads, "But it seemed good to Silas to remain there" (several manuscripts, including C, read αυτουσ for αυτου, i.e. "But it seemed good to Silas that they should remain"). Codex Bezae presents a still more expanded reading. "But it seemed good to Silas that they remain, and Judas journeyed alone."

The insertion, whether in the longer or shorter version, was no doubt made by copyists to account for the presence of Silas at Antioch in ver. 40. [IBID.; P. 439]

Could it be that the verse is there because the author (Luke) wished to account for the presence of Silas at Antioch? The reasoning of the "insertionists" could be the reasoning of the author. There is more reason therefore to accept the passage than to omit it.

Does Acts 28:29 Belong in the New Testament?

Acts 28:29 was omitted by the Westcott/Hort, Nestle's, United Bible Societies Greek Texts, the American Standard Version, the New American Standard, the New International Verison, the Revised Standard Version, the New English Bible, and single-bracketed by Today's English Version.

Passage	TR	W/H	NT	UBS	MT	KJV	ASV	RSV	TEV	LB	NAS	NIV	NKJ	CEB	ESV
Acts 28:29	-	O	O	O	-	-	O	O	S	O	O	O	-	O	O

The evidence utilized will be that found in the critical apparatus of the UBSIII.

ANTIQUITY OF THE WITNESSES

In the 2ND Century, the HARCLEAN SYRIAC VERSION WITH AN ASTERISK (dated 2ND to 7TH Century) included the verse. The PESHITTA SYRIAC VERSION (dated 2ND to 7TH Century) omitted the verse and the HARCLEAN SYRIAC VERSION is included in the witnesses against the verse.

In the 3RD Century, no witnesses include the verse, while THE SAHIDIC AND THE BOHAIRIC COPTIC VERSION [3RD – 7TH CENTURIES] omit the verse.

In the 4TH Century, the CLEMENTINE VULGATE includes the verse, while two uncials (SINAITICUS {ALEPH}, VATICANUS {B}) and the WORDSWORTH-WHITE VULGATE, along with THE ARMENIAN VERSION omit the verse.

FOR	AGAINST
2ND CENTURY	
Harclean Syriac version (w/variant) (II-VII)	Peshitta Syriac version (II-VII)
	Harclean Syriac version (II-VII)
3RD CENTURY	
	Sahidic Coptic (III-VII)

4TH CENTURY

Clementine Vulgate version

Aleph Sinaiticus uncial

B Vanticanus uncial

Wordsworth-White Vulgate version

Armenian version

The evidence from the first four centuries shows that the verse has testimony as to its antiquity, although the evidence tilts towards omission.

NUMBER

Twenty-one Greek manuscripts include the verse, while fourteen manuscripts omit it.

Seven versions include the verse, and ten versions omit it.

Three early writers quote the verse, while no early writers omit it.

The BYZANTINE MANUSCRIPTS include ACTS 28:29.

FOR   AGAINST

GREEK MSS.	VERSIONS	EARLY WRITERS	BYZ. MSS.	TEXT	BYZ. MSS	EARLY WRITERS	VERSIONS	GREEK MSS.
21	7	3	+	Acts 28:29	-	0	10	14

The Greek manuscripts include the verse at a ration of three to 2 (3/2), the versions omit the verse ten to seven (10/7), the early writers include the verse three to zero (3/0), and the Byzantine manuscripts favor its inclusion. The number of witnesses tilts in favor of the inclusion of the verse.

Continuity

In the 2ND Century, the HARCLEAN SYRIAC VERSION WITH AN ASTERISK (dated 2ND to 7TH Century) included the verse. The PESHITTA SYRIAC VERSION (dated 2ND to 7TH Century) omitted the verse and the HARCLEAN SYRIAC VERSION is included in the witnesses against the verse.

In the 3RD Century, no witness includes the verse while the SAHIDIC COPTIC VERSION and CERTAIN THE BOHAIRIC COPTIC VERSION (both dating from the 3RD to 6TH Century) omit the verse.

In the 4TH Century, the CLEMENTINE VULGATE includes the verse, while two uncials (SINAITICUS {ALEPH}, VATICANUS {B}), the WORDSWORTH-WHITE VULGATE, AND THE ARMENIAN VERSION omit the verse.

In the 5TH Century, two early writers (CHRYSOSTOM, EUTHALIUS) include the verse. Two uncials (ALEXANDRINUS {A} AND 048) and THE GEORGIAN VERSION omit the verse.

In the 6TH Century, no witnesses include the verse. One Ethiopic version (PELL PRATT AND PRAETORIUS) and two Old Latin versions (LAUDIANUS, BOBIENSIS) omit it.

In the 7TH Century, no witnesses includes the verse, and one papyrus (P. BODMER XVII {P74}) omit it.

In the 8TH Century, no witness includes the verse, and two uncials ({E} LAUDIANUS, and Y

{VII/IX}) omits the verse.

In the 9TH Century, two uncials (**049**, {Π} WOLFENBUTTEL) and the ARDMACHANUS OLD LATIN VERSION include the verse, and one minuscule (**33**) omits it.

In the 10TH Century, two uncials (**056, 0142**) includes it, and one minuscule (**1739**) omits it.

In the 11th Century, five minuscules (**436, 451, 945, 1505, 104**) and THEOPHYLACT include the verse, while two minuscules (**181, 81**) and one lectionary (**L60**) omit it.

In the 12TH Century, six minuscules (**88, 326, 330, 1241, 2127, 2412**) and two OLD LATIN VERSIONS (PHILADELPHIENSIS, COLBERTINUS dating either 12TH or 13TH Century) include the verse. No Witnesses omit the verse.

In the 13TH Century, two minuscules (**614, 2492**) and two Old Latin versions (the GIGAS, PERPINANENSIS) include the verse, and one lectionary (**L6**) omits it.

In the 14TH Century, four minuscules (629, **630, 1877, & 2495** {XIV/XV}) includes the verse, and one Latin minuscule (**629**) omits it.

THE EVIDENCE FOR ACTS 28:29

FOR	AGAINST
2ND CENTURY	
Harclean Syriac version (w/variant) (II-VII)	Peshitta Syriac version (II-VII)
	Harclean Syriac version (II-VII)
3RD CENTURY	
	Sahidic Coptic (III-VII)
	Bohairic Coptic (III-VII)
4TH CENTURY	
	Aleph Sinaiticus uncial
	B Vanticanus uncial
Clementine Vulgate version	Wordsworth-White Vulgate version
	Armenian version
5TH CENTURY	
Chrysostom	A Alexandrinus uncial
Euthalius	Georgian version
	048 uncial
6TH CENTURY	
	Pell Pratt and Praetorius Ethiopic version
	Laudianus Old Latin version
	Bobiensis Old Latin version
7TH CENTURY	

P74 P. Bodmer XVII

E Laudianus uncial

Psi uncial (VIII/IX)

049 uncial

Ardmachanus Old Latin version

33 minuscule

P Wolfenbuttel uncial

056 uncial

0142 uncial

1739 minuscule

436 minuscule

451 minuscule

945 minuscule

181 minuscule

1505 minuscule

81 minuscule

104 minuscule

L60 lectionary

Theophylact

88 minuscule

326 minuscule

330 minuscule

1241 minuscule

2127 minuscule

2412 minuscule

Philadelphiensis Old Latin version

Colbertinus Old Latin version

614 minuscule

2492 minuscule

L6 lectionary

Gigas Old Latin version

Perpinanensis Old Latin version

629 (Greek) minuscule

630 minuscule

1877 minuscule

2495 minuscule (XIV/XV)

629 (Latin) minuscule

The majority of the lectionaries in the Synaxarion (the so-called "moveable year" beginning with Easter) and in the Menologian (the "fixed year" beginning with September 1) include Acts 28:29.

The majority of the Byzantine manuscripts include Acts 28:29.

The early evidence for the inclusion of Acts 28:29 is thin, with no evidence for the 6th, 7th and 8th centuries. However, beginning in the 9th century the inclusion of the verse dominates the evidence. Although outnumbering the evidence to include the verse, the evidence is not overwhelming in either direction until the 11th century in terms of numbers. There is not a Greek manuscript which includes the verse until 056 and P Wolfenbuttel in the 9th century. On the other hand, Sinaiticus, Alexandrinus, 048, Papyrus 74, and Laudianus bear witness to the verse being omitted from the 4th through the 8th century. From the 12th century on, there are only one manuscript and one lectionary which omit the verse. There is no question as to its antiquity, nor of its obvious position in the text from the 9th century on. The tilt must be given to inclusion on the basis of continuity.

CONTEXT

And when they had appointed him a day, there came many to him into his lodging; to whom he expounded and testified the kingdom of God, persuading them concerning Jesus, both out of the law of Moses, and out of the prophets, from morning till evening. And some believed the things which were spoken, and some believed not.

And when they agreed not among themselves, they departed, after that Paul had spoken one word, Well spake the Holy Ghost by Esaias the prophet unto our fathers, Saying, Go unto this people, and say, Hearing ye shall hear, and shall not understand; and seeing ye shall see, and not perceive: For the heart of this people is waxed gross, and their ears are dull of hearing, and their eyes have they closed; lest they should see with their eyes, and hear with their ears, and understand with their heart, and should be converted, and I should heal them. Be it known therefore unto you, that the salvation of God is sent unto the Gentiles, and that they will hear it.

And when he had said these words, the Jews departed, and had great reasoning among themselves.

And Paul dwelt two whole years in his own hired house, and received all that came in unto him, Preaching the kingdom of God, and teaching those things which concern the Lord Jesus Christ, with all confidence, no man forbidding him. (ACTS 28:23-31 KJV)

The verse does no violation to the context, and helps the transition to the following verses. The context indicates that the verse belongs.

INTERNAL EVIDENCE

There is nothing about the internal evidence which indicates the verse does not fit.

CONCLUSION

Metzger says, giving the verse a {B} rating –

The Western expansion (represented by 383 614 it^{gig,p} vg^{mss} syr^{h with *}) was adopted by the Byzantine text and lies behind the AV rendering, "And when he had said these words, the Jews departed, and had great reasoning among themselves." The addition was probably made because of the abrupt transition from ver. 28 to ver. 30. [Ibid., p. 502]

It was thought to be an addition which bridged verses 28 to 30. Why could it not be an original reading which bridged these verses? The evidence in early times is scarce, but it is there. The conclusion of later years is overwhelming.

- This verse belongs in the New Testament.

DOES ROMANS 16:24 BELONG IN THE NEW TESTAMENT?

Romans 16:24 is omitted from the Westcott/Hort, Nestle/Aland, and the United Bible Society III Greek texts; and, it is omitted from the American Standard Version, the New American Standard Version, the New International Version, the Revised Standard Version, the Common English Bible, and the English Standard Version. The verse is included in the Textus Receptus and the Majority Text Greek texts, and is included in the King James Version and the New King James Version.

TEXT	TR	WH	N	BS	MT	KJV	ASV	NAS	NIV	RSV	NKJV	CEB	ESV
Romans 16:24	--	O	O	O	--	--	O	O	O	O	--	O	O

ANTIQUITY OF THE WITNESSES

In the 2ND Century, two Syriac versions (PESHITTA, HARCLEAN -- dated 2ND to 7TH Century) included the verse.

In the 3RD Century, no witnesses include the verse, while the Chester Beatty papyrus (P76), THE SAHIDIC AND THE BOHAIRIC COPTIC VERSION [3RD – 7TH CENTURIES], and Origen omit the verse.

In the 4TH Century, the CLEMENTINE VULGATE, THE GOTHIC, AND THE ARMENIAN VERSIONS include the verse, while two uncials (SINAITICUS {ALEPH}, VATICANUS {B}) and the WORDSWORTH-WHITE VULGATE omit the verse.

FOR	AGAINST
2ND CENTURY	
Harclean Syriac version (II-VII)	
Peshitta Syriac version (II-VII) after 16:27	

3RD CENTURY

P76 Chester Beatty papyrus

Sahidic Coptic version

Bohairic Coptic version

Origen (Latin)

4TH CENTURY

Clementine Vulgate version	Aleph Sinaiticus uncial
Gothic version	B Vaticanus uncial
Armenian version after 16:27	Wordsworth-White Vulgate version

The evidence from the first four centuries shows that the verse has testimony as to its antiquity, although the evidence tilts towards omission.

NUMBER

Twenty-five Greek manuscripts include the verse, while fourteen manuscripts omit it.

Fourteen versions include the verse, and five versions omit it.

Five early writers quote the verse, while one early writer omit it.

The BYZANTINE MANUSCRIPTS include ROMANS 16:24.

FOR   AGAINST

GREEK MSS.	VERSIONS	EARLY WRITERS	BYZ. MSS.	TEXT	BYZ. MSS	EARLY WRITERS	VERSIONS	GREEK MSS.
25	14	5	+	Ro. 16:24	-	1	5	14

The Greek manuscripts include the verse at a ratio of almost two to one (25/14), the versions include the verse at a ratio of almost three to one (14/5), the early writers include the verse five to one (5/1), and the Byzantine manuscripts favor its inclusion. The number of witnesses is in favor of the inclusion of the verse.

Continuity

In the 2ND Century, the HARCLEAN SYRIAC VERSION (dated 2ND to 7TH Century) included the verse, while the Peshitta Syriac Version (dated 2nd to 7th Century) includes it at a different location.

In the 3RD Century, no witness includes the verse while the Chester Beatty papyrus (P76), the SAHIDIC COPTIC VERSION and THE BOHAIRIC COPTIC VERSION (both dating from the 3RD to 6TH Century), and Origen (Latin) omit the verse.

In the 4TH Century, the CLEMENTINE VULGATE, THE GOTHIC VERSION, AND THE ARMENIAN VERSION (AFTER 16:27) include the verse, while two uncials (SINAITICUS {ALEPH}, VATICANUS {B}), and the WORDSWORTH-WHITE VULGATE omit the verse.

In the 5TH Century, one Old Latin version (CLAROMONTANUS) and three early writers (CHRYSOSTOM, THEODORET, EUTHALIUS) include the verse. Two uncials (ALEXANDRINUS {A} AND EPHRAEMI RESCRIPTUS {C}) omit the verse.

In the 6TH Century, no witnesses include the verse. One uncial (Claronomtanus {D}) and one Ethiopic version (PELL PRATT AND PRAETORIUS) include the verse, while the ROME ETHIOPIC VERSION OMITS IT.

In the 7TH Century, no witnesses include the verse, or omit it.

In the 8TH Century, one uncial (☐) and one early writer (JOHN – DAMASCUS) include the verse, and one papyrus (P. COLT 5 {P61}) and the HARLEIANUS LAUDINIENSUS OLD LATIN omit the verse.

In the 9TH Century, two uncials (G BOERNERIANUS AND P AFTER 16:27), one minuscule (33 after 16:27) and five Old Latin versions (SANGERMANENSIS, BODLEIANUS, AUGIENSIS, BOERNERIANUS, ARDMACHANUS) include the verse, and no witnesses omit it.

In the 10TH Century, no witnesses include it, and one minuscule (1739) omits it.

In the 11th Century, six minuscules (181, 451, 1837 AFTER 16:27, 256 AFTER 16:27, 436 AFTER 16:27, 104 AFTER 16:27) include the verse, while four minuscules (1838, 1962, 623, 81) omit it.

In the 12TH Century, five minuscules (88, 326, 330, 1241, 1319 AFTER 16:27) include the verse. One minuscule (2127) omits the verse.

In the 13TH Century, one minuscules (614) and two Old Latin versions (the GIGAS, DEMIDOVIANUS) include the verse, and one minuscule (263) omits it.

In the 14TH Century, six minuscules (629, 630, 1877, 1881, 1984, 2495) includes the verse, and one minuscule (5) omits it.

In the 15th Century, no witnesses include or omit the verse.

In the 16th Century, one minuscule (1985) includes the verse. No witnesses omit the verse.

THE EVIDENCE FOR ROMANS 16:24

FOR	AGAINST
2ND CENTURY	
Harclean Syriac version (II-VII)	
Peshitta Syriac version (II-VII) after 16:27	
3RD CENTURY	
	P76 Chester Beatty papyrus
	Sahidic Coptic version

Bohairic Coptic version

Origen (Latin)

4TH CENTURY

Clementine Vulgate version

Aleph Sinaiticus uncial

Gothic version

B Vaticanus uncial

Armenian version after 16:27

Wordsworth-White Vulgate version

5TH CENTURY

Claromontanus Old Latin version

Chrysostom

A Alexandrinus uncial

Theodoret

C Epraemi Rescriptus uncial

Euthalius

6TH CENTURY

D Claromontanus uncial

Rome Ethiopic version

Pell Pratt and Praetorius Ethiopic version

7TH CENTURY

8TH CENTURY

Psi uncial

P61 (P. Colt 5) papyrus

John – Damascus

Harleianus Laudiniensis Old Latin version

9TH CENTURY

G Boernerianus uncial

P uncial after 16:27

33 minuscule after 16:27

Sangermanensis Old Latin version

Bodleianus Old Latin version

Augiensis Old Latin version

Boernerianus Old Latin version

Ardmachunus Old Latin version

10TH CENTURY

1739 minuscule

11TH CENTURY

181 minuscule

451 minuscule   1838 minuscule

1837 minuscule after 16:27   1962 minuscule

256 minuscule after 16:27   623 minuscule

436 minuscule after 16:27   81 minuscule

104 minuscule after 16:27

12TH CENTURY

88 minuscule

326 minuscule

330 minuscule   2127 minuscule

1241 minuscule

1319 minuscule after 16:27

13TH CENTURY

614 minuscule

Demidovianus Old Latin version   263 minuscule

Gigas Old Latin version

14TH CENTURY

629 minuscule

630 minuscule

1877 minuscule

1881 minuscule   5 minuscule

1984 minuscule

2495 minuscule

1985 minuscule

The majority of the lectionaries in the Synaxarion (the so-called "moveable year" beginning with Easter) and in the Menologian (the "fixed year" beginning with September 1) include Romans 16:24.

The majority of the Byzantine manuscripts include Romans 16:24.

There is a break in the continuity of the witnesses in the 3rd, 7th, 10th, and 15th Centuries in including the verse. The 16th Century yields only one witness for the inclusion.

There is a break in the continuity of the witnesses omitting the verse in the 2nd, 7th, 9th and 15th Century, and scant evidence after the 5th Century except for the 11th Century. The 6th, 10th, 12th, 13th and 14th Century yield only one witness each for the omission of the verse.

When the lectionaries and the Byzantine manuscripts are included, the evidence declares in favor of the continuity of the verse.

CONTEXT

Timotheus my workfellow, and Lucius, and Jason, and Sosipater, my kinsmen, salute you.

I Tertius, who wrote this epistle, salute you in the Lord.

Gaius mine host, and of the whole church, saluteth you.

Erastus the chamberlain of the city saluteth you, and Quartus a brother.

<u>The grace of our Lord Jesus Christ be with you all. Amen.</u> (Romans 16:21-24 KJV)

The context flows similar to the ending of Paul's other epistles.

INTERNAL EVIDENCE

There is nothing about the internal evidence which indicates the verse does not fit.

CONCLUSION

Metzger says,

The earliest and best witnesses omit ver. 24. [Ibid., p. 540]. (see verse 20)

Metzger as well as the Committee display their preferential treatment of the Westcott/Hort theories in these comments. Upon what basis are these the best? And upon their own statements the witnesses to the text are as ancient.

The verse belongs in the New Testament.

DOES
1ˢᵗ JOHN 5:7
BELONG IN THE
NEW TESTAMENT?

> *One of the things which honesty requires is to follow the evidence wherever it leads.*
> *Although there may be those who disagree with my conclusion,*
> *following the same logic and chain of evidence as with other passages,*
> *I could not come to any other conclusion.*
>
> *In the name of equity,*
> *two articles from other authors presenting a different conclusion*
> *will be presented after my article.*

1 John 5:7 is omitted by Westcott/Hort, Nestle's, United Bible Societies and the Majority Text Greek Texts, the American Standard Version, the New American Standard, the New International Version, the Revised Standard Version, the New English Bible, the Living Bible, Today's English Version, the Common English Bible, and the English Standard Version. It is included in the Textus Receptus, the King James Version, and the New King James Version.

TEXT	TR	WH	N	BS	MT	KJV	ASV	NAS	NIV	RSV	NKJV	CEB	ESV
1 Jn. 5:7	--	O	O	O	O	--	O	O	O	O	--	O	O

ANTIQUITY OF THE WITNESSES

In the 2ND Century, no witnesses include the verse two Syriac versions (PESHITTA, HARCLEAN -- dated 2ND to 7TH Century) omit the verse.

In the 3RD Century, no witnesses include the verse, while THE SAHIDIC AND THE BOHAIRIC COPTIC VERSION [3RD – 7TH CENTURIES], and **Irenaeus, Clement, Tertullian, Hippolytus. Origen, Cyprian,and Dionysius** omit the verse.

In the 4TH Century, Clementine Vulgate (mss) version, Speculum or Ps-Augustine Old Latin version, Varimadum and Priscillian include the verse, while two uncials ({Aleph} Sinaiticus,

{B} Vaticanus). Twp versions (Wordsworth-White Vulgate, Armenian version [IV/V]), and eight early writers (Hilary, Lucifer, Athanasius, Basil. Faustinus, Gregory – Nazianzus, Ambrose and Didymus) omit the verse.

THE EVIDENCE FOR1 JOHN 5:7

FOR	AGAINST
2ND CENTURY	
	Peshitta Syriac version (II-VII)
	Harclean Syriac version (II-VII)
3RD CENTURY	
	Sahidic Coptic version (III-VI)
	Bohairic Coptic version (III-VI)
	Irenaeus
	Clement
	Tertullian
	Hippolytus
	Origen
	Cyprian
	Dionysius
4TH CENTURY	
	Aleph Sinaiticus uncial
	B Vaticanus uncial
Clementine Vulgate (mss) version	Wordsworth-White Vulgate version
Speculum or Ps-Augustine Old Latin version	Armenian version (IV/V)
Varimadum	Hilary
Priscillian	Lucifer
	Athanasius
	Basil

Faustinus

Gregory – Nazianzus

Ambrose

Didymus

The evidence from the first four centuries shows that the verse has testimony as to its antiquity, although the evidence overwhelmingly favors omission.

NUMBER

Four Greek manuscripts include the verse, while thirty-two manuscripts omit it.

Seven versions include the verse, and ten versions omit it.

Eight early writers quote the verse, while twenty early writers omit it.

The BYZANTINE MANUSCRIPTS omit 1 JOHN 5:7.

FOR   AGAINST

GREEK MSS.	VERSIONS	EARLY WRITERS	BYZ. MSS.	TEXT	BYZ. MSS	EARLY WRITERS	VERSIONS	GREEK MSS.
4	7	8	-	1 Jn. 5:7	+	20	10	32

The Greek manuscripts omit the verse at a ratio of almost eight to one (32/4), the versions omit the verse at a ratio of ten to seven (10/7), the early writers omit the verse twenty to eight (20/8), and the Byzantine manuscripts favor its omission. The number of witnesses is in favor of the omission of the verse.

Continuity

In the 2ND Century, two Syriac versions (Peshitta, HARCLEAN SYRIAC VERSION [dated 2ND to 7TH Century]) omit the verse. No witnesses include the verse.

In the 3RD Century, no witnesses include the verse, while THE SAHIDIC AND THE BOHAIRIC COPTIC VERSION [3RD – 7TH CENTURIES], and Irenaeus, Clement, Tertullian, Hippolytus. Origen, Cyprian, and Dionysius omit the verse.

In the 4TH Century, Clementine Vulgate (mss) version, Speculum or Ps-Augustine Old Latin version, Varimadum and Priscillian include the verse, while two uncials ({Aleph} Sinaiticus, {B} Vaticanus). Twp versions (Wordsworth-White Vulgate, Armenian version [IV/V]), and eight early writers (Hilary, Lucifer, Athanasius, Basil, Faustinus, Gregory – Nazianzus, Ambrose and Didymus) omit the verse.

In the 5TH Century, three early writers (Cassian, Ps-Vigilius, Vitonvita [manuscripts according to] include the verse. Two uncials (ALEXANDRINUS {A} AND 048) and five early writers (EPIPHANIUS, CHRYSOSTOM, JEROME, AUGUSTINE, CYRIL OF ALEXANDRIA) omit the verse.

In the 6ᵀᴴ Century, two writers (Ps-Athanasius, Fulgentius) include the verse. The Ethiopic version include the verse.

In the 7ᵀᴴ Century, the Monacenus Old Latin includes the verse, no witnesses omit it.

In the 8ᵀᴴ Century, one early writer (ANSBERT) include the verse, and one uncial (☐ {VIII/IX}) omits the verse.

In the 9ᵀᴴ Century, no witnesses include the verse, and three uncials (K, Π, 049), one minuscule (33) and one Old Latin version (ARDMACHANUS) omit it.

In the 10ᵀᴴ Century, no witness includes it, and two uncials (056, 0142) one minuscule (1739) omit it.

In the 11th Century, one minuscule (635[MARGIN]) includes the verse, while four minuscules (181, 436, 451, 945, 81, 1505, 104) and one lectionary (L598) omit it.

In the 12ᵀᴴ Century, one minuscule (88 [MARGIN]) and one Old Latin version (Colbertinus) include the verse. Six minuscules (88[text], 326, 330, 1241, 2127, 2412) omits the verse.

In the 13ᵀᴴ Century, three Old Latin versions (DEMIDOVIANUS, DIVIONENSIS, PERPINIANENSIS) include the verse, and two minuscule (614, 2492) omits it.

In the 14ᵀᴴ Century, one minuscule (629) includes the verse, and four minuscules (630, 1877, 1881, 2495) omit it.

In the 15th Century, no witnesses include or omit the verse.

In the 16th Century, one minuscule (61) includes the verse. No witnesses omit the verse.

THE EVIDENCE FOR 1 JOHN 5:7

FOR	AGAINST
2ND CENTURY	
	Peshitta Syriac version (II-VII)
	Harclean Syriac version (II-VII)
3RD CENTURY	
	Sahidic Coptic version (III-VI)
	Bohairic Coptic version (III-VI)
	Irenaeus
	Clement
	Tertullian
	Hippolytus

	Origen
	Cyprian
	Dionysius

4TH CENTURY

	Aleph Sinaiticus uncial
	B Vaticanus uncial
	Wordsworth-White Vulgate version
	Armenian version (IV/V)
Clementine Vulgate (mss) version	Hilary
Speculum or Ps-Augustine Old Latin version	Lucifer
	Athanasius
Varimadum	Basil
Priscillian	Faustinus
	Gregory – Nazianzus
	Ambrose
	Didymus

5TH CENTURY

	A Alexandrinus uncial
	048 uncial
Cassian	Epiphanius
Ps-Vigilius	Chrsostom
Manuscripts according to Victonvita	Jerome
	Augustine
	Cyril of Alexandria

6TH CENTURY

Ps-Athanasius	
Fulgentius	Ethiopian version

7TH CENTURY	
Monacensus Old Latin version	

8TH CENTURY	
Ansbert	Psi uncial (VIII/IX)

9TH CENTURY	
	K uncial
	P uncial
	049 uncial
	33 minuscule
	Ardmachanus Old Latin version

10TH CENTURY	
	056 uncial
	0142 uncial
	1739 minuscule

11TH CENTURY	
	181 minuscule
	436 minuscule
	451 minuscule
	945 minuscule
635 minuscule (margin)	81 minuscule
	1505 minuscule
	104 minuscule
	L598 lectionary

12TH CENTURY	
	88 minuscule (text)
88 minuscule (margin)	326 minuscule
Colbertinus Old Latin version	330 minuscule

	1241 minuscule
	2127 minuscule
	2412 minuscule

13ᵀᴴ CENTURY

Demidovianus Old Latin version	614 minuscule
Divionensis Old Latin version	2492 minuscule
Perpinianensis Old Latin version	

14ᵀᴴ CENTURY

	630 minuscule
	1877 minuscule
629 minusucle	1881 minuscule
	2495 minuscule

15ᵀᴴ CENTURY

16ᵀᴴ CENTURY

61 minuscule

The majority of lectionaries in the Synaxrion (the so-called "moveable year" beginning with Easter) and in the Menologion (the "fixed year" beginning with September 1) omit 1 John 5:7.

The majority of the Byzantine manuscripts omit 1 John 5:7.

There is a break in the continuity of the witnesses in the 2nd, 3rd, 9th, 10th, and 15th Centuries in including the verse. The 7th, 8th, 11th, 14th, and 16th Century yields only one witness for the inclusion.

There is a break in the continuity of the witnesses omitting the verse in the 7th, 15th and 16th Century. The 6th and 8th Century yield only one witness each for the omission of the verse.

When the lectionaries and the Byzantine manuscripts are included, the evidence declares against the continuity of the verse.

CONTEXT

This is he that came by water and blood, even Jesus Christ; not by water only, but by water and blood. And it is the Spirit that beareth witness, because the Spirit is truth. <u>For there are</u>

three that bear record in heaven, the Father, the Word, and the Holy Ghost: and these three are one. And there are three that bear witness in earth, the Spirit, and the water, and the blood: and these three agree in one. If we receive the witness of men, the witness of God is greater: for this is the witness of God which he hath testified of his Son. [1 John 5:6-9 KJV]

Jesus' ministry began with water, and ended with blood, with water and blood flowing from His side through the puncture of the Roman spear. Baptized (immersed) by John in the Jordan River (water), Jesus began His ministry by "fulfilling all righteousness" in obedience to the command of the Father. Beaten, crowned by thorns, and crucified (blood) ended His ministry in obedience to the requirements of the Father. When His side was pierced by the Roman spear, *and forthwith came there out blood and water. (John 19:34 KJV)*

There remain two institutions which bear witness to who Jesus is -- baptism (immersion) in water, in the likeness of His death, burial and resurrection; and the cup of the Lord's Supper representing His blood. Thus, water and the blood continue to bear witness.

In addition, the Spirit bears witness through the Word of God which He inspired.

Verse 8 repeats for emphasis the three witnesses upon the earth.

Verse 7 expands upon the end of verse 6. The Spirit bears witness, but the Father and the Word bear witness in heaven, as well. There is nothing in this verse which is not contained in other Scripture.

IV. The argument against the passage from the external proof is confirmed by internal evidence, which makes it morally certain that it cannot be genuine.

(a.) The connexion does not demand it. It does not contribute to advance what the apostle is saying, but breaks the thread of his argument entirely. He is speaking of certain things which bear "witness" to the fact that Jesus is the Messiah; certain things were well known to those to whom he was writing--the Spirit, and the water, and the blood. How does it contribute to strengthen the force of this to say that in heaven there are "three that bear witness"--three not before referred to, and having no connexion with the matter under consideration?

(b.) The language is not such as John would use. He does, indeed, elsewhere use the term Logos, or Word, o logov Joh 1:1,14 1Jo 1:1, but it is never in this form, "The Father, and the Word;" that is, the terms "Father" and "Word" are never used by him, or by any of the other sacred writers, as correlative. The word Son--o uiov--is the term which is correlative to the Father in every other place as used by John, as well as by the other sacred writers. See 1Jo 1:3; 2:22-24; 4:14; 3:9; and the Gospel of John, passim. Besides, the correlative of the term Logos, or Word, with John, is not Father, but God. See Joh 1:1. Comp. Re 19:13.

(c) Without this passage, the sense of the argument is clear and appropriate. There are three, says John, which bear witness that Jesus is the Messiah. These are referred to in 1Jo 5:6; and in immediate connexion with this, in the argument, (1Jo 5:8,) it is affirmed that their testimony goes to one point, and is harmonious. To say that there are other witnesses elsewhere, to say that they are one, contributes nothing to illustrate the nature of the testimony of these three--the water, and the blood, and the Spirit; and the internal sense of the passage, therefore, furnishes as little evidence of its genuineness as the external proof. It is easy to imagine how the passage found a place in the New Testament. It was at first written, perhaps, in the margin of some Latin manuscript, as expressing the belief of the writer of what was true in heaven, as well as on earth, and with no more intention to deceive than we have when we make a marginal note in a book. Some transcriber copied it into the body of the text, perhaps with a sincere belief that it was a genuine passage, omitted by accident; and then it became too important a passage in the argument for the Trinity, ever to be displaced but by the most clear critical evidence. It was rendered into Greek, and inserted in one Greek manuscript of the 16th century, while it was wanting in all the earlier manuscripts....

(1.) Even on the supposition that it is genuine, as Bengel believed it was, and as he believed that some Greek manuscript would yet be found which would contain it; yet it is not wise to adduce it as a proof-text. It would be much easier to prove the doctrine of the Trinity from other texts, than to demonstrate the genuineness of this.

(2.) It is not necessary as a proof-text. The doctrine which it contains can be abundantly established from other parts of the New Testament, by passages about which there can be no doubt.

(3.) The removal of this text does nothing to weaken the evidence for the doctrine of the Trinity, or to modify that doctrine. As it was never used to shape the early belief of the Christian world on the subject, so its rejection, and its removal from the New Testament, will do nothing to modify that doctrine. The doctrine was embraced, and held, and successfully defended without it, and it can and will be so still.

* Mill. New Test., pp. 379-386; Wetstein, II. 721–727; Father Simon, Crit. Hist. New Test.; Michaelis, Intro. New Test. iv. 412, seq.; Semler, Histor. und Krit. Sammlungen uber die sogenannten Beweistellen der Dogmatik. Erstes Stuck uber, 1 John v. 7; Griesbach, Diatribe in locum, I John v. 7, 8, second edit., New Test., vol. II., appendix 1; and Lucke's Commentary.

■ **Barnes**

INTERNAL EVIDENCE

See the quotation from Barnes above.

CONCLUSION

Metzger says,

After μαρτυρουντεσ *the Textus Receptus adds the following:* εν τω ουρανω ο Πατηρ, ο Λογοσ, και το Αγιον Πνευμα: και ουτοι οι τρεισ εν εισι. (8) και τρεισ εισιν ο ι μαρτυρουντεσ εν τη γη. *That these words are spurious and have no right to stand in the New Testament is certain in the light of the following considerations.*

(A) EXTERNAL EVIDENCE. (1) The passage is absent from every known Greek manuscript except four, and these contain the passage in what appears to be a translation from a late recension of the Latin Vulgate. These four manuscripts are ms. 61, a sixteenth century manuscript formerly at Oxford, now at Dublin; ms. 88, a twelfth century manuscript at Naples, which as the passage written in the margin by a modern hand; ms. 629, a fourteenth or fif-

teenth century manuscript in the Vatican; and ms. 635, an eleventh century manuscript which has the passage written in the margin by a seventeeth century hand.

(2) The passage is quoted by none of the Greek Fathers, who, had they know it, would most certainly have employed it in the Trinitarian controversies (Sabellian and Arian). Its first appearance in Greek is in a Greek version of the (Latin) Acts of the Lateran Council in 1215.

(3) The passage is absent from the manuscripts of all ancient version (Syriac, Coptic, Armenian, Ethiopic, Arabic, Slavonic), except the Latin; and is not found (a) in the Old Latin in its early form (Tertullian Cyprian Augustine), or in the Vulgate (b) issued by Jerome (codex Fuldensis [copied a.d. 541-46] and codex Amiatinus [copied before a.d. 716] or (e) as revised by Alcuin (first hand of codex Vercellensis [ninth century]).

The earliest instance of the passage being quoted as part of the actual text of the Epistle is in a fourth century Latin treatise entitled Liber Apologeticus (chap. 4), attributed either to the Spanish heretic Priscillian (died about 385) or to his follower Bishop Instantius. Apparently the gloss arose when the original passage was understood to symbolize the Trinity (through mention of three witnesses; the Spirit, the water, and the blood), an interpretation which may have been written first as a marginal note that afterwards found its way into the text. In the fifth century the gloss was quoted by Latin Fathers in North Africa and Italy as part of the text of the Epistle, and from the sixth century onwards it is found more and more frequently in manuscripts of the Old Latin and of the Vulgate. In these various witnesses the wording of the passage differs in several particulars. (For examples of other intrusions into the Latin text of 1 John, see 2.17; 4.3; 5.6, and 20.)

(B) INTERNAL PROBABILITIES. (1) As regards transcriptional probability, if the passage were original, no good reason can be found to account for its omission, either accidentally or intentionally, by copyists of hundreds of Greek manuscripts, and by translators of ancient versions.

(2) As regards intrinsic probability, the passage makes an awkward break in the sense.

For the story of how the spurious words came to be included in the Textus Receptus, see any critical comentary on 1 John, or Metzer, The Text of the New Testament, pp. 101 f., cf. also Ezra Abbot, "I.John v.7 and Luther's German Bible," in The Authorship of the Fourth Gospel and Other Critical Essays (Boston, 1888), pp. 458-463. [IBID., PP. 714-6]

When you weigh the evidence for and against 1 John 5:7, honesty compels the conscience to reject the verse's validity. There is not a single category where the evidence favors the inclusion of this verse. Although familiarity, and emotion tend to lean toward the inclusion, the evidence cannot be ignored. This verse does not belong in the New Testament.

*Attached are two defenses of the inclusion of this verse. Although I believe both of them fall short of making their case, they present about as good a case as can be given. Therefore, I include them for your perusal.

1 John 5:7 (Johannine Comma) - "These Three Are One"

"For there are three that bear record in heaven, the Father, the Word, and the Holy Ghost: and these three are one."

The passage is called the *Johannine Comma* and is not found in the majority of Greek manuscripts. [1] However, the verse is a wonderful testimony to the Heavenly Trinity and should be maintained in our English versions, not only because of its doctrinal significance but because of the external and internal evidence that testify to its authenticity.

The External Support: Although not found in most Greek manuscripts, the Johannine Comma is found in several. It is contained in 629 (fourteenth century), 61 (sixteenth century), 918 (sixteenth century), 2473 (seventeenth century), and 2318 (eighteenth century). It is also in the margins of 221 (tenth century), 635 (eleventh century), 88 (twelveth century), 429 (fourteenth century), and 636 (fifteenth century). There are about five hundred existing manuscripts of 1 John chapter five that do not contain the *Comma*. [2] It is clear that the reading found in the Textus Receptus is the minority reading with later textual support from the Greek witnesses. Nevertheless, being a minority reading does not eliminate it as genuine. The Critical Text considers the reading *Iesou* (of Jesus) to be the genuine reading instead of *Iesou Christou* (of Jesus Christ) in 1 John 1:7. Yet *Iesou* is the minority reading with only twenty-four manuscripts supporting it, while four hundred seventy-seven manuscripts support the reading *Iesou Christou* found in the Textus Receptus. Likewise, in 1 John 2:20 the minority reading *pantes* (all) has only twelve manuscripts supporting it, while the majority reading is *panta* (all things) has four hundred ninety-one manuscripts. Still, the Critical Text favors the minority reading over the majority in that passage. This is common place throughout the First Epistle of John, and the New Testament as a whole. Therefore, simply because a reading is in the minority does not eliminate it as being considered original.

While the Greek textual evidence is weak, the Latin textual evidence for the Comma is extremely strong. It is in the vast majority of the Old Latin manuscripts, which outnumber the Greek manuscripts. Although some doubt if the Comma was a part of Jerome's original Vulgate, the evidence suggests that it was. Jerome states:

In that place particularly where we read about the unity of the Trinity which is placed in the First Epistle of John, in which also the names of three, i.e. of water, of blood, and of spirit, do they place in their edition and omitting the testimony of the Father; and the Word, and the Spirit in which the catholic faith is especially confirmed and the single substance of the Father, the Son and the Holy Spirit is confirmed. [3]

Other church fathers are also known to have quoted the Comma. Although some have questioned if Cyprian (258 AD) knew of the Comma, his citation certainly suggests that he did. He writes: "The Lord says, 'I and the

Father are one' and likewise it is written of the Father and the Son and the Holy Spirit, 'And these three are one'." [4] Also, there is no doubt that Priscillian (385 AD) cites the Comma:

As John says "and there are three which give testimony on earth, the water, the flesh, the blood, and these three are in one, and there are three which give testimony in heaven, the Father, the Word, and the Spirit, and these three are one in Christ Jesus." [5]

Likewise, the anti-Arian work compiled by an unknown writer, the *Varimadum* (380 AD) states: "And John the Evangelist says, . . . 'And there are three who give testimony in heaven, the Father, the Word, and the Spirit, and these three are one'." [6] Additionally, Cassian (435 AD), Cassiodorus (580 AD), and a host of other African and Western bishops in subsequent centuries have cited the Comma. [7] Therefore, we see that the reading has massive and ancient textual support apart from the Greek witnesses.

Internal Evidence: The structure of the Comma is certainly Johannine in style. John is noted for referring to Christ as "the Word." If 1 John 5:7 were an interpretation of verse eight, as some have suggested, than we would expect the verse to use "Son" instead of "Word." However, the verse uses the Greek word *logos*, which is uniquely in the style of John and provides evidence of its genuineness. Also, we find John drawing parallels between the Trinity and what they testify (1 John 4:13-14). Therefore, it comes as no surprise to find a parallel of witnesses containing groups of three, one heavenly and one earthly.

The strongest evidence, however, is found in the Greek text itself. Looking at 1 John 5:8, there are three nouns which, in Greek, stand in the neuter (Spirit, water, and blood). However, they are followed by a participle that is masculine. The Greek phrase here is *oi marturountes* (who bare witness). Those who know the Greek language understand this to be poor grammar if left to stand on its own. Even more noticeably, verse six has the same participle but stands in the neuter (Gk.: *to marturoun*). Why are three neuter nouns supported with a masculine participle? The answer is found if we include verse seven. There we have two masculine nouns (Father and Son) followed by a neuter noun (Spirit). The verse also has the Greek masculine participle *oi marturountes*. With this clause introducing verse eight, it is very proper for the participle in verse eight to be masculine, because of the masculine nouns in verse seven. But if verse seven were not there it would become improper Greek grammar.

Even though Gregory of Nazianzus (390 AD) does not testify to the authenticity of the Comma, he makes mention of the flawed grammar resulting from its absence. In his *Theological Orientations* he writes referring to John:

. . . (he has not been consistent) in the way he has happened upon his terms; for after using Three in the masculine gender he adds three words which are neuter, contrary to the definitions and laws which you and your grammarians have laid down. For what is the difference between putting a masculine Three first, and then adding One and One and One in the neuter, or after a masculine One and One and One to use the Three not in the masculine but in the neuter, which you yourselves disclaim in the case of Deity? [8]

It is clear that Gregory recognized the inconsistency with Greek grammar if all we have are verses six and eight without verse seven. Other scholars have recognized the same thing. This was the argument of Robert Dabney of Union Theological Seminary in his book, *The Doctrinal Various Readings of the New Testament Greek* (1891). Bishop Middleton in his book, *Doctrine of the Greek Article,* argues that verse seven must be a part of the text according to the Greek structure of the passage. Even in the famous commentary by Matthew Henry, there is a note stating that we must have verse seven if we are to have proper Greek in verse eight. [9]

While the external evidence makes the originality of the Comma possible, the internal evidence makes it very probable. When we consider the providential hand of God and His use of the Traditional Text in the Reformation it is clear that the Comma is authentic.

[1] The first and second editions of Erasmus' Greek text did not contain the Comma. It is generally reported that Erasmus promised to include the Comma in his third edition if a single manuscript containing the Comma could be produced. A Franciscan friar named Froy (or Roy) forged a Greek text containing it by translating the Comma from the Latin into Greek. Erasmus was then presented with this falsified manuscript and, being faithful to his word, reluctantly included the Comma in the 1522 edition. However, as has now been admitted by Dr. Bruce Metzger, this story is apocryphal (*The Text Of The New Testament*, 291). Metzger notes that H. J. de Jonge, a respected specialist on Erasmus, has established that there is no evidence of such events occurring. Therefore, opponents of the Comma in light of the historical facts should no longer affirm this report.

[2] Kurt Aland, in connection with Annette Benduhn-Mertz and Gerd Mink, *Text und Textwert der griechischen Handschriften des Neuen Testaments: I. Die Katholischen Briefe Band 1: Das Material* (Berlin: Walter De Gruyter, 1987), 163-166.

[3] *Prologue To The Canonical Epistles.* The Latin text reads, "*si ab interpretibus fideliter in latinum eloquium verterentur nec ambiguitatem legentibus facerent nec trinitatis unitate in prima joannis epistola positum legimus, in qua etiam, trium tantummodo vocabula hoc est aquae, sanguinis et spiritus in ipsa sua editione ponentes et patris verbique ac aspiritus testimoninum omittentes, in quo maxime et fides catholica roboratur, et patris et filii et spirtus sancti una divinitatis substantia comprobatur.*"

[4] *Treatises* 1 5:423.

[5] *Liber Apologeticus.*

[6] *Varimadum* 90:20-21.

[7] Some other sources include the *Speculum* (or *m* of 450 AD), Victor of Vita (489 AD), Victor Vitensis (485 AD), Codex Freisingensis (of 500 AD), Fulgentius (533 AD), Isidore of Seville (636 AD), Codex Pal Legionensis (650 AD), and Jaqub of Edessa (700 AD). Interestingly, it is also found in the edition of the Apostle's Creed used by the Waldenses and Albigensians of the twelfth century.

[8] *Fifth Orientation the Holy Spirit.*

[9] Actually the 1 John commentary is the work of "Mr. John Reynolds of Shrewsbury," one of the ministers who completed Matthew Henry's commentary, which was left incomplete [only up to the end of Acts] at Henry's death in 1714.

The Johannine Comma

The standard Greek text of I John 5:7-8 may be rendered literally:

Because there are three who testify, the Spirit and the water and the blood; and these three are unto one.

The symbolism in the passage is obscure, as we have seen in the Commentary; and so it is no surprise that there have been attempts to clarify and that these have left marks upon the text in the course of transmission. The most famous, which refers to three heavenly witnesses, is known as the Johannine Comma and consists of the words italicized below:1

Because there are three who testify *in heaven. Father, Word, and Holy Spirit; and these three are one; and there are three who testify on earth:* the Spirit and the water and the blood; and these three are unto one.

The Comma offers some explanation for the Spirit, the water, and the blood (footnote 31 below) but leaves unexplained the exact witness that is borne. It is not surprising then that in the late eighth century, Heterius and Beatus in their response to the Archbishop of Toledo2 glossed the Comma by supplying information about the contents of the witness. But with or without further explanation the Comma is not pellucid.

Isaac Newton, who was interested in the Bible as well as in mathematics, remarked of the Comma, "Let them make good sense of it who are able; for my part I can make none." Without yielding to such despair, one may recognize that, even were the textual evidence for the Comma stronger, one could be suspicious on several scores that the Comma did not belong to I John. The terms "Holy Spirit" and personified "Word" are not found elsewhere in I John. Even in the GJohn Prologue the personified Word is not joined with the "Father" as in the Comma—the GJohn Prologue says, "The Word was with *God.*" The Comma awkwardly has the Spirit a both an earthly and a heavenly witness, and the latter idea is foreign to the Johannine picture where the Spirit/Paraclete bears witness on earth and within the Christian. No other passage in the NT betrays the trinitarian sophistication of the Comma, which mentions not only three divine entities (as does Matt 28:19) but also that they are one. And while such a statement of unity among the three divine figures would have been helpful in the trinitarian debates of the fourth century, it is awkward in the first-century context of I John where a plurality of witnesses was needed to give force to the argument. (In the undisputed Greek text of I John the three witnesses are "unto one," i.e., of one accord; but they are not one witness.) Today scholars are virtually unanimous that the Comma arose well after the first century as a trinitarian reflection upon the original text of I John and was added to the biblical MSS. hundreds of years after I John was written. Nevertheless, the Comma has had such an important place in the history of textual criticism and in theology that it must be ...

A. *The Textual Evidence before 1500*

The key to the Comma lies in the history of the Latin Bible in Spain, but first let us discuss the non-Latin evidence (or lack thereof) pertinent to the Comma.

1. The Non-Latin Evidence

The italicized words above that constitute the Comma appear in only eight among some five thousand known Greek biblical MSS. and lectionaries; and in none of the eight can they be dated before A.D. 1400. In four of the eight the Comma appears in the text; in the other four it is a marginal addition serving as an alternative or variant reading. The eight are as follows according to the Gregory enumeration:

• 629: the Codex Ottobonianus at the Vatican. It is of the fourteenth or fifteenth century and has a Latin text alongside the Greek, which has been revised according to the Vulgate.

• 918: an Escorial (Spain) MS. of the sixteenth century.

• 2318: a Bucharest (Rumania) MS. of the eighteenth century influenced by the Clementine Vulgate.

• 88vl: a variant reading of the sixteenth century added to the twelfth-century Codex Regius at Naples.

• 22lvl: a variant reading added to a tenth-century MS. in the Bodleian Library at Oxford.

• 429vl: a variant reading added to a sixteenth-century MS. at Wolfenbüttel

• 636vl: a variant reading added to a fifteenth-century MS. at Naples.

3 I am indebted to Professor B. M. Metzger for information about these MSS. (see also his TCGNT 716−18), all of which are listed in the apparatus of the 26th edition of the Nestle-Aland Greek NT (1979). I have omitted Codex Ravianus (Tischendorf w110), preserved in the Royal Library of Berlin. It is of the sixteenth century and has merely copied from the *printed* Complutensian Polyglot of 1514.

4 Seemingly the scribe was a Franciscan monk named Froy(e) or Frater Roy (d. 1531). As we shall see, this was the codex that forced Erasmus to change his Greek text of the NT, and perhaps the Comma was translated from Latin to Greek and inserted into a Greek codex in order to bring about

that change.

It is quite clear from a survey of this evidence that the Comma in a form probably translated from the Latin was added very late to a few Greek MSS. by scribes influenced by its presence in Latin MSS.

Within the uncontaminated Greek tradition, the Comma is never quoted by a Greek author of the first Christian millennium. This silence cannot be dismissed as accidental; for the genuine Greek text of I John 5:7 is quoted (e.g., three times by Cyril of Alexandria) without the Comma. And there is no reference to the Comma by the Greeks even in the midst of the trinitarian debates when it would have been of help were it known. Indeed, the first instance of the appearance of the Comma in Greek seems to have been in a translation of the Latin *Acts of the IV Lateran Council* (1215). Later Manuel Kalekas (d. 1410), who was heavily influenced by Latin thought, translated the Comma into Greek from the Vulgate.

If we turn from the Greek to ancient versions other than the Latin, we note that the Comma is absent from all pre-1500 copies of the Syriac, Coptic, Armenian,5 Ethiopic, Arabic, and Slavonic translations of the NT — an incredible situation if it were once part of the original Greek text of I John.

The Oriental church writers do not seem to know the Comma before the thirteenth century. Let us be more specific, however, about the Aramaic/Syriac tradition. There were no Catholic Epistles in the Palestinian Syriac version. By the mid-fourth century three of the seven Catholic Epistles (I Peter, James, I John) began to be accepted in the Syriac-speaking churches. Nevertheless, all the old copies of I John in the Peshitta and Harclean Syriac lack the Comma. Where it appears in the later Syriac MSS., it has been translated from the Latin Vulgate. While absent from the first 1555 edition of the Syriac NT by Widmanstadt, it is found in the margin of the 1569 Tremellius edition; and by the next century it is incorporated into the body of the text with the supposition that it was original but had been excised by the Arians.

6 No clear knowledge of the Comma appears among the great church writers in Syriac, although a debate has arisen about Jaqub of Edessa (d. 708). In the Borgia collection of the Vatican Library there are two copies (133, *159)* of a commentary "On the Holy [Eucharistic] Mysteries" attributed to Jaqub, albeit written in a style very different from his other works. In them there is a reference to: "The soul and the body and the mind which are sanctified through three holy things: through water and blood and Spirit, and through the Father and the Son and the Spirit." Baumstark, "Citat" 440-41, discusses the possibility that Jaqub knew a Latin or Greek (from Latin?) MS. that had the

Comma. Yet a reference to Father, Son (note: not Word), and Spirit need not reflect a knowledge of the Comma—the mention of *three* witnesses in the standard text of I John 5:7—8 led many Western church writers to think of the Father, Son, and Spirit in Matt 28:19. Indeed, as we shall see below, the Comma probably arose through allegorical reflection on what the three witnesses (Spirit, water, blood) of I John 5:7 might symbolize in relation to the Trinity, especially on the basis of texts in GJohn. Thus we are far from certain that Jaqub was an exception to the Syriac ignorance of the Comma.

2. The Latin Textual Tradition

The two great textual traditions of the Bible in Latin are the Old Latin (OL) and Jerome's Vulgate (Vg). In the instance of the Catholic Epistles, Jerome did not revise the OL; and although

1 The word "comma" in this usage means part of a book or sentence. The Latin witnesses show variance as to the exact text of the Comma, e.g., most read the heavenly witnesses before the earthly ones, but early Instances such as Priscilllan, *Contra Varimadum,* Cassiodorus, and the Palimpsest of León have the opposite order. (Information about these authors and works will be given below under Al and C.) Kunstle, *Comma* 48, argues for a variant line 3 of the Comma as stated by Priscillian and the Palimpsest of León: "and these three are one in *Christ Jesus"—a* variant that appears in the genuine text of I John 5:7-8 as well (footnote 9 below). Occasionally "Son" is read for "Word" in the Comma (e.g., Cassiodorus).

2 *Ad Elipandum epistolam* 1.26; PL 96, 909B. discussed in a serious commentary on the Johannine Epistles. This will be done under three headings: A. The Textual Evidence before A.D. 1500; B. Important Discussions since 1500; and C. The Origins of the Comma.

3 • 61: the Codex Montfortianus (Britannicus), an early-sixteenth-century MS. at Trinity College, Dublin.

4 This codex was copied from an earlier Lincoln (Oxford) Codex (326) that did not have the Comma. Insertions elsewhere in Montfortianus have been retroverted from the Latin.

5 While the Comma is totally absent from Coptic and Ethiopic NT MSS.. It appears in a few late Armenian witnesses under Latin Influence. In the Armenian edition of Oskan (1662), which he conformed to the Latin Vulgate, the Comma appears marked with an asterisk. The Comma (with variants known in the Latin) entered into debates of the thirteenth and fourteenth centuries between the Armenian and Roman churches over unification and the use of water In the chalice at Mass. See Bludau, "Orientalischen Übersetzungen" 132-37.

6 Bludau, *Ibid.*, 126–32 eventually a revision appeared in the Vg, we are not certain of the date of origin. In both the OL and the Vg, before the appearance of the Comma, the translation of the Greek of I John 5:7–8 was almost literal.

7 However, in the course of Latin textual transmission, independently of the Comma, variants appeared that show that the passage was the subject of reflection and "improvement" by scribes. (Some of these would be retained when the Comma was introduced.) For instance, Facundus of Hermiane (*ca.* 550) reads I John as saying "There are three who give testimony *on earth*" (*Pro Defensione Trium Capitulorum ad Iustinianum* 1.3.9; CC 90A, 12; also inferior MSS. of Bade). If that addition was an older tradition, it may have facilitated the creation of the Comma with its corresponding witnesses in heaven. Instead of the masc./fem. numeral for "three" (*tres*) corresponding to the mixed masc. and fern, genders of the Latin nouns for "Spirit, water, and blood," the neuter *tria* appears. This neuter may reflect trinitarian reflection.

8 Still another variant occurs at the end of the passage, after "these three are one," when a phrase Is added, whether it be "in Christ Jesus"

9 or "in us."

10 *As* for the Comma itself, in the MSS. known to us it does not appear in the OL until after A.D. 600, nor in the Vg until after 750, although obviously these MSS. reflect an already existing tradition.

Even then its appearance is geographically limited, for until near the end of the first millennium the Comma appears only in Latin NT MSS. of Spanish origin or Influence.11 These include:

• Palimpsest of León Cathedral: OL-Vg, seventh century, Spanish origin.

• Fragment of Freising: OL-Vg, seventh century, Spanish.

• Codex Cavensis: Vg, ninth century, Spanish.

• Codex Complutensis: Vg, tenth century, Spanish.

• Codex Toletanus: Vg, tenth century, Spanish.

7 *Quonlam (quia) tres runt qul testimonium dant, Spiritus (et) aqua et sanguis, et tres unum sunt.* The *quonlam* ("that, because") and *quia* ("because") are alternative translations of *hoti*. The "three are one," for the awkward Greek "are unto [into] one," is a change that ultimately facilitated trinitarian reflection.

8 See below how Tertullian makes a point of the neuter "one." Some early Latin NT MSS. must

have had *tres* and some must have had *tria* in the opinion of Riggenbach, "Comma" 381-85. The neuter appears In Priscillian, who is *the* first clear witness to the Comma.

9 Cassiodorus (?), *Speculum,* and the Palimpsest of León. We can see the roots of this addition in the *Adumbratines* of Clement of Alexandria: after citing "these three are one," he says, "For *in the Savior* are those saving virtues."

10 In *Contra Varimadum.* Another variant Is Priscillian's "water, *flesh,* and blood." The replacement of "Spirit" with "flesh" may have had sacramental overtones, e.g., "water" is baptism, and "flesh and blood" is the eucharist.

11 However, it is still absent In some tenth-century Spanish MSS. (Legionensis and Valvanera), and in a Catalan witness (Farfensis) which is a recension based on earlier witnesses. The Comma Is not attested before the tenth century in Lath biblical MSS. with a pure Italian, French, or British lineage. It Is absent, for Instance, In the following Latin codloes:

Fuldensis (LD. 546, Italian origin); Amiatinus (early eighth century, Northumbrian); Vallicelllanus* (ninth century, Alcuin tradition); Sangermanensia (ninth century, French); and in the Lectionary of Luxeuil (sixth-seventh century, French).

• Codex Theodulphianus: Vg eighth or ninth century, Franco-Spanish.

• Some Sangallense MS&: Vg, eighth or ninth century, Franco-Spanish.

If we try to go back beyond the evidence of our extant MSS.,12 It is not clear that the Comma was Included in the text of I John when St. Peregrinus edited the Vulgate In Spain in the fifth century. After a stage when the Comma was written in the margin, it was brought into the Latin text in or before the time of Isidore of Seville (early seventh century), In the period of the Spaniard Theodulf (d. 821), who served in France as bishop of Orleans, the Comma was brought from Spain and made its way into some of the copies of the Vg written in the Carolingian era. Nevertheless, in a survey of some 258 MSS. of the Vg in the National Library of Paris, among those predating the twelfth century more lacked the Comma than had it.13

B. *Important Discussions since 1500*

Granted the poor textual attestation of the Comma, It would merit a historical footnote, not an appendix, were it not for some curious events related to it that have occurred since 1500. It was absent from Erasmus' first Greek NT edition (1516) and from his second edition (1519). D. Lopez de Zuñiga (Stunica), the editor of the Complutensian Polyglot Bible of Cardinal Ximenes (NT printed *1514,* published 1522), criticized Erasmus for omitting it and included it in his own work (wherein the

Greek form of the Comma was translated from the Latin!). Another critic of Erasmus was the Englishman E. Lee In 1520, and Erasmus replied to Lee that he would have inserted the Comma In his editions of the Greek NT If he had found a Greek MS. that had ft.13a Between May 1520 and June 1521 it was pointed out to Erasmus that the Comma existed in Greek In the Codex Montfortianus (In which, almost surely, the Comma had been translated into Greek from the Vulgate in order to embarrass Erasmus).

Reluctantly and not believing that it was original, Erasmus inserted the Comma into the third edition of his Greek NT (1522); and it remained in the fourth (1527) and fifth (1535) editions. Erasmus' reputation for scholarship lent support to the contention that the Comma must be genuine; and the Parisian printer Robert Estienne the Elder (Stephanus) included the Comma (conformed to the form in the Complutensian Polyglot) in his third Paris edition (1550) of the Greek NT. Finally the Comma found its way into the Textus Receptus (Elzevir, 1633) which served for centuries as the standard Greek NT. On both sides of the Reformation it won acceptance. Although it was absent at first from Luther's NT,14 It was inserted by editors at Frankfurt after 1582. Although Zwingli rejected the Comma, Calvin accepted

12 For a list of post-tenth-century MSS. containing the Comma, see Brooke, *Epistles* 156—58.

13 See Ayuso Marazuela, "Nuevo estudio" 220-21.

13a Usually this is referred to as a promise by Erasmus, but see H. de Jonge, "Erasmus and the Comma Johanneum," ETL 56 (1980) 381—89.

14 Luther commented on I John 5:7—8 in the years 1522—24 and again in *1543-45.* In his earlier remarks he stated that the Comma had been inserted secondarily into the Greek Bible; in his later remarks he commented upon the meaning of it with hesitation. On the Catholic side, the Comma appeared in both the Sixtine (1590) and the Clementine (1592) editions of the Vulgate, the latter of which became the official Bible of the Roman Catholic Church.

15 Although Tyndale placed the Comma in brackets in the English NT, ultimately it was accepted by both the KJV and Rheims translations. Even if the Comma had won the battle for acceptance in the sixteenth and seventeenth centuries, the war was not over; for in 1764 J. S. Semler challenged it, thus opening a new campaign of rejection. Doubts increased, and since the nineteenth century no recognized authority upon the Greek text of the NT has accepted the authenticity of the Comma.

16 In Roman Catholicism still another battle remained to be fought over the Comma. On January 13, 1897, the Sacred Congregation of the Inquisition in Rome issued a declaration (confirmed by Pope Leo XIII on January *15)* that one could not safely deny or call into doubt the authenticity of

the Comma.

Such an extraordinary intervention of church authority on a matter of textual criticism produced consternation; and very quickly Cardinal Vaughan wrote to Wilfrid Ward[17] with the assurance (which he said was officially sanctioned) that the declaration was not meant to end discussion or discourage biblical criticism. This was confirmed by H. Janssens (who was to become Secretary of the Roman Pontifical Biblical Commission) writing in 1900, as well as by the absence of hostile Roman reaction to Künstle's *Comma* published in Freiburg in 1905 (with the Archbishop's *imprimatur*), which attributed the origin of the Comma to the Spanish heretic Priscillian in the fourth century. How could one reconcile such freedom with the declaration of the Inquisition? One explanation was that the declaration was disciplinary, not doctrinal. A more popular explanation was that the Inquisition was not speaking about the *genuineness* of the Comma (i.e., that it was written by the author of I John) but about its *authenticity* as Scripture.[18] The latter would have to be judged by the norms of the Council of Trent, which declared (DBS 1504) to be holy and canonical those books or parts of books that were customarily used in church over the centuries and belonged to the Latin Vulgate.[19] However, the authenticity of the Comma could scarcely meet such criteria: It was totally ignored for the whole first millennium of Christianity by all but a small section of the Latin Church, and it was not part of Jerome's original Vg. *De facto* the nonauthenticity of the Comma for Roman Catholics may now be regarded as settled; for Rome has permitted church translations of the NT from the Greek rather than from the Latin, and naturally such recent Catholic translations, including those approved for use In the liturgy (NAB, JB), omit the

15 Ayuso Marazuela, "Nuevo estudio" 99, traces the roots of the Clementine form of the Comma to the usage in a Parisian family of thirteen Vg MSS.

16 For the history of the Comma in the printed Greek NT, see Bludau, "Im Jahrhundert" 280—86.

17 The *Guardian* of *June* 9, 1897, and RB 15 (1898) 149.

18 This interpretation was confirmed on June 2, 1927, by a declaration of the Holy Office (the renamed successor to the Congregation of the Inquisition) stating that, while scholars were free to discuss and deny the genuineness of the Comma, only the Church could decide whether it was authentically a part of Scripture, A good example of the distinction Is supplied by the story of the adulteress in John *7:53-8:11*. Like other scholars, Roman Catholic exegetes recognize that It was not written by the evangelist but added to GJohn by scribes (thus, not genuine). However, they would also recognize that it Is authentic Scripture according to the norms of the Council of Trent, which did *not* make authorship a criterion of canonicity.

19 There was discussion at Treat of certain disputed scriptural passages the authenticity of which participants wanted affirmed. However, the Comma was not one of these.

Comma. All recent Roman Catholic scholarly discussion has recognized that the Comma Is neither genuine nor authentic.

C. *The Origins of the Comma*

Granted that the Comma was not written by the author of I John, when, where, and how did it originate? The first clear appearance of the Comma is in the *Liber apologeticus* 1.4 (CSEL 18, 6) of Priscillian who died in 385.21 Priscillian seems to have been a Sabellian or modalist for whom the three figures in the Trinity were not distinct persons but only modes of the one divine person. Seemingly he read the Comma ("Father, Word, and Holy Spirit; and these three are one Christ Jesus]") in that sense; and because the Comma fits Priscillian's theology many have surmised that he created it. Before commenting on that, let me survey the subsequent history of the Comma among Latin writers before its appearance two hundred or three hundred years later in the extant MSS. of the NT, as discussed above.

1. The Comma in Writers after Priscillian (A.D. 400-650)

Whether or not modalist in origin, the Comma could be read in an orthodox trinitarian manner. For instance, it was invoked at Carthage in 484 when the Catholic (anti-Arian) bishops of North Africa confessed their faith before Huneric the Vandal (Victor of Vita, *Historia persecutionis Africanae Prov.* 2.82 ; CSEL 7, 60). Indeed, in the century following Priscillian, the chief appearance of the Comma is in tractates defending the Trinity. In PL 62, 237 — 334 there is a work *De Trinitate* consisting of twelve books. Formerly it was attributed to the North African bishop Vigilius of Thapsus who was present at the Carthage meeting; it has also been designated Pseudo-Athanasius; but other guesses credit it to a Spanish scholar such as Gregory of Elvira (d. 392) or Syagrius of Galicia (*ca.* 450).

22 Recently the first seven books have been published (CC 9, 3 — 99) as the work of Eusebius of Vercelli (d. 371), but not without debate (see CPL #1O5). In any case, the work Is probably of North African or Spanish origin; and its parts may have been composed at different times, e.g., Books 1 — 7 written just before 400, and 8 — 12 at a period within the next 150 years. In Books 1 and 10 (PL 62, 243D, 246B, 297B) the Comma is cited three times. Another work on the Trinity consisting of three books *Contra Varimadum* has also been the subject of speculation about authorship and dating,23 but North African origin *ca.* 450 seems probable. The Comma is cited in *1.5* (CC 90, 20 — 21). Victor, the bishop of Vita in North Africa toward the end of the Vandal crisis (*Ca.* 485), wrote the *Historia*

persecutionis Africanae Provinciae in the course of which he cited the Comma as representing the testimony of John the evangelist (2.82 In CSEL 7, 60; 3.11 in PL 58, 227C). Early in the next century the Comma was known as the work of John the apostle as we hear from Fulgentius, the bishop of Ruspe in North Africa (d. 527), in his *Responsio*

20 See Rivière, "Authenticité" 303-9.

21 Occasionally ft has been attributed to his follower Instantius. Priscillian founded a sect with ascetic (Manichean? gnostic?) leanings in southern Spain *ca.* 375. He was consecrated bishop of Avila but aroused the strong opposition of Ithacius of Ossonoba. In 385 Priscillian was executed in Trier for heresy and magic by the usurper Emperor Maximus, despite the intervention of St. Martin of Tours. The persecution of his followers continued after his death.

22 Ayuso Marazuela, "Nuevo estudio" 69.

23 Implausible are the attributions to Augustine (by Cassiodorus), to Athanasius (by Bede), to Vigilius of Thapsus, to Idacius of Clarus (or Hydatius, a Spanish bishop *ca.* 400). The editor of CC 90 (p. vii) thinks that the unknown North African author may have gone into exile in Naples whence came the later knowledge of the Comma in Italy by Cassiodorus. *contra Arianos* (*Ad* 10; CC 91, 93), and in his *De Trinitate* (1.4.1; CC 91A, 636). The Vandal movements in the fifth century brought North Africa and Spain into close relationship, and the evidence listed above shows clearly that the Comma was known in those two regions between 380 and 550. How and when was it known elsewhere?

To the period before 550 belongs a *Prologue to the Catholic Epistles,* falsely attributed to Jerome, which is preserved in the Codex Fuldensis (PL 29, 827–31). Although the Codex itself does not contain the Comma, the *Prologue* states that the Comma is genuine but has been omitted by unfaithful translators. The *Prologue* has been attributed to Vincent of Lerins (d. 450) and to Peregrinus (Künstle, Ayuso Marazuela), the fifth-century Spanish editor of the Vg. In any case, Jerome's authority was such that this statement, spuriously attributed to him, helped to win acceptance for the Comma.

In Italy Cassiodorus (d. *ca.* 583) cited the Comma in his commentary *In Epistolam S. Joannis ad Parthos* (10.5.1; PL 70, 1373A), although it is not clear that he thought it belonged to the Bible and was written by John. The work of Cassiodorus was a channel through which knowledge of the Comma came also to France. As for England, no MS. of the commentary on the Catholic Epistles by Venerable Bede (d. 735) was thought to show knowledge of the Comma, although two inferior MSS. had the phrase "on earth" after "testify" in the standard text of I John 5:7–8. C. Jenkins has now found a late-twelfthcentury MS. (177 at Balliol, Oxford) that does contain the Comma, but by that date it may well have been read into Bede from the Latin Bible.

Overall, then, the evidence from the writers of the period 400-650 fits in with the evidence of the Latin Bible where the Comma begins to appear after 600 in the MSS. known to us. (Isidore of Seville, d. 636, who shows knowledge of the Comma *in his Testimonia divinae Scripturae* 2 [PL 83, 1203C], if the work is genuinely his, may have served as a bridge to the biblical MSS., for his name is connected with editorial work on the Latin Bible.) The Comma was known in North Africa and Spain, and knowledge of it elsewhere was probably derivative from North African and Spanish influence.

2. The Comma In Writers before Priscillian (A.D. 200-375)

Let us now look in the other direction to see if there was pre-Priscillian knowledge of the Comma. On the one hand, del Alamo ("Comma" 88−89) gives evidence to show that Priscillian was quite free with biblical texts and might well have shaped the Comma himself by combining the original I John passage with the reflections of the North African church writers (e.g., Cyprian) on the Trinity. On the other hand, as we saw in A2 above and also in the INTRODUCTION (VI B), there were early Latin additions to I John for which there is little or no support in Greek MSS.; and one may wonder if the origins of the Comma are to be divorced from such earlier Latin textual expansions.24 Moreover, Riggenbach (*Comma* 382−86) argues on the basis of variants that Priscillian's was only one form of the Comma which, therefore, must have antedated him. (However, Lemmonyer, "Comma" 71−72, points out that variants would have arisen when the Comma was still a meditation on I John *5:7−8* and before it became part of the Latin biblical text.) One way to control these theoretical observations is to check through the church writers before Priscillian for knowledge of the Comma; and because of subsequent history, particular attention must be paid to North Africa.

24 Thiele, "Beobachtungen" 72-73, argues that since some Latin additions to I John may have been translated from lost Greek originals, we cannot deny the possibility of a Greek original for the Comma. I judge this quite implausible − see Al above.

25 These may be seen from comparing the Comma In Priscillian's *Liber apologeticus,* in *Contra Varimadum,* and in the Palimpsest of León. In Tertullian's *Adversus Praxean* (25.1; CC 2, 1195), written *ca.* 215, he comments on John 16:14 in terms of the connection among the Father, the Son, and the Paraclete: "These three are one thing [*unam*] not one person [*unus*] as it is said, 'My Father and I are one' [John 10:30]" This is scarcely a reference to the Comma, but it should be kept in

mind as we turn to Cyprian (d. 258), another North African.

26 In *De ecclesiae catholicae unitate* 6 (CC 3, 254) Cyprian states, "The Lord says, 'The Father and I are one [John 10:30],'and again of the Father, Son, and Holy Spirit it is written, 'And three are one.'"

27 There is a good chance that Cyprian's second citation, like the first, is Johannine and comes from the OL text of I John *5:8*, which says, "And these three are one," in reference to the Spirit, the water, and the blood. His application of It to the divine trinitarian figures need not represent a knowledge of the Comma, but rather a continuance of the reflections of Tertullian combined with a general patristic tendency to invoke any scriptural group of three as symbolic of or applicable to the Trinity. In other words, Cyprian may exemplify the thought process that gave rise to the Comma. That Cyprian did not know the Comma Is suggested by its absence In the early Pseudo-Cyprian work *Dc rebaptismate* which twice (15 and 19; CSEL 38, 88, 92) cites the standard text of I John *5:7_.8.29* Similarly other church writers, even in North Africa, who knew Cyprian's work show no knowledge of the Comma. In particular, the mid-sixth-century African, Facundus of Hermiane, in his *Pro Defensione Trium Capitulorum ad Iustinianum* (1.3.9—14; CC 90A, 12—14), cites I John *5:7—8* without the Comma (which he does not seem to know) as proof for the Trinity—the trinitarian references are derived from the significance of the Spirit, the water, and the blood. Facundus then goes on to quote Cyprian in the same vein, thus understanding Cyprian to have given a trinitarian interpretation of the *standard* I John text.

Augustine (d. 430) was a North African bishop a generation after the time when Priscillian was a bishop in Spain. A serious debate centers on whether or not Augustine knew the Comma. He never cites it; but in his *De civitate Dei* (5. 11; CC 47, 141) he speaks of Father, Word, and Spirit and says "the three [neuter] are one" To jump from that to ta knowledge of the Comma is hasty, for all that it shows is that Augustine mediated in a Trinitarian way on the "three" of I John. We see this clearly in *Contra Maximinum* 2.22.3 (PL 42, 794—95) where he says that I John *5:7—8* (standard text without the Comma) brings the Trinity to mind; for the "Spirit" is the Father (John 4:24), the "blood" is the Son (see

26 It has been argued seriously by Thiele and others that Cyprian knew the Comma, a knowledge which would make second- or third-Century North Africa the most probable area of origin. I would rather speak of area of formation.

27See also Cyprian's *Epistula* 73.12 (CSEL 32, 787) where the same "three are one" statement is applied to God.

Christ, and the Spirit without a reference to Scripture.

28 Somewhat favorable to Cyprian's knowledge of the Comma is that he knew other Latin additions to the Greek text of I John, e.g., the addition to 2:17 (NOTE on 2:17e). Unfavorable to knowledge of the Comma is his use of "Son" instead of "Word," although that is an occasional variant in the text of the Comma, e.g., Fulgentius, *Contra Fabianum* (Frag. 21.4; CC 91.4, 797), applies the "three are one" to the Divine Persons, and speaks of the "Son." while in his *Responsio contra Arianos* (cited above) he speaks of the "Word."

29 The Pseudo-Cyprianic *Sermo de Centesima*, published by L Reitzenstein, ZNW 15 (1914) 60 – 90, is attributed by H. Koch, ZNW 31(1932) 248, to fourth-century Africa and (possibly) to a follower of Priscillian, drawing upon Cyprian's works. It speaks of Father, Son, and Holy Spirit as "three witnesses" without any reference to I John (PL Supp 1, 65; Reitzenstein, 87).

His commentary on I John does not reach beyond 5:3.

John *19:34 – 35)*, and the "water" is the Spirit (John 7:38 – 39). Such reflection on the symbols of I John in light of other Johannine symbolic usage may have been exactly what gave rise to the wording of the Comma.

Fickermann, "Augustinus," has recently raised the possibility that in fact he did know the Comma but rejected it (and for that reason never quoted it). Fickermann points to a hitherto unpublished eleventh-century text which says that Jerome considered the Comma to be a genuine part of I John— clearly a memory of the Pseudo-Jerome *Prologue* mentioned above. But the text goes on to make this claim: "St. Augustine, on the basis of apostolic thought and on the authority of the Greek text, ordered it to be left out." No known text of Augustine substantiates this, and yet it is strange that a medieval writer would dare to invent a testimony of Augustine against what was being widely accepted as a text of Scripture and which seemingly had Jerome's approval.32 Could the Comma have come from Spain to North Africa and have been rejected by him? Such an explanation would mean that the Comma was not part of the Latin Bible known to Augustine33 and would make it most unlikely that the Comma was known to have had Cyprian's approval.

Without seeking to be exhaustive, I should mention that, besides never being quoted in Jerome's writings, the Comma Is absent from the writings of the following major Latin theologians: Hilary of Poitiers (d. 367) who wrote on the Trinity; Ambrose (d.. 397) who cited I John 5:7 – 8 four times; Leo the Great (d. 461); and Gregory the Great (d. 604).

* * *

The following picture emerges from the information drawn from the church writers. In North Africa in the third and fourth centuries (a period stretching from Tertullian to Augustine), the threefold witness of the Spirit, the water, and the blood in I John 5:7—8 was the subject of trinitarian reflection, since the OL translation affirmed that "these three *are one.*" Woven into this reflection were statements In GJohn offering symbolic identifications of each of the three elements, plus John 10:30, "The Father and I are one." Eventually, in the continued debates over the Trinity, the modalist Priscillian or some predecessor took the Johannine equivalents of Spirit, water, and blood, namely, Father, Spirit, andWord, and shaped from them a matching statement about another threefold witness that was also one. If

31 In PG 5, 1300 Claudius Apollinaris of Hierapolis (late second century) interprets the "blood" and "water" of John 19:34—35 as Word and Spirit. Bucherius of Lyons (d. 450), living just after Augustine, makes no reference to the Comma but interprets the water, blood, and Spirit In John 19:30-35 as references to Father, Son, and Spirit who testify (*Instructionum I: De Epistula Iohannis* CSEL 31, 137—38). A century later Facundus of Hermiane was applying the three elements of I John to Father, Son, and Holy Spirit without clearly indicating he knew the Comma

32 Invention would have been all the more difficult because there were then in circulation spurious works of Augustine (thought to be genuine) that cited the Comma, e.g., *Liber de divinis Scripturis sive Speculum* (CSEL 12, 314—a work from fifth-century Africa?).

33 Thiele, "Beobachtungen" 71-fl, would argue that Augustine's silence in reference to the Comma (which is not as serious as his rejection of it) does not necessarily tell us whether the Comma was already present in the OL text of North Africa, for Augustine used a Lath text more closely revised according to the Greek. However, Augustine seems to know some Latin readings of I John not found in the Greek. and the history of Latin MSS. narrated in A2 above does nothing to support the thesis of such an early presence of the Comma in the OL

34 Harnack. "Textkritik" 572-73, argues that the trinitarlan modallsm of the Comma is close to that of the so-called Symbol of Sardica (343) sometimes attributed to the Western bishops under the leadership of Hosius of Cordoba, and he and Julicher and Thiele would move the formation of the Comma back into the third century. The evidence, in my judgment, shows the formative process at work in the third century, but we do not know that the Comma existed before the fourth century; and we remain uncertain how soon after its formation it found its way Into biblical texts.

The phrase "on earth" had already appeared in the OL reference to the Spirit, the water, and the blood, the counterpart "in heaven" was obvious for the added threefold witness of the divine figures. At first this added witness was introduced into biblical MSS. as a marginal comment on I John 5:7—8, explaining it; later it was moved into the text itself. Some who knew the Comma may have resisted it as an innovation, but the possibility of invoking the authority of John the Apostle on behalf of Trinitarian doctrine won the day In the fifth-century debates against the Arians and their Vandal allies. The close connection of Spain to North Africa explains that the Comma appeared first in Latin biblical texts of Spanish origin. In summary, Greeven[35] phrases it well: "The Johannine Comma must be evaluated as a dogmatic expansion of the scriptural text stemming from the third century at the earliest in North Africa or Spain."

BIBLIOGRAPHY PERTINENT TO THE JOHANNINE COMMA

Abbot, E., "I John V. 7 and Luther's German Bible," *in The Authorship of the Fourth Gospel and Other*

Critical Essays (Boston: Ellis, 1888) 458–63.

Ayuso Marazuela, T., "Nuevo estudio sobre ci 'Comma Ioanneum,'" *Biblica* 28 (1947) 83–112, 216–

35; 29 (1948) 52–76.

Baumstark, A., "Ein syrisches Citat des 'Comma Johanneum," *Oriens Christianus* 2 (1902) 438–41.

Bludau, A., "Das Comma Johanneum (I Job. 5, 7) in den orientalischen Übersetzungen und

Bibeldruchen," *Oriens Chrlstlanus* 3 (1903) 126-47.

_____."Das Comma Johanneum (1 Io 5, 7) im 16. Jahrhundert," BZ 1 (1903) 280–302, 378–407.

_____."Das Comma Johanneum (1 lo 5, 7) in den Sebriften der Antitrinitarier und Socinianer des 16. und 17. Jahrhunderts," BZ 2 (1904) *275–300.*

_____."Richard Simon und das Comma Johanneum," *Der Katholik* 84 (1904) 29–42, 114–22.

_____."Dan Comma Johanneum bei den Oriechen," BZ 13 (1915) *26–50,* 130–62, 222–43.

_____."Das Comma Ioanneum (I Joh *5,7)* in den Glaubensbekenntnis von Karthago vom Jabre 484,"TG 11(1919) 9–15.

_____."Der hl. Augustinus und I Joh *5, 7–8,"* TG 11(1919) 379–86.

_____."Das 'Comma Johanneum' bei Tertullian und Cyprian," TQ 101 (1920) 1–28.

_____. "Der Prolog des Pseudo-Hieronymus zu den katholischen Briefen," BZ 15 (1918–1921) 15–34, 125–38.

35 "Comma Johanneum" RGG 1,1854.

_____. "The Comma Johanneum in the Writings of English Critics of the Eighteenth Century," 1TQ 17 (1922) 66—67.

del Alamo, M., "El 'Comma Joaneo," EstBib 2 (1943) 75—105.

Fickermann, N., "St. Augustinus gegen das 'Comma Johanneum'?" BZ 22 (1934) 350—58.

Fischer, B., "Der Bibeltext in den pseudo-augustinischen 'Solutiones diversarium quaestionum ab haereticis obiectarum," _Biblica_ 23 (1942) 139—64, 241—67, cap. 263—64.

Jenkins, C., "A Newly Discovered Reference to the 'Heavenly Witnesses' (I John v., 7,8) in a Manuscript of Bede," ITS 43 (1942) 42—45.

Künstle, K., _Das Comma Joanneum auf seine Herkunft untersucht_ (Freiburg: Herder, 1905).

Lemmonyer, A., "Comma Johannique," DESup 2 (1934) 67—73.

Martin, J. P., _Introduction_ a _la critique textuelle du Nouveau Testament: Partie Pratique_ (5 vols.; Paris:

Maisonneuve, 1884—86) vol. 5.

Metzger, B. M., _The Text of the New Testament_ (New York: Oxford, 1964) 101—2.

Riggenbach, E, _Das Comma Johanneum_ (Beiträge zur Forderung christlicher Theologie 31; Gütersloh:

Bertelsmann, 1928) 367—405 (or _5—43_).

Rivière, J., "Sur 'l'authenticité' du verset des trois témoins," _Revue Apologétique_ 46 (1928) 303—9.

Thiele, W., "Beobachtungen zum Comma Johanneum (I Joh 5, 7f.)," ZNW 50 (1959) 61—73.

CPSIA information can be obtained
at www.ICGtesting.com
Printed in the USA
LVHW010052081019
633404LV00001B/194